THE GURU'S
GUIDE TO SELF-MANAGED
SUPER FUNDS

GRANT ABBOTT

ISBN: 978-1-925681-14-7
Published by Vivid Publishing
A division of Fontaine Publishing Group
P.O. Box 948, Fremantle
Western Australia 6959
www.vividpublishing.com.au

October 2017 edition

Cataloguing-in-Publication data is available from the National Library of Australia

CONTENTS

Chapter Three: The Keys to SMSF Strategy

Chapter Four: What is a SMSF and a Foreign SMSF?

Chapter Five: The New SMSF — A Strategic Revolution

Chapter Six: Setting up a SMSF from the Get Go

Chapter Seven: The Ups and Downs of Bankruptcy

Chapter Eight: Contributions

Chapter Nine: Excess Contributions Rules

Chapter Ten: SMSF Contribution and Investment Strategies

Chapter Eleven: Compliance with the Super Laws

Chapter Twelve: Lending, SMSF Borrowing and the In-House Assets Test

Chapter Thirteen: Accessing Superannuation

Chapter Fourteen: Superannuation Benefits

Chapter Fifteen: The Taxation of a SMSF

Chapter 16: SMSF Estate Planning

Chapter 17: The Glossary - SMSF Terms and Meanings

THE GURUS GUIDE TO SMSFS
– A BIG WORD OF WARNING

This book is all about knowledge, ideas and strategy in the field of SMSFs. It should come as no surprise that there are more than 3,000 pages of law, explanatory memorandum, regulatory guidelines, state laws and so much more that apply to Trustees of SMSFs and more importantly, their advisers.

The Gurus Guide to SMSFs is for educational purposes only. It is a guide prepared by someone who has a lot of experience, practical and theoretical, and who has spent tens of thousands of hours thinking, speaking and writing about SMSFs. One thing that I know and teach those who have completed my specialist SMSF adviser courses, is that every circumstance, transaction and SMSF is unique. So, when using this book use it as a guide only as you cannot rely on it for any specific advice or application to a set of personal facts. It is general advice only as that term is defined in the Corporations Act 2001 and not personal advice - as I have no knowledge of your personal circumstances.

I have also spent a lot of time and effort on this book so please respect it's copyright. I do not mind you using small or large parts of text, however ask beforehand so I know what context it is going to be used. I would hate to see it being used to promote an investment product (for example) without my knowledge. As I said above, it is an educational guide only so I cannot warrant the application of the laws to any specific circumstance.

Finally, education is an on-going journey so please keep up to date and for those who have had their passion ignited by this book, please go to www.ilovesmsf.com or contact us at support@ilovesmsf.com to see how we can help your career or personal circumstances.

ACKNOWLEDGEMENTS

It is impossible to start on the journey of writing a book, particularly one that covers the field of SMSFs, without help along the way. *The Guru's Guide to SMSFs* is a snapshot of where I have been and who I have become on my journey. So, there are a lot of people to thank for getting here and also a lot who have helped me shape this book.

I don't have enough space to acknowledge everyone – this has been a 25-year journey for me and would consist of an entire book of its own. However, a particular thank you goes to former **Prime Minister Paul Keating** for introducing the Superannuation Guarantee Levy in 1992. It created a financial backbone for Australia and has got the Australian economy through good and bad times. In addition, I would also like to thank and recognise former **Treasurer Peter Costello** for cutting through the complexity of super and making Super Simpler in 2007. It gave all Australians tax free superannuation post age 60 – a wonderful retirement gift for everyone and an incentive to be a self-funded retiree.

Then there are all those who have seen, read or listened to me over the years. I truly thankyou as you have given me a wonderful career filled with challenge, fun and most of all, longevity. It would be so easy to kick back and retire but I have had a couple of two-year sabbaticals in my life and I am here to tell you, SMSF advising beats retirement by 100%. As long as I have my sanity, my mental acuity and health, I will be SMSF advising until the day I die and I hope that with this book and my teachings many of you will to.

I would also like to thank my parents, **Barb and Pete** who gave me the wanderlust of looking for new things all the time and to my grand-mother who told me to never say no – figure it out. Without this I would not be such a great strategist. Also to my daughters, **Tiana and Sophia** who push me higher in their own ways and give me insights into new ideas and fields I have never experienced. Let's face it if you are not learning, you are going backwards.

Now to the book. A very big and heartfelt thank you to **Ashleigh Jaremyn,** who is the smartest yet most demanding person I have ever met – but whose great wisdom, insight and push to make this book the best it can be has created the start of something big. With the ability to self-publish and digital printing, *The Guru's Guide to SMSFs* that you have in your hands is only the start. It will grow, change, grow, change – just like the seasons and superannuation laws.

And to all those people who have helped editing from **Amelia Stuckey, Ian Fehlberg, Dean Hutchins, Katrina Brown** and so many more along the way – thank you. Thank you so much.

Finally, I would like to acknowledge that part in me that has given me strength, courage and tenacity through many of my personal ups and downs, and enabled me to use my career as my backbone – my guiding light so to speak. Who would ever have thought that one day this little Adelaide boy would be writing his 5th book on Self-Managed Super Funds?

How to Best Use
"The Guru's Guide to SMSFs"

"Self-Managed Super Funds, SMSFs for short, have transformed so many Australian families financially and also provided the rock for the Australian share market in troubled times. With more than 700,000 Funds holding on average $1.2M, it is a great success story. With little or no tax, flexible investment choices from property to gold, shares and start-ups, those who have broken away from industry and retail super funds to start a SMSF, don't look back." – Grant Abbott

1. Introduction

Let's face it, most of us here in Australia have superannuation some-where. At last count, there were 14.8 million Australians with super-annuation accounts amounting to more than $2.3 trillion. For many innocent employees, unaware of their power to change, it is probably tucked away in two or three superannuation accounts. In fact, I am so, so surprised when I do presentations, and I have done more than 1,500 on superannuation and Self-Managed Super Funds (SMSFs) over the years, that couples in their 20's and 30's, and embarrassingly in their 40's, do not know where all their super is or how much they have. But with a little investigation they find, particularly those in the mid-30's up that they have $100,000+ in their superannuation and when combined with their spouse this tidies up into a nice little amount of capital. Yet, like the GST, it is hidden and most people don't take responsibility for it – even though it is a forced direct deduction from their salary and wages. And the banks, fund managers and industry funds love ripping the fees from the accounts of members that don't take that responsibil-ity. As they say – "use it or lose it".

So at talks, to inspire a little passion in super ownership, I play the following game and you might want to play along with me.

And if you already have a SMSF then still play the game to see how you would go with some freewheeling monopoly ideas - but don't use the figures shown in the game - use the total amount sitting in your own SMSF for all members which may include your spouse. As Trustee of your Fund and investment controller, you have complete control of where to invest – so let's see how you go.

2. The Super Monopoly Game

STRATEGY

Game One: Let's say that I handed over $150,000 to you right now and told you that you could only invest this money, and that it was not for general spending purposes.

But I gave you only one minute to choose no more than 1 to 3 investments – what would they be?

_____

_____

_____

_____

Game Two: Let's say that each month your employer deducts 9.5% of your salary and places it into the same investment account – again to be untouched and used only for investment. But because of these employer contributions, your local bank will lend you $300,000 to buy a property – enabling you to buy a $450,000 investment property. Where would you buy right now if I gave you one minute to choose the location of your investment property?

_____

_____

_____

_____

How did you go and did your mind start racing around all of the possibilities? There is nothing like being free minded on investing money – having all the choices in the world.

Game Three: I am going to give you the same $150,000 plus deduct 9.5% of your salary each month – but you have to immediately give all of it to a bank or union controlled institution to invest it for you. Well not exactly for you, they take your money and place it in a pool of millions of others like you – some very old, some younger – the they choose a portfolio of investments in shares here and around the world, plus some big property conglomerates. And for the last ten years, on average, the returns that they make for you have been around 5% per annum – depending on the institution – some more and some less. Now sometimes they win and sometimes they lose, but it doesn't matter, because they are going to take 1% or more of all the money you have invested each year as a fee for investing on your behalf.

You have one minute to choose which Fund your hard-earned salary goes into – what are your three choices?

....

....

....

....

3. Don't have a SMSF? – Read this...

I make no bones about it – I Love SMSFs and have seen them change so many people's lives. In fact I love them so much that I named my company after them – www.ilovesmsf.com and Facebook: I Love SMSF. But I do admit they are not for everybody – have a look at the videos on the ATO website – www.ato.gov.au and to be truthful they can scare the living daylights out of you when it comes to choosing what to do with your investment (sorry I mean your super) money. But if you are remotely curious in what a SMSF can do, then devour this book and make a choice – don't just stay with the faceless establishment - make your own decision whether a SMSF is for you. I will be covering the basics – like how to set up a Fund, receive wise advice from SMSF professionals and experts on how much you need to set up a Fund, what you can and cannot invest in, the tax benefits of a Fund and much more.

4. For those with a SMSF

Now this is not called *"The Guru's Guide to SMSFs"* for nothing. By the time you have finished reading this book you will be a SMSF Guru amongst your friends. And don't stop at one reading – underline the key bits and continue to improve and learn – it is your financial destiny. I love this comment by Tony Robbins and it has always stood me in good stead throughout my life and will do for you as well:

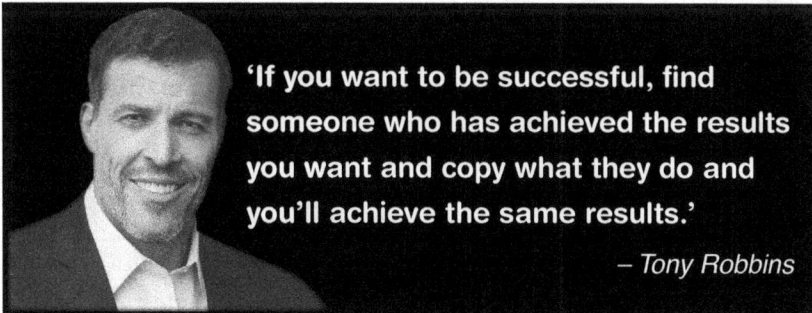

'If you want to be successful, find someone who has achieved the results you want and copy what they do and you'll achieve the same results.'

– Tony Robbins

Now the game above about investing your super was to get the, hopefully 14.8 million Australians with super, but not a SMSF, to consider the full breadth of what is possible with a SMSF. And to be brutally honest, if you have a SMSF, I would bet you $100 you don't even know 25% of the treasure trove of opportunities, strategies and possibilities you are sitting on. For me, I see, a SMSF as a long-term, family wealth creation and transfer vehicle that is tailored to the needs of your family. This is why I call a well-structured, planned and strategic SMSF, a Family Super Fund. And with the broad changes to SMSFs and superannuation on 1 July 2017 – the need for a Family Super Fund over the basic DIY Super Fund and the SMSF has increased tenfold.

From all of the research undertaken by the Australian SMSF Members Association, 90% of SMSF members and Trustees get into a SMSF to control their investments. Particularly when their super funds are going backwards because of investment markets. And that's what the Super Monopoly game is all about – it's your super money after all. What do you really want to do with it? But really that is the tip of the iceberg and if it is the sole reason you have gotten into a SMSF, it is a great start but there is so much you are missing out on – so, so much.

That is why I am writing this book, and don't think of it as just a book, look at it as an experiential journey – one we are on together. Now if you have a SMSF, I will be throwing a lot of strategies, ideas, short cuts and knowledge at you, but – *words without action mean nothing.* So get involved!

As we go through the book and you see a strategy that might suit you, go to your adviser, accountant or a SMSF specialist to see whether there are any technical or legal issues, and more importantly how to put it together. Believe me, there are no dumb questions and only you know your family – like how do I keep my super away from my daughter in law when I die, or can I invest in my mate's new invention that is going to be the next Facebook. And when it comes to questions, I have seen them all – including investing in ostriches, abalone, New York apartments and well so much more. Please don't get years down the track and then remember reading about the strategy knowing that you should have put it in place when you saw it here first. Particularly with the new way of looking at super and SMSFs post July 2017 – the new SMSF Version 2.0.

5. Testing your SMSF Knowledge

For the past twenty years I have been the Adviser to the Advisers, some have even called me the Grandfather of SMSFs. And I have loved the opportunity. There have been so many great SMSF specialists who I have trained and helped with developing ideas and strategies for their clients. In May 2017 I had the opportunity of training more than 500 on the latest changes to the SMSF and superannuation laws post July 2017, giving my opinions on where strategies will go over the next five years, and the big switch from super to SMSFs for those under 50 when the share market and big super fund returns dive. For many of you, you are lucky to have received this book from an experienced professional who wants you to increase your knowledge and understanding of your SMSF – because the more you know, the more strategies you can create for your own Fund and for your family, with their specialist help.

Design, build, change and deliver are the constant themes running through Family SMSFs. Your goal – read, get expert advice and tailor the Fund to your family's circumstances. And that, my friends, is why no two SMSFs are ever the same – ever. That I can guarantee. But pity the Trustees of a SMSF without a great adviser and more importantly, who haven't read this book.

Anyway, before we get into the ideas, strategies and SMSF knowledge, I thought I would start with another test so you can objectively assess your SMSF strategy level. And even for those that do not have a SMSF, it is important to complete this assessment – it will show you what you know and what you should or must know. And for those advisers reading this book, it is just as important for you to complete it also – you don't want your client SMSF Trustees to outshine you.

6. The SMSF Knowledge Test

This is a simple test and all you have to do is tick the True or False box.

STATEMENT	TRUE	FALSE
• 34% of Australians in retirement live below the poverty line.		
• 9.5% of an employee's salary is transferred into a superannuation Fund by their employer.		
• The Australian Super System has more than $2,000 billion in assets.		
• A SMSF can have no more than 4 members.		
• There are more than 1 million SMSF members.		
• The average member balance for SMSF members over age 60 is more than $150,000.		
• Superannuation can be used as a deposit for an investment property in a superannuation fund		
• As owner of the Fund and Trustee I have a responsibility to invest for my retirement.		
• My SMSF can buy an office or farm and let me use it, provided market value rent is paid.		
• The Trustee of a SMSF can invest in Australian and overseas stocks and shares.		
• A member's Will is the key document that controls the ultimate distribution of a member's superannuation benefits.		
• When a person loses their mental capacity they must be removed as Trustee and member		
• An overseas director of an Australian SMSF Trustee company is illegal.		

• The Trustee of a SMSF invests in a start-up company and loses all its money but the investment strategy for the Fund stated the Fund could only invest in cash. The Trustee can recover losses against the Fund's auditor.		
• The Commissioner of Taxation is the regulator for SMSFs.		
• The Commissioner's ruling on property investments says that borrowed funds can be used to renovate a kitchen.		
• Any person recommending that another person set up a SMSF to buy real estate must be licensed.		
• A Trustee of a SMSF is exempt from the Corporations Act 2001 (CA) requirements in relation to giving advice to its members regarding commencing a pension.		
• Mum and Dad are members of the Fund and their son and daughter in law join their SMSF. Dad dies and without any binding directions as to what happens to his super, the son takes all his father's super?		
• The Trustee of a Fund is very careful about his super and only wants his bloodline family to be members of his Fund, even when he dies and this includes any benefits passing on his death. Can this be done?		
• A Trustee can claim a tax deduction for membership fees to I Love SMSF?		
• The Trustee of a SMSF invests in property and a tenant slips on the property and breaks their back. They sue the Trustee. If the Trustee is an individual the tenant can sue them individually while a director of a corporate Trustee is protected by the company structure.		

As part of the I Love SMSF mentorship programs, I run regular webinars addressing the answers to these questions - visit www.ilovesmsf.com to learn more.

7. For the SMSF Professionals

As a SMSF professional, whether you are an accountant, financial planner, administrator, auditor, SMSF specialist or new to the game, this book is for you. I have written the book in a conversational style as the next generations – Generation X, Gen Y and the Millennials, are the next group to enjoy the love we have for SMSFs. It is my goal to get this book distributed widely so that more and more people see the light and take responsibility for their super with their SMSF. As you know, SMSFs are not suited for everyone, but with a good adviser – and I use that term to cover all professionals working in the SMSF field – the task of building a strong, strategic and lasting SMSF is a given. It is an impossibility for the SMSF Trustee – except for perhaps 1,000 out of 1 million + members (most of them professionals) to understand, and more importantly, implement the range of strategies contained in this book.

But I have not left you out. Although the book is written in conversational tones, there are lots and lots of strategies and plenty of case studies that cover the four generations plus, lots of section references, taxation rulings, tax determinations and cases. Educational for all reading this and more importantly, great learning for all advisers on how I review facts, build strategies and put them into play.

It is my hope that you will send this book to your clients, friends, family and also your colleagues. I am passionate about SMSFs and in fact I Love SMSFs – it is in all of our interests and also for Australia, that more and more super members get great SMSF advice – whether starting out or moving along the natural strategy time line of a SMSF.

CHAPTER ONE

Setting the SMSF Scene

"My Dad left work at age 55 with $400,000 in super, lived off $80,000 a year for the next 28 years, travelled the world and at age 83 has $800,000 left – hasn't paid tax for 25 years, gets a tax refund and a Government health care card. How is that possible? Four words my friend – self managed super fund – the greatest wealth creation vehicle in the world – period. So let me ask you – are you in or out?"

1.1 **Introduction**

Hi! I'm Grant Abbott, SMSF lover, teacher and author and I'd like to introduce you to the world of self-managed superannuation funds (SMSFs). Now that is a mouthful so we are going to shorten it to SMSFs – roll that around your tongue a few times because you are about to have a life -long love affair with them. So get used to saying it – SMSF, SMSF, SMSF. Sometimes in the Guru's Guide we will use the word Fund when discussing a member's SMSF or if you are lucky – your SMSF. This is different to a retail or industry superannuation fund.

Now let me go out on a limb here – I have seen more people using SMSFs to become millionaires than any property, share or other investment scheme anywhere in the world. So, humour me for a while and I am going to show you that choosing a SMSF is the best financial decision of your life for those with one and those not yet with one, why and how you are missing out.

Anyway, at this point are you in or out? For those already with a SMSF, then I am going to show you strategies that will take your excitement and passion meter to a 10 out of 10. Particularly with the new stuff – the laws creating the new SMSF Version 2.0 post June 2017. For those without a SMSF – I hope that I shake up your system so you wonder why you have missed out on it for so long.

1.2 **How I know whether you are SMSF suitable**

First off let me confess – I have been called many things when it comes to SMSFs. From the SMSF Guru, the Grandfather of SMSFs, Australia's top SMSF Adviser and so it goes on, but one of the ones I love is that I am too far out there. And why do I love that? Well let me show you something, something that will tell you and me together where you are someone who takes opportunities in life and you are SMSF suitable. It's called – *dramatic pause here* – **The Change Chart.**

Diagram One – The Change Chart

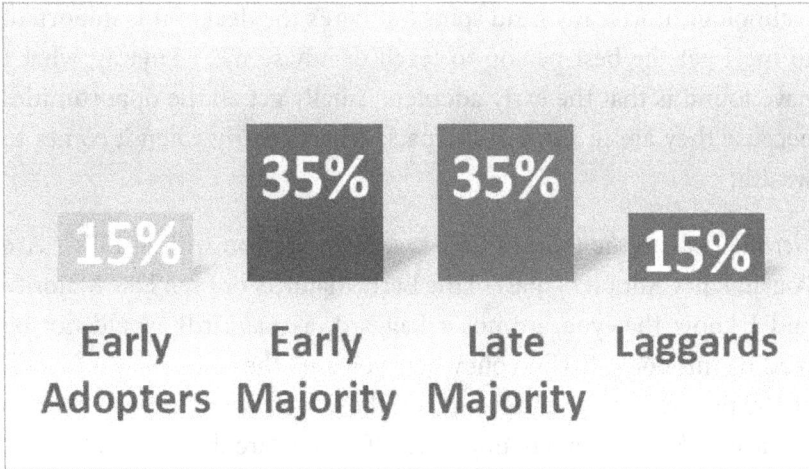

So what is the Change Chart? Well I've been around the block a few times and have lots of experience in the ups and downs in life - *as we all have.* Even my 15 year old daughter tells me life is too hard when her favourite fashion brand – which happens to be from the US, does not ship to Australia – love her but what a first world problem! Anyway, one thing I've seen in life is how people adapt to change or take on new ideas. This can be products, services, strategies, knowledge, and really anything that challenges us and or is new to us.

For example, the Apple iPhone came out in June 2007 in the US – so how long did it take you to get one? Look at the Change Chart - where were you on the Change Chart when it comes to an iPhone or smart phone? Were you an early adopter or did you wait for everyone else to get one before you did. It's funny, a good friend of mine who runs several publications in the financial services industry still has a Black-berry he got in 2004 and is very, very proud of it. Have a look at the Change Chart – where would he be? LAGGARD!

I got my iPhone in 2008 when it first came to Australia so I was an early adopter and for many things, particularly technology, I always will be. I don't want to be like my mum who at age 79 used the ATM for the first time. It gets too hard to keep up. Even now with some things technological wise my head spins but here's the deal, if it is important to me I get the best person to teach or advise me. Anyway, what I have found is that the early adopters usually get all the opportunities because they are in front of the pack – particularly when it comes to wealth.

Getting back to the Change Chart. Where are you with SMSFs? Are you an Early Adopter – part of the Early Majority or even Late Majority and I know that you are not a Laggard, as Laggards would not be reading this book. To find out where you are - the easiest way is to look at 100 people in your age group. Of those, you would expect 10 or so to have a SMSF if you are under age 40 – they are the Early Adopters. However, people under 40 aren't ripe and ready for SMSFs just yet so that demographic is not fully into the Early Majority stage yet, maybe just starting from my research. For those between 40-55, there would be a full complement of Early Adopters – 15 and another 15 to 20 from the Early Majority. Over 55 and well, all the Early Adopters and Early Majority have been in for more than a decade and made some great money and wealth. That demographic is well into the Late Majority, but here's the problem. The Late Majority generally don't like change and move only when they are forced to or when everyone else is doing it. With 14.8 million Australians with super, according to the Australian Taxation Office website, and only 1 million SMSF members, the Late Majority will never make it to SMSFs.

1.3 Change and Missed Opportunity

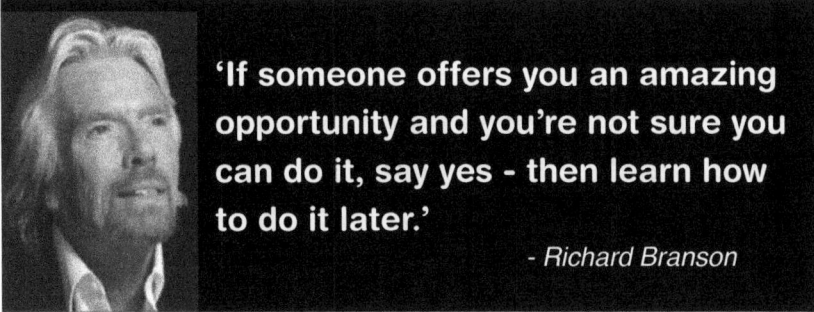

'If someone offers you an amazing opportunity and you're not sure you can do it, say yes - then learn how to do it later.'

- Richard Branson

Can I tell you a funny story? You are going to think I am so dumb because I flinched at a big opportunity. So big that if I had followed it through, these words would not be on this page because I would be hanging out with Richard Branson on his private island.

Well the year was 1999 and I was preparing a key note opening presentation for the Financial Planning Association of Australia's Sydney conference which was to be attended by 3,000 financial planners, fund managers and accountants. I was doing my usual thing and crystal ball gazing on what financial services would be like in 2020. Part of my brief was to go the US and interview key people in the industry and find out their views on the impact of the internet on financial services – this was the era of the Dot Com. Great gig and very interesting. Well I thought why not go to the heart of innovation and see what the views were of the venture capitalists in Silicon Valley and who better to predict trends. Anyway I was lucky to get 15 minutes with Michael Moritz a partner with famed venture capitalist Sequoia Capital. He was very frank and saw a vision of artificial intelligence helping us with all our financial services needs – dealing with banks, loans, wealth products and so much more.

As we were packing up, I asked him what were the best investments his company made - and remember they are start-up investors so they get in at the best valuation – the real money makers. By the time a stock gets to list there is not a huge upside like there is in the start-up space anymore – but of course there is also not the potential of a major flop. So here we go – picture young Grant sitting with one of the world's top start up investors:

"Just out of curiosity Mr Moritz what are some of the latest investments that you have got into?" I asked. As he took the microphone from his lapel and gave it to the cameraman, he looked me in the eyes and said, "Well six weeks ago we invested in some new technology that is going to change searching on the internet and we are pretty excited about it."

Of course I followed up with "What is the name of the company?" He stood up, paused and said "Google". Firsts investor in Google – can you hear my screams from where you are?

I should have grabbed his leg and begged him to let me invest – can you imagine what that initial investment would be worth now? Oh well that was me being a dumb laggard when it comes to investing. Now I am more savvy – well sometimes.

1.4 Why a SMSF – What's your Story?

The industry leading market survey firm CoreData puts out a lot of information on SMSFs and why people make a change to an SMSF. So what are some of the reasons given?

Grant's Note: My experience shows that when the markets crash, because retail and industry super funds are generally well invested in shares, super fund returns take a real hiding. And when a member of a super fund sees their account balance going down – even when their employer contributions are being made into the fund the overarching comment is "Well if I am going to lose money, I may as well do it myself." Watch what happens with the next stock market rout – for three years after that the number of SMSFs set up will reach record proportions and more importantly introduce a new generation to SMSFs.

Diagram Two: SMSF Trustee Survey - Why a SMSF?

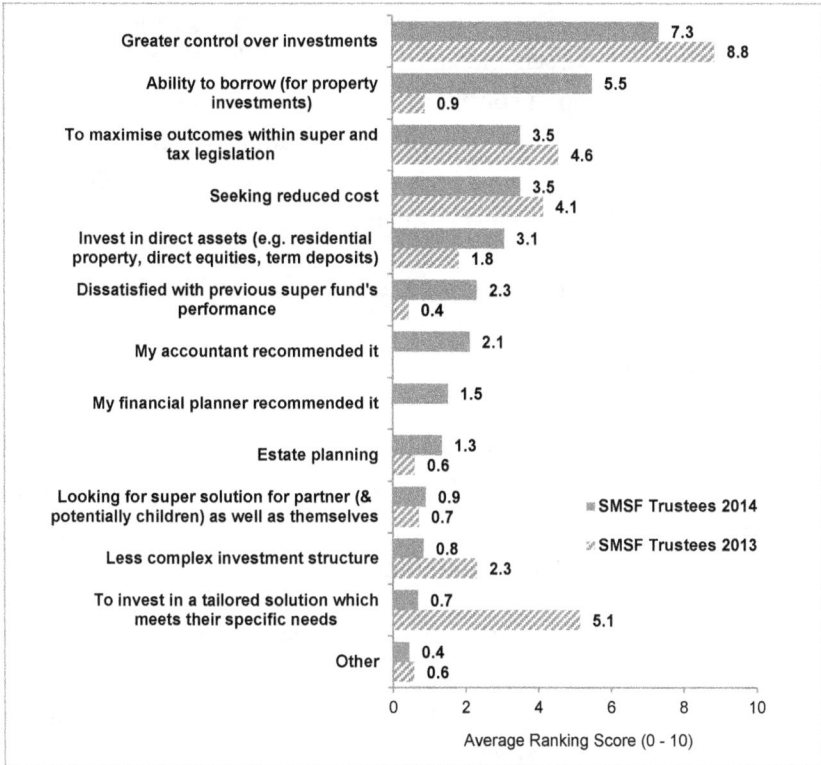

Category	2014	2013
Greater control over investments	7.3	8.8
Ability to borrow (for property investments)	5.5	0.9
To maximise outcomes within super and tax legislation	3.5	4.6
Seeking reduced cost	3.5	4.1
Invest in direct assets (e.g. residential property, direct equities, term deposits)	3.1	1.8
Dissatisfied with previous super fund's performance	2.3	0.4
My accountant recommended it	2.1	
My financial planner recommended it	1.5	
Estate planning	1.3	0.6
Looking for super solution for partner (& potentially children) as well as themselves	0.9	0.7
Less complex investment structure	0.8	2.3
To invest in a tailored solution which meets their specific needs	0.7	5.1
Other	0.4	0.6

SMSF Trustees 2014
SMSF Trustees 2013

Average Ranking Score (0 - 10)

1.5 Are there Risks with a SMSF?

If I am out and about telling everyone how good SMSFs are, why isn't everyone doing it? Well this is the only time I am going to say this in relation to SMSFs – they are not set and forget like a retail or industry based super fund. You have to own them and work them and be responsible for them. It is like having your own special little investment bank and believe me that is not for everyone – consider some of the risks.

1. **You are the controller of the Fund** – legally, and so you must abide by all the rules that apply to controllers, who are called Trustees of

the Fund. I suggest that once you have read this book or if you are the Late Majority, go the ATO website and see the videos on "Thinking about a self-managed super." As the ATO video says – You are the person in control and, if you make a mistake there can be serious penalties. Don't jump in without considering the risks and if you ask me get in touch with a good accountant, financial planner or SMSF specialist to help you.

2. **Time Involved** – Like anything, this is not a fly by night decision – once you are in, you are in for life so make sure that you have the time to spend on choosing your investments, liaising with your accountant to get your income and compliance returns done on time, listening to the ATO and of course viewing my videos on the latest laws and strategies. Time is usually one of the reasons that the Late Majority never make it into a SMSF – it is easier to give it to an Industry or Retail super fund.

3. **Costs** – For some, running a SMSF can be done on a shoestring – the so-called DIY Funds, but for many, outsourcing the stuff you are not good at to an accountant or professional SMSF administrator saves time, prevents stuff ups but of course costs money. I can only tell you whenever I need help I research and look for the best of the best. It will cost more but at the end of the day, you will make more money and have a lot less headaches.

4. **Investments** – You cannot use the investments in the Fund for your own use – the only exception is property used in your own business. A SMSF is not a play thing and people have been imprisoned for not abiding by the laws So when you invest you should stick to property, shares, cash, fixed interest and other stuff that we will talk about along the way. The good thing with SMSFs is, you are not out to get rich quick, as you can't touch it until preservation age anyway, so as I say – become a SMSF Millionaire slowly.

'Someone's sitting in the shade today because someone planted a tree a long time ago'

- Warren Buffet

1.6 How much do you need to set up a SMSF?

This is the typical question everyone asks – particularly when motivated to move. Let's start at the start and *make sure you read all of this*.

The Australian and Securities Investment Commission (ASIC) has released guidelines for financial planners and other licensed persons - INFO201 that states:

"In many cases, a recommendation for a retail client to set up an SMSF with a starting balance of $200,000 or below is unlikely to be in the client's best interests. The costs of establishing and operating an SMSF with a balance of $200,000 or below are unlikely to be competitive, compared to a fund regulated by the Australian Prudential Regulation Authority (APRA)." Now Rice Warner, an actuary representing the super funds industry – not SMSFs, made a submission in the Financial Systems Inquiry in 2013 that the average cost of having a superannuation account in Australia (again not a SMSF) is 1.12%. So for a SMSF with $200,000 there is an assumption that the administration and other running fees are above $2,200 per annum.

SMSF Friends and Professionals - Simon Makeham and Myself

Now I took the $200,000 thing up with Simon Makeham, who appeared on behalf of SMSF members at a consultative meeting of the drafters of ASIC's INFO201. We were sitting together having a red wine after a presentation that he and I gave together on SMSFs.

"So Simon tell me about your experience with ASIC and this $200,000 limit?"

Simon, who has a very successful financial planning business laughed, "Well there were a few of us in the room and some of us had read the Rice Warner report and one of the other consumer advocates, a practising actuary, took the report to task" Simon said, "Now that is not my expertise but I asked them how they could be so prescriptive when there are administration services out there that offer compliance and tax for SMSFs for $500, and in some cases much less, when the Trustees of the Fund are doing a lot of the investment and accounting work."

I took a sip of wine, it was Simon's shout, "Were they really listening to you and the actuary – after all, you represent the consumers, not the professionals at the big end of town."

Again he laughed, "No way. Because I said to them, based on the Rice Warner statistics, that a Fund of $50,000 in a retail or industry super fund environment which was paying in excess of $500 in fees could also be in a SMSF. And if the Trustees did their own work and got an independent audit, so the fees were even lower, then the start-up amount for a SMSF could be much smaller."

"And what was the reaction?" Although I already knew. After all you never set up an enquiry unless you know the answers.

"To tell you the truth, their mind was made up because the directive was made for licensees, not people wanting to set up their own Fund, who are exempt from licensing. I figure they just wanted to make sure accountants did not steer people into Funds with smaller super balances and charge them high accounting fees."

"So what is the real amount needed to set up a Fund?"

Simon looked at me, took a tilt at his wine and said "Well it depends on your age and how long you are going to be in the Fund. If you are a young couple aged 30 or thereabouts, happily married and have combined super in a retail fund of $100,000 then that is a great deposit on residential investment property. Banks and some building societies, provided you have stable employment, will lend up to 75% of the value of the property so the couple could set up a Fund and acquire a tidy little $350,000 one."

I asked him "What are the benefits of that strategy?"

Simon smiled, "Well the most obvious benefit is that you are using monies sitting in a retail or industry fund to buy a long, long term investment being property. Now you may never need to sell that property as it is for retirement purposes. But the good thing is it is yours – you can't live in it, but your tenants rent and contributions you make will go into paying that off quick smart. Of course, the large funds don't want that to go too far and wide because they don't offer that investment option. But if it is your Fund, so you can."

So there is the real SMSF set up answer from one of Australia's most prominent SMSF Advisers. Remember the negatives but here's my advice – read this book, do your research and make your decision. It's your money and you have a right to do with it as you see fit – within the rules and laws of course.

1.7 **Are you likely to start a SMSF?**

Again, CoreData have a lot going on in the research side and have looked at the likelihood of members of various super funds switching to a SMSF. Not a huge switching component but there has been a long time since the Global Financial Crisis when super fund returns were smashed. I would love to see these charts one year after the next share market correction. Anyway, if you are not in a SMSF now – where are you? And by the way make me a promise. Read this book cover to cover and come back and see where you are? Is that a deal?

Diagram Three: Likelihood of switching to a SMSF

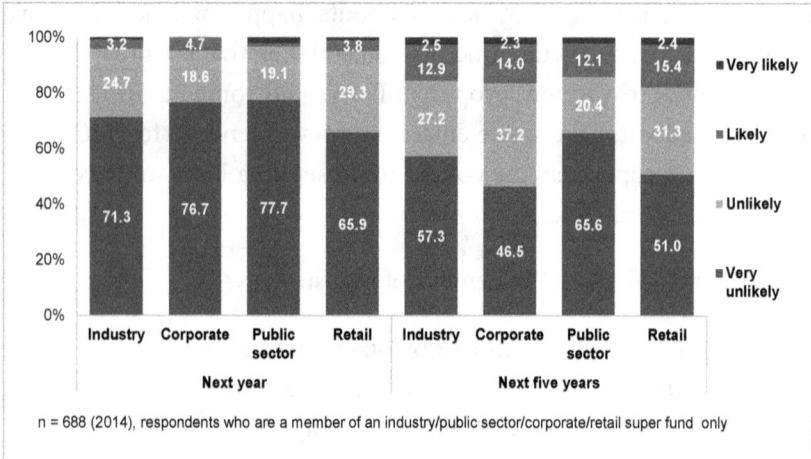

n = 688 (2014), respondents who are a member of an industry/public sector/corporate/retail super fund only

Source: Coredata 2014 Investor Survey

1.8 **What do SMSF Members think?**

SMSF members acting as Trustees are a powerful influence in the Australian economy. ATO Statistics show that only 2% of SMSF wealth is invested overseas, so to say that SMSF members like to stay close to home is an understatement. It is also fair to say that they are heavily engaged in the growth and protection of their SMSF. When the Government announced limits on the amount a superannuation member can use to acquire a pension, SMSF members were vocal. Here are a couple of responses to the Government changes in a SMSF members survey:

"Please do not change current arrangements with respect to lump sum withdrawals without penalty. Respect the fact that many self-funded retirees have provided for themselves without being on above average salaries/wages by being very frugal and undertaking often less than pleasant employment in order to maintain themselves and their families."

"Do not make any changes to the current SMSF rulings that will disadvantage retired and those nearing retirement. We have worked hard over many years to contribute to our funds in order to be completely self-funded in retirement, thereby saving the government and community many thousands of dollars in pension payments. We appreciate the benefits the Howard government provided and this is how we repay that advantage."

"The government and the opposition need to get together and create an independent commission to look after super. Plus future policies should only be made with bipartisan agreement. You cannot trust any one party with the vast wealth of the super industry."

However it is not only changes that SMSF members are vocal about – they are also engaged when it comes to the BIG issues impacting the Australian economy.

1. Long Term Infrastructure and Energy

SMSF members were asked the following question:

If the Government provided a long term bond - 10+ years, that was used to provide infrastructure investment across Australia, given the right terms and conditions would you invest?

It may come as a surprise for many, but SMSF members crave for long term secure cash flow and if targeted, genuinely to nation building. The response to this question was 74% positive and be on the lookout for infrastructure and energy bonds specifically built for SMSF Trustees.

2. Solving the Housing Affordability Crisis

The housing affordability crisis is one that is not going to go away. Government and councils are moving as fast as they can to get new stock but the entry level pricing in the major capital cities is frightening. There are many parents who either have their children living with them while they are trying to save for retirement or have to use non-super savings to help or provide a deposit for their child. With more than one child that is a significant financial burden.

We asked SMSF members the following:

Housing affordability for the younger generation is at crisis levels. Should we be looking at how superannuation and SMSFs can solve this crisis?

SMSF members were not as positive as the long term infrastructure bonds, possibly because many of them are in their retirement years and have children that are well and truly in their own home. But for some it is a big issue and that is borne by the fact that 56% believed that SMSFs could be used to solve the housing affordability crisis.

In the past I have advocated for the use by senior SMSF members, parents to provide second mortgage funding for the acquisition of a child's first home including the use for the payment of a deposit.

1.9 So who is Grant Abbott?

I talked a bit about myself above but it is important, before I give you some insights and my best SMSF strategies, that you know who you are dealing with. I have always made sure, whenever I am dealing with investments, finances and absolutely the law, to get the best advice. Even if you have to pay for it.

Education wise, I completed a dual Bachelor of Economics and Bachelor of Laws degree at Sydney University before taking on the role as the Tax Research Director at the Taxation Institute of Australia. I was lucky in that role to have the time to complete a Master of Laws specialising in international business and taxation studying under some legendary tax professors. Following my time at the Taxation Institute my next home was at KPMG as a tax manager in the wealth management and superannuation divisions. At KPMG my interest in superannuation was really sparked by the introduction of the Superannuation Industry Supervision Act 1993 ("SISA") and also the superannuation guarantee. The forecast of $ trillions pouring into super over the next few decades sold me on super being the place to be.

After a stint as superannuation manager at Rothschild and then opening my own business providing advice and training to financial planners and accountants – the rest is really history. To cut a long story short, I was there at the beginning of SMSFs, way back when they started and even before then when I made submissions to Government on SISA.

Since that time:

- I have written more than 1 million words on SMSFs;

- Written four SMSF books - "The Guide to Self Managed Super Funds", which retails for $120 and is now in its third edition as well as "The SMSF Strategy Guide" both published by professional publisher CCH;

- Presented on the subject of SMSFs to Trustees, Financial Planners, Accountants and Lawyers – even Judges for more than 3,000 hours;

- Trained more than 600 professionals to become specialist SMSF advisers and to meet the standards required for competency to provide advice on SMSFs under ASIC guidelines;

- Founded, with some other professionals, the SMSF Professionals Association in 2001, now known as the SMSF Association;

- Founded, along with a number of Trustees, the Australian SMSF Members Association in 2011; and

- Have advised a whole range of financial institutions including Westpac, NAB, ANZ, MLC, AMP, TAL, Citibank; investment product providers such as BT, Macquarie, Barclays, State Street, Vanguard, ASX and numerous advisory groups including Hillross, Pattersons, AMP, Sentry, Count, Countplus ... the list goes on .... forever.

Anyway, I thought this was a great opportunity for me to sit down and write a book for those Australians with a SMSF and show them how to maximise what they have, and also for super members who are under age 55 contemplating a SMSF. And more importantly, for all super and SMSF members to learn the best and latest strategies from someone who has been right in the thick of it. A book that in 15 years from now my daughters can say – "actually he did know his stuff". You know how kids are, they never think much of their parents or find it hard to describe what they do for a living.

1.10 My Promise to You

You may have a SMSF or you may not – either way I still have the same promise. You see, I know my stuff when it comes to SMSFs and have dreamt up, created and reviewed thousands of strategies and client files in my past 24 years as a SMSF Specialist, Author, Trainer, Presenter and Teacher. Now I am going to give you my best strategies, short cuts, hacks and direction to get you up to speed-lightning fast.

And this book is a great start but if you are like me, you will want more. So if you want to know more, then keep up to date with our regular strategy updates through the I Love SMSF Facebook page. And if that is not enough, then come to one of my webinars or face to face trainings where we can explore and innovate SMSF Strategies. For more information go to www.ilovesmsf.com

1.11 Working through The Guru's Guide to SMSFs – for Professionals and advanced Trustees

The last chapter of the *Guru's Guide* includes a glossary of major terms used in the *Guru's Guide to SMSFs*. These help tie the discussion to relevant legal terms and also should replicate the terms in the Fund's trust deed and governing rules. If your Fund's trust deed does not have these terms, then there is a good chance that your deed needs updating and is strategically limited. For a list of trust deeds that I have authored, please contact support@ilovesmsf.com

My advice is to start at Chapter 17 and go through all the terms first so that when you encounter them throughout the book you will have a deeper insight into the discussion or strategy.

CHAPTER TWO

The Benefits of a SMSF
and even better – a Family SMSF

2.1   The ten BIG benefits of a SMSF

2.2   Introducing the Family Super Fund – the SMSF with Smarts

2.3   Now for the simple long term SMSF strategy – Guru style

2.4   Time to meet Peter and Barbara Abbott

2.5   SMSF Strategy Alert

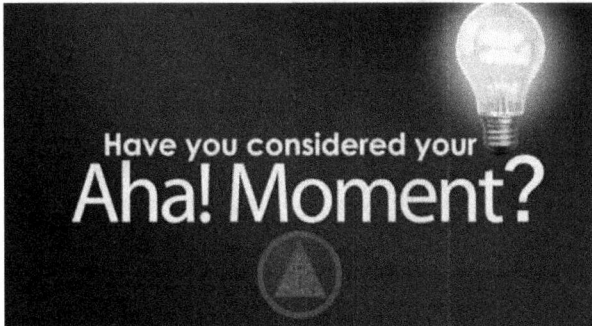

Have you considered your
Aha! Moment?

"It is an amazing experience to witness a person's "aha" moment when it comes to SMSFs. And when it does, irrespective of when or how they made it into a SMSF – it is time for gratitude that one decision can make a profound life difference."

So far so good – we are all learning and in this chapter, we want to see the benefits of a SMSF and also a type of SMSF that I designed back in 1999 – the Family SMSF. Essentially a Family SMSF is a SMSF with expanded options that enables up to four members of a family to participate in the Fund. And to cap things off I want to tell you my Mum and Dad's SMSF story because it is a cracker and has made such an important difference in their lives. Through the power of their SMSF, they were able to travel to Bali and other exotic destinations 8 weeks a year, every year for 20 years. They never had to go without, they funded their children into businesses, and their friends - who started with more wealth than them outside of a SMSF, have ended up on the Age Pension.

And finally, I want to share with you my Dad's "aha" moment with the Abbott Family SMSF.

2.1 The Ten BIG Benefits of a SMSF

We are going to look at the ten benefits of a SMSF but theory is theory. The only way to learn, grow and turbocharge your super is to put the ideas and strategies you find in the Guru's Guide into practice for your benefit. But remember my goal is to make things simple – but with thousands of pages of laws it is my recommendation that you find a great SMSF adviser to help you put your ideas and strategies, along with their input, into practice.

Benefit One: A SMSF lets you look after your Family

For the majority of people, their family is the most important aspect in their lives. I don't know about you but I love my kids and it is great to see them grow and blossom in this marvellous world we live in. Stressful yes but filled with opportunity. And as their Dad I take my responsibilities, particularly financial very seriously. I have made sure that if something happens to me they are well looked after, but more importantly, protected from financial predators – parents if you get my drift. Bloodline protection the whole way down the line. Now that is a real Family SMSF Estate Plan and erupts from my Family SMSF if I die.

In this way, a SMSF provides members with an opportunity to lay down the foundations to provide a comfortable retirement income stream for their immediate family and possibly generations to come. This opportunity has been increased with the Super Reform proposals where a member of a SMSF can leave their superannuation benefits in the Fund until their death.

Benefit Two: Providing a Secure Income in Retirement
The major reason for establishing a SMSF is to ensure that, when an individual ceases work or business they will have a stable, secure alternative to keep the lifestyle that they are accustomed to. That income stream, if it comes from super is called a pension and is a very popular strategy for SMSF members once they retire. The big benefit is, if the member is over age 60 when receiving the pension then the pension income is tax free in the hands of the member. Moreover, if this is a member's only source of income, being tax free they will not have to lodge a personal tax return. Can you imagine that? Being out of the Commissioner of Taxation's clutches for the first time in your life. Plus, the Trustee of the SMSF paying the pension will not pay tax on income or capital gains earned on pension assets in the Fund[1].

Benefit Three: Offering a financial helping hand if your Health Deteriorates
Health is one of those things that can never be taken for granted. I know as 2016 was a bad year for my parents and also myself. Old age and dementia hit my Dad, stress my mum and myself, and well it was good to put it behind us. But knowing that when the chips are down we can use the SMSF along with health insurance is a blessing.

---

1 There is a Pension Transfer Balance Limit of $1.6M per member. This limits the amount of accumulated super monies that a member may use to acquire a pension. Any excess must be kept in the member's accumulation account where the Trustee is taxed on income at a rate of 15%.

So if an individual's health declines, he or she needs to have access to a safe, secure income that takes the financial worry out of becoming seriously ill or even incapacitated. A SMSF allows members access to a range of benefit options in times of sickness and ill-health. This is the case even where the sickness is of a temporary nature. Temporary and Permanent Disabilities inflict great change and superannuation benefits are able to be accessed during these times of trouble.

Warning – the Demented Trustee
As I have found out in my own family, once one of the Trustees has dementia, they have to bow out of the running of the Fund and the person with their Enduring Power of Attorney may take their place as Trustee of the Fund – even though they may not be a member of the Fund. Do you have an Enduring Power of Attorney in place? This is a vital cog in a well-structured SMSF – if you haven't my advice is do it now!

Benefit Four: Investment Choice
The large majority of people or families who find their way into SMSFs want to have some say as to how they invest overall weatlth — including their superannuation. As Trustee of a SMSF, the power of choosing investments for the Fund resides with the Trustee; however, great care needs to be taken to ensure that the Trustee meets the relevant superannuation laws in terms of investment choice. These laws include the need to draft and successfully implement an investment strategy as well as ensure that, within confined limits, no asset of the Fund is used by a member of the Fund, their relatives or any entity related or closely associated with them or their family. But the choice of investments is broad – residential investment property, commercial property, shares, government bonds, gold, overseas investments, start-ups, Early Stage Investment companies, syndicates and the list goes on.

Benefit Five: Low Taxation fully sanctioned by the Government

Taxation in Australia is significant, but the Government has chosen to save on future welfare payments by providing tax incentives for its people to become self-funded retirees. And particularly given that employees are forced to transfer over 9.5% of their salary into their choice of superannuation – self funded retirement is a goal for most employees. Members of SMSFs have the best opportunity to simply reduce the taxation burden in their retirement lives. For example, the tax-free nature of a private pension and lump sum arrangements for a member of a SMSF post age 60 is one of the key benefits to a secure lifestyle retirement income.

Grant's Note: Don't expect the low tax ride to last forever. A member in a $3M SMSF who is living on tax free retirement income receives a huge amount of actual tax benefits to someone with $3M outside of super, let alone a person with $100,000 in a retail super fund. The Government changed the pension limits in 2017 to claw back some tax from the wealthy SMSF members and this is just the start. So expect ongoing tinkering with tax in superannuation but make sure that you are up to date and in front of any changes, not left behind asking "What happened?"

Benefit Six: Looking after your Family when you Die

The SMSF is by far the most flexible, most targeted and most tax-effective vehicle to provide lump sums or income streams to a member's spouse, children or grandchildren when the member dies — and it lets the member control the process without fear of legal challenge. Importantly where a member puts in place a strategic SMSF estate planning strategy, it resides outside the member's will. This is not known to many SMSF members, and Trustees who forget to put in place a SMSF estate plan are missing out on highly valued taxation concessions, and also opening the deceased member's benefits to the lawyers and in some cases the Public Trustee.

Benefit Seven: Access to the Age Pension
The Age Pension is available for persons over age pension age – currently age 65 and a half. However, it is subject to an Income and Assets test. A member's benefits in a SMSF once a member reaches age pension age are generally included for Assets Test purposes, as is income withdrawn from the Fund. Changes to the Assets Test have seen a drastic reduction in the Assets Test limit, but for many SMSF members with less than $830,000 who have a family home (exempt from the Assets Test), they may be entitled to an age pension. In addition, they may be entitled to other important benefits including the Health Care Card but as this is a complex area, specialist financial planning advice should be sought.

Benefit Eight: Protection from Creditors
This is a sleeper and, for most people, is not used at all. However, where a person gets into serious financial difficulty, the Government has provided rules in the bankruptcy laws that broadly protect a member's benefits in the Fund from creditors with the exception of any retirement income. This can be a relief when unfortunate financial events occur.

Benefit Nine: Transition to Retirement Income Stream ("TRIS")
The biggest bug bear for most people when it comes to compulsory superannuation is not having access to their super until they retire. There are a number of exceptions such as temporary and permanent incapacity, certain compassionate grounds and financial hardship.

One important exception introduced in 2005 was the Transition to Retirement Income Stream. The TRIS enables a working member of a super fund, who has reached their preservation age to access their superannuation as an income stream. The TRIS requires the member to withdraw at least 4% of their TRIS account balance each year and no more than 10%.

What is a Member's Preservation Age?

A member's preservation age can be found at the Superannuation Industry Supervision Regulations 1994 ("SISR") 6.01and is as follows:

Date of birth	Preservation age (years)
Before 1 July 1960	55
1 July 1960 – 30 June 1961	56
1 July 1961 – 30 June 1962	57
1 July 1962 – 30 June 1963	58
1 July 1963 – 30 June 1964	59
After 30 June 1964	60

From a tax perspective, if the TRIS is received when a member is under age 60, the TRIS income will form part of the member's assessable income - however it will attract a 15% tax offset. From age 60 any TRIS income from a member of a SMSF will be tax free.

STRATEGY So while working, an employee, small business owner, professional or other person with a SMSF may access pension income - much like salary - that is extremely tax effective. At the same time, they may contribute their pre-tax salary or business profits into their SMSF (subject to certain limits). This means that if they can set in place a "transition to retirement" pension as their key source of living expenses while contributing salary into a SMSF, a reduction in overall personal taxation may arise. As will be seen later in the Guru's Guide, generally income and capital gains earned on assets held for pension purposes is tax free but this excludes a TRIS which is also not counted in the $1.6M transfer balance cap (as the earnings on the investments used to support them are no longer tax exempt from 1 July 2017).

Benefit Ten: Superannuation Contributions Splitting
Under the laws, it is possible for a member of a superannuation fund to split their benefits with their spouse. Spouse includes a de facto spouse under the superannuation laws. The advantages of this is where both spouse members of the Fund are between the ages of 55-60 and using the transition to retirement strategy, then the benefits of the 15% tax rebate is maximised. Further where one member is older than the other and will thus reach the tax-free pension and/or lump sum status before the other, then it makes strategic sense to split any contributions for the younger spouse to the older spouse. However, it is only the employer or deductible superannuation contributions that can be split and then to a maximum of 85%.

2.2 Introducing the Family Super Fund – the SMSF with Smarts

There are more than 600,000 SMSFs in Australia controlling more than $700 Billion – so on average each Fund holds more than $1.2M. As we saw from the CoreData research, the majority of these Funds have been established for one reason only and that is to enable members of the Fund to control the investment of their superannuation monies. Many have become sick and tired of leaving their retirement dreams in the hands of faceless money managers. Although this is a powerful driver, this single focus often limits that strategic possibilities of the Fund and misses the whole point of these powerful vehicles.

a) What type of SMSF do you have or want?
Having worked in the SMSF industry for over 24 years, I have found that there is a wide range of SMSF clients - those that want to do every-

thing themselves (the DIY'ers), the SMSF'ers and those that are happy to build their Fund into a strong, strategic Family SMSF. Let's have a look at each of these types of small four member superannuation Funds:

i) *The DIY Super Fund*

This is a super Fund where there is a strong hands-on focus by the Trustees of the Fund - the true Bunnings DIY style of Fund. The Trustee generally does the accounts of the Fund using an accounting program such as MYOB. All bank reconciliations, income receipts and expenses are accounted for and the management of the investments are undertaken by the Trustee. Due to the complexity of the superannuation and taxation laws, the Trustee will need an accountant to compile the tax return and must have an independent audit under the SIS Act 1993. As you can imagine, unless the Trustee is only investing in one or two simple property investments, there is a lot of work that must be done by the Trustee – for a Trustee trading shares it is a full-time job.

You are going to witness throughout this book a lot of strategies, and also, the unveiling of SMSF Version 2.0. 99% of these strategies are not used by DIY Super Fund Trustees. Not knowing or using common tax and superannuation strategies can end up costing thousands in the long run.

ii) *Self Managed Super Fund*

This is the next level above the DIY superannuation fund and one that the majority of SMSFs run. Again the focus is on investments but the Trustees of a SMSF generally have the advantage of tax and superannuation advice from their accountants and financial planners. Strategy in a SMSF may be around pensions, estate planning, maybe some insurance and taxation strategies. The strategic input will depend on the SMSF skills of the advising professional and the willingness of the Trustee to learn and enquire what is possible within their Fund.

iii) *The Family SMSF (also known as the Family Super Fund)*

This SMSF is the same tax structure as a DIY super Fund and a SMSF but the key focus is on the family. Surprisingly, of all the SMSFs in Australia that have the opportunity of bringing up to four members of a family into the Fund, only 10% have chosen to do so. 20% of SMSFs have only one member with 70% having only two members. This is a great loss of opportunity – can anyone imagine what it would be like to establish a family trust with only one or two beneficiaries? No accountant in their right mind would recommend this course of action.

To see the difference between the Family Super Fund and the DIY or SMSF Fund, consider some of the following Family Super Fund strategies:

- An adult child member in the Fund has an accident and spends six months off work. The Trustees of the Family Super Fund can begin to pay out salary continuance benefits to the incapacitated member to ensure that their salary and wages are kept to a level they were, before the accident.

- The retiree members of the Fund use some of their super-annuation benefits to fund a deposit on a property that is acquired with a loan from a bank. However, the younger members of the Fund pay off the loan with on-going salary sacrifice contributions made by their employer. When the property is ultimately sold any capital gain is split between the members relevant to their capital investments.

- Mum is the sole remaining parent member of the Fund and has been diagnosed with dementia. The adult child members are in the Fund guiding her superannuation benefits towards the best in health and psychological care for their mother.

- The retiree pension members of the Fund invest in Austra-lian shares with imputation credits. These credits are used by the Trustee of the Fund to reduce any of the Fund's tax liabilities including any contributions tax liability of the younger members of the Fund that salary sacrifice.

In short, these unique super Funds have a very special place in Australia, and for that matter the world. If designed and used properly - they allow the aggregation and investment of a family's superannuation benefits, as well as providing a pool of monies and assets to look after family members including children and grandchildren at the time of an accident, sickness, permanent disability, death, pre-retirement and retirement. To make the most of your SMSF, turn it into a Family SMSF.

b) Let's look as some important Frequently Asked Questions regarding a Family Super Fund.

Q: I have a SMSF – can this be turned into a Family Super Fund or do I have to get some more documentation or a different trust deed?

Provided you are using a trust deed which has in-built Family SMSF strategies and options, there is nothing preventing you and your family using your SMSF as a Family SMSF. I have authored a number of trust deeds to ensure they meet the strict guidelines of a Family SMSF. To see those I have authored, visit www.ilovesmsf.com or email support@ ilovesmsf.com

Q: I don't want to bring my children into the Fund and then they take control when I get older.

This is a key benefit of the Family SMSF trust deeds I have written. When a child, brother, sister or grandchild becomes a member of the Fund, they must become a Trustee of the Fund or director of the Fund's corporate Trustee, if the Fund has one. For child members under the age of 18, one of their parents can act as a Trustee or director on their behalf. A corporate Trustee is where a company acts as Trustee of the SMSF rather than individual members. But as a Trustee, each member must be involved in the decision-making process which means each member must be a director – except if the member is a child.

As an aside, the Commissioner of Taxation recommends the use of a company acting as Trustee of a SMSF. Under section 17A of the Superannuation Industry Supervision Act (SISA) this means that each member must be a director. Where there is a child member then the Corporations Act 2001 (CA) will not allow the appointment of a child director. In these circumstances, one of the parents of the child, who is already a director of the SMSF corporate Trustee will act on the child's behalf.

Under a smart Family SMSF trust deed, each Trustee is given the same number of votes for each $1 sitting in the account balance of the member they represent. This means that, although an adult child may be a member, their voting power when it comes to investments and major decisions of the Fund is limited. For example if they have $10,000 in their superannuation account then that will be 10,000 votes. But if the main member of the Fund has $900,000 then they will have 900,000 votes.

Q: I have three children. How do I get all of them into the Fund?

The limitation of these small superannuation structures is that only four members can reside in the Fund at any one time. This means that the controllers of a Family SMSF - generally the parents - need to choose who is best to occupy the Fund at that point in time. As with children living at home, at some stage a child's benefits and personal family circumstances may see them commencing their own Family SMSF with their spouse and children - this may leave an opening in the parent's Fund which may be filled by another child. Alternatively, for sizable Funds it may be wise to consider two or more Family SMSF to cover the immediate and possibly the extended family.

2.3 Now for Simple Long Term SMSF Strategy – Guru Style

In my career I have created and developed thousands of SMSF strategies and you will get to see how I do it later. Now I have to stop there

– many lawyers and others want me to keep these strategies secret but SMSFs have been an absolute love of my life for the past 24 years. They have given me an amazing life and I've seen strategies change and transform not only members of Funds, but also transform families. And it's been an exciting opportunity for me to not only give as much as I can to those that read, listen or watch me, but also to see exactly how much difference my strategies can make to people's lives.

2.4 Time to Meet Peter and Barbara Abbott

Peter Abbott, my father, retired at age 55 from a successful insurance management career of 40 years. A 55 year old retirement age was, in my opinion, well and truly too young – so be careful - when you are retired, you are really retired. For me, as long as someone reads my strategies, turns up to my webinars and goes to my presentations – I will continue to do what I am best at – creating passion with SMSFs. So I have at least 20 more years of SMSF strategising and helping people, particularly those in retail and industry super funds, see the light on the hill.

Dad's super story starts on the day of Peter's retirement when he accessed $400,000 under the company's superannuation plan. He was extremely lucky to be part of a life insurance company that, for a number of years, set aside money for his superannuation, or re-tirement funding. Most people at that time in Australia – before the introduction of the Superannuation Guarantee Scheme for employees in 1992, were not provided with any superannuation or retirement funding. Being a relatively cautious man, finance wise, Dad went and received advice from an actuary on how long his savings would last. The actuary did the computer modelling and claimed without doubt that at age 55, with his life expectancy around age 80 and my mother Barbara with a life expectancy of 85 that the money wouldn't last to his 80th year and that to live comfortably he needed at least $800,000. Given that Mum and Dad's parents lived to a ripe old of 84 and my grandma spent ten years in a nursing home, it was certainly a great way to stress out a newly retired executive. Like many executives who had given up a powerful position at work but now had an idle mind – guess what he was constantly thinking about? You guessed it - money. And right in the front of his mind was how he was going to run out of it. Stressful – you bet.

And did that cause some fights. How often was I on the phone to mum – it was STD charge in those days (remember those days of expensive trunk calls) and I could hear Dad telling Mum to get off the phone because of the charges. He was also very tight with his budgeting. Poor Mum was allowed to use the credit card to buy groceries and the like but only spend a maximum $50 per week and well, forget about non-food necessities and herself. The future looked bleak for a number of years but then they started their own SMSF and slowly things began to turn around for the better. And looking back, their SMSF was easily the best financial decision that they ever made – with a bit of their son's help of course.

Dad and Myself at his Retirement Home – his SMSF paid for that!

So as I sit here are write this book - Dad is 85 and Mum is 82. They still live in Adelaide – Mum at home and Dad in a nursing home that costs $80,000+ a year and guess what, they still have plenty in their Family Super Fund. So how have they managed to keep a strong SMSF while living off $80,000 with Dad in a great nursing home? There are two reasons:

1. *Great Investments* and in particular the luck of the draw getting into an amazing technology stock at the right time – wait until you hear this story; and

2. *Being in a SMSF* for a long time. I often tell people that it is the time in a SMSF that counts – the longer the wealthier. And particularly in Mum and Dad's super Fund where the Fund did not pay any tax on capital gains on share sales or income tax either. Plus any dividend they received on share investments in banks and retail stocks had 30% franking credits (underlying company tax passed back to the share-holder – the Trustee of the SMSF) with the franking credits paid back to the Fund as a refund.

A simple equation of good returns and no taxation. We will look at taxation later in the Gurus Guide as it is always changing however I promise you will be up to speed with the latest taxation strategies. But in terms of getting great investment returns – that is not my game so I suggest that if you are serious – get a good financial planner or stock broker to help you out.

STRATEGY **Strategy Alert:** One of the best strategies that I love at the moment are Early Stage Innovation Companies ("ESIC") but mind you they are risky, have lots of upside potential and great tax incentives. So, the way the strategy goes is that a member of a SMSF contributes their employer contributions into super – pre-tax but as we will see later, it is included in the Fund's assessable income and taxed at 15%. For example, a $20,000 contribution would have $3,000 of tax payable by the Trustee of the SMSF not the employee/member. The same goes for self-employed business owners. An investment in an ESIC provides a great 20% tax offset for the capital invested which on the $20,000 contribution above, if fully ESIC invested will give a tax credit of $4,000 easily offsetting the contributions tax. The remaining $1,000 tax offset in the Fund can be used to cover tax on income such as interest and dividends so a pretty good deal – using your employer super contributions to get into one of more start-ups. And there are a range coming on line through crowd funding platforms – all very exciting. But the best of all if the ESIC company is held for a period greater than a year and less than ten years when it is sold there is NO CGT!!! Great tax relief, good upside relief – just pick your start-ups well through a good crowd funding platform AND make sure that they are ESIC guaranteed – *No ESIC = No Tax incentives.*

My Mum watching while I write the Guru's Guide

Back to Mum and Dad: On the investment side, Dad was fortunate enough to have a great stockbroker that looked after him with some great share advice plus, and this is the big one, he was also smart enough to get out of the markets a year before they fell. The two big times he exited the market were before the Dot Com crash in September 2000 and the GFC in October 2007. Knowing when to be in cash, and for that matter what type of assets to invest in and when has made a huge difference to their wealth – along with the great tax or as we have seen the no tax regime that they experienced in a SMSF. And, being a bit selfish - hopefully, if there's some left over, they might pass it onto the children.

So what were the good investments? Well the typical bank and retail stocks have always done well pre-market corrections. But the real kicker for their Fund was a technology investment in a company called Computershare that ran the share registration business of the Australian Stock Exchange and ultimately many exchanges around the world. With good technology and an overseas expansion plan the company took off during the period from 1998 to 2007.

The Fund's or really Dad's initial investment into the stock was $13,000 in 1997. The shares took off like a rocket to $220 and due to the high price in 1999 they had a four for one share split which saw four shares issued for every one share. This is a practice usually done for big companies overseas like Apple, Microsoft and Google, to stop their share price looking beyond the reach of the normal investor. Now it wasn't a big part of Dad's portfolio, but its rapid growth cast a great richness over his financial life – he ended up making over $800,000 alone from that technology investment. But to his credit as Trustee of the Fund, Dad knew he had to sell and was worried about taxation. But if you don't sell then there is no capital gain. And how many times I have seen investors not sell an investment because they were worried about taxation issues only to hold out too long and not realise the gain because the market dropped or worse, collapsed. That almost happened to the Family Super Fund if it wasn't for a chance and choice conversation between Dad and myself.

Picture this. We were sitting around the family home in Adelaide after one of my SMSF Strategy roadshows which I still do to this day and hope that you make it to one of my next ones. After a big dinner and a few choice South Australian shiraz we started talking about the stock markets and of course the topic moved to Computershare:

"How is Computershare going now?" I asked Dad. Investments were one of our favourite conversations and a great way to bond together.

Dad looked up from the television – one of the greatest loves of his life, "Well they had a four for one share split so they are still tracking really well. I was looking to sell some but my broker says I should stay the course as there is still a lot of upside and they are doing some good things overseas."

I could tell though there was something more, "So why do you want to sell?"

"Well I have had an amazing run on them and I am just worried from all my research about technology and other stocks going down."

"So how much do you want to get rid of and what is stopping you?"

"Ideally I would like to get rid of a lot of my portfolio because if the market goes down I can buy it again at a cheaper price and there is not much more growth left in over the next 18 or so months. I have had a good run – it will be time to bargain hunt soon."

"Well do it." I said with as much strength as I could muster dealing with Dad.

"I would but there is a lot of capital gains, particularly on Computershare and the Fund would be up for a lot of tax."

"So if there was no tax you would go ahead with your plans. But you would take the risk of losing all your paper gains because of having to pay tax?"

Dad's shoulder slumped – he was in a bind. Of course, I was going to get him out of the tax pickle but he had to have his AHA moment.

"Dad - here's what we can do. You are now retired and so you can take a pension or income stream from the Fund. Now when you do that, the income will form part of your assessable income each year but there is a 15% tax rebate. Plus because you were in the superannuation system prior to 1983 it means that 75% of your pension income will be tax free so you can effectively take up to $75,000 a year tax free.' By this time the Fund had grown to well into the early $1M's – not bad for a $400,000 start-up amount.

Dad looked perplexed, "But I am comfortable taking money in lump sums as and when I need it from the Fund." I laughed, "Well that is all well and good Dad. But living off lump sums in retirement means that you have chosen to stay in the accumulation side of the Fund. By age 65 you will have to take a pension – your own private pension anyway. But here is the thing. If you move all your investments to start this pension because you are retired and able to, then when you sell the shares you don't pay any tax on the capital gains."

Now I had his interest and said, "So, say I start a pension tomorrow and sell my shares in the next few months, the Fund does not have to pay any tax?"

I nodded, "That's right. Even though a lot of the capital gain has been earned when you were in the taxed accumulation phase of the Fund. It is where it is held at the time of the sale that determines the tax position and particularly if you hold those assets in a segregated account for pension purposes."

Dad was ear to ear smiling now, "How long does it take to set up one of these private pensions?"

"All you have to do is talk to your accountant and he can do all the paperwork pretty quickly I would say – maybe at most a week. And the other benefit is all the income you receive - both interest and dividends will be tax free."

Dad got out of his chair and went upstairs to his office and as he walked out of the room I asked him, "Where are you going in such hurry?"

He turned around with a big smile, "To see how much tax I will save. It will be close to $90,000 I think."

Dad had his "aha" moment. If you are in a SMSF already, when was yours. If you are not in one, I suggest that at some time when you are reading this book and you look at all that superannuation of yours in a retail or industry super fund – you will have your "aha" moment.

STRATEGY 2.5 SMSF Strategy Alert – Watch out for this Sign

"Throughout the Guru's Guide to SMSFs you will see this sign – it is the SMSF Strategy Alert. Now when you see this, it means I am about to explain a key feature or arrangement that, if used properly, can make a huge difference to your superannuation and your SMSF."

But sometimes it will be much, much more than that. Over the past 20 years I have received countless number of adviser questions - and many of them extremely complex - but that is the nature of SMSF strategy and why and how I have had the opportunity of building up my skills to the current Guru level of expertise. And you will see this in the book as there will be a few occasions where we will look at an adviser question and my detailed response to it. Much of this will include legislative references and an analysis of ATO rulings and guidelines – so it is a MUST READ for accountants, advisers and financial planners. For Trustees, get in as far as you can to see what the real deal is when it comes to SMSF strategy and how much a good SMSF adviser needs to know, understand and most importantly, apply.

CHAPTER THREE

The Keys to SMSF Strategy

3.1   Keep up to date and get professional help

3.2   The five Steps for SMSF Strategy Success

3.3   Big Strategy Hint: Learn from the Commissioner
      of Taxation

"Strategy – investment or tax is the key to SMSF success. That is why great SMSF advisers charge so much to create and implement an estate planning, tax reduction, restructuring, pension or family strategy. Above all investment markets come and go, but strategy remains true to the end. No strategy and well, why bother with a SMSF?"

3.1 **Introduction**

The best way that I can put it is that a SMSF is an absolute financial thoroughbred compared to an industry or retail superannuation fund. So many SMSFs were started at the behest of their accountant or financial planner years ago, some in excess of a decade since formation. And for many SMSF members they will tell you that it has been the best financial decision they have ever made. Sure the laws keep changing and for that reason, it is important to:

a) **Keep up to date with legal changes as a Trustee** – the Commissioner of Taxation states this clearly on the ATO website in terms of setting up a SMSF and his general warning is a good one:

"If you set up a self-managed super fund (SMSF), you're in charge – you make the investment decisions for the Fund and you're held responsible for complying with the super and tax laws. It's a major financial decision and you need to have the time and skills to do it. There may be better options for your super savings."

If you are looking at going it alone, then I strongly suggest that you read the "Guru's Guide to SMSFs" and use it as your handbook. I also recommend that you join one of our I Love SMSF membership programs where there is monthly education and strategies. But as I have stated already and will continue to do so, for even professionals that look at SMSF laws and client situations day in and day out, it is hard to keep up. So don't go it alone – it will cost you.

b) **Get Professional Help** – This is for both Trustees and accountants, financial planners and professionals when it comes to tough cases. We will see throughout this book there are so many laws that apply to SMSFs – over 2,500 pages and to prevent overwhelm and meltdown, it is important to get help. As an aside, it is mandatory to get an auditor to check on the Fund's compliance status each year – but for my part, the auditor is the ATO's lookout so don't rely on them for advice. The Commissioner of Taxation states the following: "It's best to see a qualified, licensed professional to help you decide. The Australian Securities and Investments Commission website has information about choosing a financial adviser."

SMSF Warning: Don't fall foul or try to flout the law – particularly if you are a professional, it can cost you dearly in terms of financial penalties and more importantly resources in investigating and defending any action plus your all-important reputation.

To see a disaster in the making – look at the case of *Australian Prudential Regulation Authority v Holloway* [2000] FCA 579. In that case a very experienced accountant - Anthony Holloway - who had a successful accounting firm in Adelaide, provided advice to a number of his clients in relation to a specific scheme. The scheme involved his clients – essentially small business clients – to set up a SMSF, contributing money into the Fund then investing that money into a unit trust which was wholly controlled by the Fund.

As an aside, the laws in relation to investing in unit trusts, as we will see later in the investments chapter, were changed in 1999. However, the Holloway case related to the laws prior to this time which allowed an investment in a wholly owned and controlled unit trust. Anyway, once the monies were transferred to the unit trust they were then lent back to the small business – effectively generating a tax deduction for money going in and coming out again. Importantly the laws at that time prevented a Trustee of a superannuation fund from lending directly more than 5% of the assets of the Fund to a related party – the In-House Assets test in section 84 of SISA. Now, as this was through a unit trust, there was no apparent contravention of the laws as it was the Trustee of the unit trust that lent the money not the Trustee of the SMSF. However, the Court found the accountant - Mr Holloway - guilty of a breach of the anti-avoidance rules in the in-house assets test in section 85 of SISA as there was a scheme in place and clearly the intent of the scheme was to avoid the operation of the In-House Assets test in section 84.

And here is the important point for ALL advisers and Trustees. In the Federal Court, Justice Mansfield stated that "Mr Holloway gave evidence. He accepted that he, and he alone, was the mind of Holloway & Co. His evidence was that he did not think that the transactions in which he or officers working under him played a part were improper...... He did not believe that the structure led to the creation of in-house assets. Put simply, the respondents contended that APRA had not established the intention required by s 85(1)."

And here is what Justice Mansfield had to say about Anthony Holloway personally *(I have excerpted the relevant parts)*, "Mr Holloway is an experienced accountant, having worked first in the United Kingdom and from 1967 in Australia......Mr Holloway knew that a regulated superannuation fund was restricted in its ability to invest in, or lend monies to, the employer-sponsor..... He understood that direct investment in, or loans to, an employer-sponsor were restricted by the OSS regulations. He said he knew of the Act in a general way, including in 1993 when it was soon to come into force, but did not apply his mind to how it might impact upon the various transactions now under consideration...... That claimed level of ignorance is in contrast with his knowledge of other aspects of legislation relating to regulated superannuation funds, namely the levels of contributions available to employer-sponsors to attract the taxation concessions, and the inability of superannuation funds to borrow monies. It is also in contrast with his general insistence on the need for an arms-length Trustee, a matter to which almost all of the witnesses who were Trustees of superannuation funds referred."

Ouch and double ouch. To be taken to task by a Judge when you are a professional adviser is not a nice way to go – sorry. In the end, the Federal Court handed down penalties amounting to $257,000 against Adelaide accountant Anthony Philip Holloway, and his firm, for carrying out a scheme to avoid the in-house assets provisions of the SISA. Please never get caught either as a professional advising in this area or as a Trustee.

Anyway, enough of talking about breaking the law. Let me leave you with this – it is crucial for all accountants, financial planners, lawyers, auditors and SMSF Trustees to understand and know the law and the Fund's trust deed (*which forms part of the law as we will see later*) – ignorance is no excuse.

3.2 The Five Steps for SMSF Strategy Success

SMSF strategy success is dependent upon meeting compliance across the following five key areas:

Diagram One – The Five Step SMSF Strategy Success Model

a) The Trust Deed – does it allow the strategy?

We will look at the trust deed in detail shortly as it is a vital cog in the strategy wheel. To that end, section 55(1) of the SISA, the Super-annuation Laws provides that NO-ONE can breach the provisions of the Fund's Trust Deed. This means Trustee, Member, Auditor or Professional.

Here is a little test for you to see if you can read, understand an apply the rules of a SMSF. Let's say we have the Smith SMSF where the Fund's Trust Deed at Rule 2 says the following, *which is very common for SMSFs with individual Trustees*:

Rule 2 states "The Fund is for the purpose of paying old age pensions only" (as that term is seen in the Australian Constitution rather than Centrelink).

Now George Smith who is a retired member of the Smith SMSF and one of two individual Trustees of the Fund receives a lump sum of $50,000 from his accumulation account in the Fund. Can you advise me – has there been a breach of the trust deed and thereby the superannuation laws and who has breached the laws and what are the penalties?

Clearly the Trustee has breached the laws and this should not get past the auditor – although it often does. We will learn a lot more when we look at SMSF trust deeds and governing rules – the key building block for a successful SMSF a bit later.

b) The Corporations Act 2001 (CA)

Now this one is tough and I can give you a super long version – 20 pages or more but let's stick with the simple version. I will stick to the simple as the rest is so technical and better for the Corporations lawyers. Under the Corporations Act 2001, if a person recommends a financial product they must:

  a) be licensed to provide advice on the financial product;

b) provide the client with a Financial Services guide that authorises them to advise on the specific financial product;

c) review the client's specific circumstances and provide a Statement of Advice detailing how the financial product fits the client's circumstances

Unlicensed Advising: This is a big never breach unless you want your business closed down. For example, if an unlicensed accountant recommends a SMSF Trustee to invest in an Exchange Traded Fund ("ETF") there is a breach of the CA as clearly the ETF is a financial product.

So where do SMSFs fit in as they are not what you would typically call a financial product? Surely an accountant that tells their client to set up a SMSF can't get into trouble?

Well first and foremost a SMSF is not a financial product but a collection of financial products which means that it is potentially very dangerous if unlicensed advice is given. Luckily a Trustee of a SMSF is exempt from being licensed but any accountant, financial planner, auditor, real estate agent, mortgage broker, lender or in some cases a lawyer that recommends any of the following interests in a SMSF must be licensed:

- Setting up a SMSF

- Making a contribution to a SMSF

- Advising a client to rollover monies from an industry, retail or other superannuation fund to a SMSF

- Recommending any specific financial product investments like shares, unit trusts, ETFs and options

- Recommending or advising a person to become a member of a SMSF

- Advising a member to commence a pension
- Advising a member to set up a binding death benefit nomination or SMSF Will

Great care should be taken by Trustees, Licensed Advisers and Accountants where and when any transaction fits within the breadth of the Corporations Act, and the statutory requirements for a Statement of Advice under that Act.

For Unlicensed Accountants Tax Advice is okay: An unlicensed accountant may provide taxation advice on a financial product such as making a tax-deductible contribution or commencing a pension however in any advice, they must disclaim that it is not financial advice and the person should seek their own financial advice on the matter. For more on this see ASIC guidance note: *ASIC Corporations (Recognised Accountants: Exempt Services) Instrument 2016/1151.*

c) The Superannuation Industry Supervision Act 1993 (SISA)

The Guru's Guide to SMSFs covers a wide range of issues in SISA but remember there is only so much that can be covered in a book. Look what happened to the experienced accountant, Anthony Holloway – SMSFs are great but be careful.

On the basic laws, information for Trustee's can be found on the ATO website www.ato.gov.au and at www.ilovesmsf.com

Change happens, almost weekly so it is vital that any person advising a Trustee or member of a SMSF keep up to date, not only on the laws and regulations but also the latest strategies – it is better to be in front of the curve not languishing as a laggard!

d) The Income Tax Assessment Act 1997 (ITAA 1997)

A significant number of transactions undertaken by a member or Trustee of a SMSF have a tax impact. That is the very nature of a SMSF – it is a concessionally taxed superannuation fund and the government has put limits on contributions – both concessional (where a member claims a tax deduction) and also non-concessional. A non-concessional contribution is one where a member contributes their after-tax dollars into a SMSF. It also includes an in-specie, or allowed property contributions like listed shares such as NAB shares.

In addition there are limits on the amount of concessionally taxed pension income that the Trustee of a Fund may use as a transfer balance for a member from their accumulation account to a pension account. As such the Trustee AND their professional advisers must be on top of the tax side of each transaction.

More often than not I see a strategy proposed that has a particular tax angle and when I run it through the five-step compliance model, it fails one or more of the steps – in particular the trust deed and the SISA. This usually requires a rework from the ground up in order to get to the desired tax result.

e) The SMSF Transaction Documentation

This is by far the weakest point of most transactions, arrangements or undertakings by a Trustee. Wholeheartedly this is the province of the professional and the Trustee should be able to rely on the professional adviser – whether the accountant, administrator or financial planner to pull together all the requisite documents and pieces of the strategy. This includes interaction with the Regulators of various components of the transaction.

Consider the Death Benefit Flowchart overleaf for the payment of death benefits upon the death of a member – as you can see there are a number of important steps that must be completed and in exactly the right order or the whole process can be subject to a challenge.

WHAT HAPPENS ON THE DEATH OF A MEMBER OF THE FUND

STEP 01

Member's death sparks a course of action by the Adviser and the Trustee
A Obtain notification and note from the Trustee that the member is dead
B Advice to be sought dependant upon any formal requests in the Binding Death Benefit Nomination SMSF Will or Conditional Pension

STEP 02

Documentation Review – linked to the Members
A Review the SMSF Trust Deed
B Check that the lineage and any Change of Trustee documents are correct
C Review the BDBN, SMSF Will and any Pension documentation

STEP 03

Trustee/Director Appointment
A What do the Trust Deed or the Trustee Constitution require for SMSF replacements?
B What voting powers apply to the existing Trustees and Replacement Trustee/Director?
C What is the Adviser's position?
D Notify the Regulators

STEP 04

Fund-Member Insurances
A Review any Fund/Member Insurances
B Contact Life Broker to accelerate insurance payout
C Determine Insurance distribution policy

STEP 05

Determine Member Death Benefits
A Calculate death benefits in line with the trust deed – BDBN or SMSF Will
B Are there any reserve payments?
C Value assets used to pay death benefits

STEP 06

Auto-reversionary Pensions
A What does the deed state regarding the transfer of the pension?
B Review of Pension documentation for compliance and transfer of Pension Account

STEP 07

Set up Payment Schedules
A Be careful as the SIS Act requires that once the first payment is made the Replacement Trustee must step down
B Review who is to get what payment – lump sum or income steam and are there any in-specie payments?

STEP 08

Retirement of Replacement Trustee
A The laws require the retirement of the Replacement Trustee/Director
B Ensure new Members become Trustee/Director unless incapacitated

STEP 09

Ongoing payout of Pensions
A What are continuing Pension requirements?
B Is there a SMSF Guardian in place to protect further reversionaries down the line?

Diagram Two: The SMSF Death Benefit Flow Chart

An example of what can go wrong with SMSF estate planning was seen in the case of *Katz v Grossman* [2005] NSWSC 934 where the senior member of a SMSF died and instead of paying out his superannuation benefits to his Estate for equal distribution between his daughter and son – his daughter, who was the remaining member and Trustee of the Fund, refused and held the Funds back. The argument was that Ervin Katz, the father, had put in place a binding death benefit nomination for a distribution of his superannuation benefits to his estate. That was what he desired. But the NSW Supreme Court held that the death benefit nomination that was made was non-binding as it had not been approved by the Trustee – a crucial procedural step that was missed by the Trustee and advisers to the Fund. As such the remaining Trustee was authorised to make the payment to herself.

Interestingly, the son's counsel argued that the daughter - Linda Grossman - was not validly appointed as Trustee – but the Court reviewed the trust deed and relevant documentation and declared her to be a validly appointed and continuing Trustee. So when she paid all of her father's superannuation benefits to herself, the Court held that she had the absolute right – BECAUSE the advisers to the Fund did not put in place the appropriate documentation.

3.3 Big Strategy Hint: Learn from the Commissioner of Taxation

In 1999, the Commissioner of Taxation (Commissioner) became the Regulator for SMSFs and for many advisers the thought was "it is like using a sledgehammer to crack a walnut". Sorry to hark back to history but I commenced advising on SMSFs in 1993, so to me the ebbs and flows of history and the impact of strategies are crucial in a real un-derstanding of SMSF strategy, and the Commissioner has been a great friend of SMSFs. Particularly with all the guidelines, Trustee videos, in-depth rulings and determinations he publishes on a consistent basis.

For us superannuation and SMSF tax nerds, this is a great tool because the ATO rulings provide all the heavy lifting, research and analysis on a wide range of issues, like what assets can be contributed into a SMSF by a member. Therefore, if I lift some quoted passages from rulings and guidelines from the Commissioner throughout the *The Guru's Guide to SMSFs* then you know it is straight from the horse's mouth – *so to speak*. You know for sure how the Commissioner is thinking and that it is not just my thoughts.

And I am going to let you in on a little secret - some of my best strategies and ideas come from the Commissioner's rulings. For example, business real property is a big deal for SMSFs particularly as the in-house assets test that we saw in Holloway's case limits the use of Fund assets by a related party – with the exception of business real property. Further, the Trustee of a Fund cannot acquire an asset from a member or related party such as a family trust or relative. One exception is business real property provided market value consideration is used. In a similar vein, the Trustee cannot lend or lease an asset to a member or related party except for – you guessed it, business real property. So the question of what is business real property is a BIG deal. And of course, the Commissioner has published a super ruling on the subject – SMSFR2009/1. Thank-you Commissioner.

If you were doing in-depth SMSF specialist training with me, we would immerse ourselves in this ruling for a good couple of hours but we are here to learn about strategy so I am going to give you one of the best examples from the ruling. Personally, I find the examples from the Commissioner a great way to see his thoughts applied in practise, particularly at the leading edge. Take the following examples and throw them around in your mind:

Bed and breakfast - case 1 - No Business

The Ngo family own their large family home. During the school holidays, they allow guests to stay on a bed and breakfast basis. Three of the bedrooms are used for guests, while the members of the family use the remaining rooms.

The scale of this operation is not sufficient to establish the existence of a business. The property is therefore not business real property of any entity.

Bed and breakfast - case 2 - Business

Dean Lamont owns a house with 5 bedrooms and 2 living areas. He uses one of the bedrooms himself. The other four bedrooms are let year-round as part of a bed and breakfast business. One living area is set aside for the exclusive use of guests. Breakfast is included in the room cost and other meals are available by arrangement.

Dean advertises his rooms with Worldwide B&B Internet bookings agency. Dean has a business plan, pays tax, and has three permanent part time employees. The business has operated since Dean acquired the house 17 years ago.

In this case, a business is being carried on. Dean's non-business use of the property is incidental and relevant to that business. Accordingly, the property is used wholly and exclusively in the business and is business real property.

So where does AirBnB sit in this equation? Where is the dividing line between Dean and the NGO example for a SMSF to hold business real property where the members may live in the property or on the other side it breaches the in-house assets test?

CHAPTER FOUR

What is a SMSF and a Foreign SMSF?

4.1 **POP Quiz**

What am I doing in the workshop above?

Go to the end of this chapter to find the answer – most SMSF advisers would have an idea but by the end of this book, most of you will - *I promise*. A simple strategy, but very effective given the recent changes that limit transfer amounts from a member's accumulation account to their pension account (the $1.6M Transfer Balance Cap which we will discuss more later).

4.2 **What is a SMSF?**

"A self-managed superannuation fund (SMSF) is a superannuation fund created for the purpose of fulfilling the long-term retirement, estate planning and possible incapacity needs of the members of the Fund and their family." Grant Abbott

A Trustee of a superannuation fund, *excluding a SMSF*, must be licensed, and where a Trustee is not licensed, they will be subject to a fine and possibly a term of imprisonment for no more than two years[2]. So it is pretty important to get a good grip of what is and is not a SMSF. The last thing you want is to be in a SMSF that it not a SMSF and be faced with potential legal challenges.

We will also see later in the book – for taxation purposes – the difference between an Australian SMSF and a Foreign SMSF. If you get it wrong - it could be the end.

4.3 **The Seven SMSF Conditions**

Section 17A of SISA provides important rules on what is a SMSF as well as some exceptions to the broad rules. A summary of the key requirements are discussed below.

---

2 Section 29J of SISA

Condition 1: The Fund must be a Regulated Super Fund with a Trustee

The Fund must be a regulated superannuation fund requiring there to be a Trustee, and where the Trustees of the Fund are individuals, the sole or primary purpose is to pay old age pensions[3]. Where the Trustee is a company, the Trustee may pay a lump sum or pensions to members of the Fund. The Trustee may also use the Fund for estate planning purposes, as well as providing incapacity and other benefits allowed, under the superannuation laws to members of the Fund. We will see this later when we get to the necessity of having a company acting as Trustee of the Fund rather than individuals. It might be cheaper to run as individuals at the outset, but if you can't pay a lump sum when you are retired (note the difference in the definitions of an individual Trustee and a Corporate Trustee, as defined in the Commonwealth Constitution) – you are giving up a lot of flexibility and SMSFs should never be limited.

Warning – Individual Trustees and the new Pension Limit Rules

With the introduction of the $1.6M Pension Transfer Balance Limit, there is a big problem with individual Trustees. Once this limit is reached any excess superannuation may be required to leave the Fund's accumulation account as a lump sum as it cannot continue to be held in the member's accumulation account. Why? Because under section 19 of SISA a super fund with individual Trustees must be for the purpose of providing old age pensions – not lump sums. In contrast a corporate Trustee may pay lump sums and pensions.

Condition 2: Four Members Only

Don't breach this one at any time or you lose your SMSF status and the penalties for a non-complying SMSF are horrendous – up to 45% of the value of the Fund's assets and that is without any penalty tax.

---

3 As it is defined in Section 19 of SISA

As an aside to this, be careful who takes up the position of member in the Fund. I am all for family members, but if there is a relationship split then that's where the fun starts. This is precisely why Funds should be Bloodline Family SMSFs that only allow the bloodline into the SMSF, otherwise if there is a divorce or split, then the drama and expensive legal bills will start.

Condition 3: Trustees must be Members

If the Trustees of the Fund are individuals then, subject to the exceptions considered below, all Trustees must be members of the Fund and if the Trustee of the Fund is a company, all directors must be members of the Fund.

Condition 4: All Members must be Trustees

A member of the Fund must be a Trustee, a director of a corporate Trustee or the member has a replacement Trustee where they cannot be a Trustee or director due to legal incapacity such as dementia or they are under the age of 18.

Condition 5: No Employees

No member can be an employee of another member unless they are related. There is an extended meaning of employee that includes related entities and groups so be careful[4].

Condition 6: Trustee not to Profit from the Fund

No Trustee or director of the corporate Trustee can receive any remuneration from the Fund for any services or duties performed as Trustee or by the director in relation to the Fund. However, if the Trustee provides similar services to the market and they operate on an arm's length basis then it is possible to charge the Trustee. For example, an accountancy firm may be able to maintain a Fund for compliance and taxation purposes and then charge a market based fee for the service. It is best to not try and push this rule as it is very easy for the ATO to

---

4 Section 17A(6) of SISA

pick related party service fees on audit and then the Trustee has to explain a lot for a little reward. The Fund also gets a tax deduction at a 15% tax rate while transferring fee income to the business which is taxed at higher rates, which does not really make sense.

Condition 7: Single Member Funds

Where the Fund is a single member SMSF, trust law does not recognise a trust being created where the sole beneficiary of the trust is also the Trustee. The SMSF laws require any individual Trustee of a single member SMSF to appoint a further Trustee provided they are not an employee of the member/Trustee. Where there is a company Trustee, the member can either be the sole director of the company Trustee or appoint a further non-employee director[5].

4.4 **What is not a SMSF? - Trouble**

The following are some examples of what are not SMSFs:

- A superannuation fund that is not a regulated superannuation Fund. This may arise where the Fund has individual Trustees and does not pay age pensions, but pays lump sums, or uses the Fund for estate planning or incapacity benefit purposes. Again a corporate Trustee for the SMSF is the best strategic move.

- A superannuation fund that has no Trustee. This may arise where the Trustees of the Fund pass away at the same time and there is no automatic power of appointment of the executor to Trusteeship. Apart from losing SMSF status, the Fund would lose its concessional tax status, which may be costly in the terms

---

5 Section 17A(2) and please note that any deeds that I have authored the question is - if a separate Trustee comes in for single members – should they have a vote? After all they really are there only there to help out for trust law purposes. So generally most deeds provide a proportional voting rule which would see the two Trustees or directors of the company Trustee share the votes at any meeting – effectively providing each with 50% of the vote. This rule may be amended under the SMSF deeds I have written to only allow the member/Trustee or the member/director to hold any voting power at a Trustee or director's meeting.

of the payment of estate planning benefits. This is another reason to utilise a special purpose SMSF Trustee company as corporate Trustee of the SMSF.

- Where the Trustee of a Fund introduces or accepts a new member into the SMSF and this takes membership to above five or more members. The SMSF instantly loses its SMSF status and with no licence – this is a problem.

O━━ Golden Key

If the Trustee breaches one of the SMSF definitional requirements above (except for the new member rule immediately above), the Trustee generally has six months grace to correct the rule and maintain their SMSF status.

4.5 Important Exceptions to the SMSF Rule – Things you can do outside the Four Member Rule

The key rule for a SMSF is that there are no more than four members and that all members are Trustees and that all Trustees are members. However, where a member loses their mental capacity, they cannot be a Trustee or director of the Fund's corporate Trustee so a replacement Trustee or director needs to be appointed.

a) But do you really want to be a Replacement Trustee/Director?

Being a Trustee and not being a Member means all downside and no upside. If the Trustee gets sued, then the Trustee standing in on behalf of the members, is then in the firing line. What do you think happens if the Trustee of the Fund enters into a building contract for a property on a block of land that it owns and then a visitor enters the premises, falls over and sues the Trustee? Well the Trustee is up for an expensive legal claim.

Ideally the Trustee of the Fund is a director of a Corporate Trustee and is protected by the company veil. However, irrespective of a corporate Trustee, the individual Trustees of the Fund should have insurances, and not only for legal suits, but also for penalties and losses occurred through acting as Trustee of the Fund. To find some providers of Trustee insurances go to www.Ilovesmsf.com for links to the best insurers.

b) The Five Exceptions

There are a number of instances where a member of a Fund may have legal incapacity and cannot act as Trustee or director of the SMSFs company Trustee including loss of mental capacity, being a minor or simply not financially suitable. In addition where a member dies, there needs to be a mechanism for the deceased member's executor to look after the distribution of the member's benefits.

The definition of a SMSF allows the Trustee, *where the trust deed or company constitution provides*, to appoint another person as a replacement Trustee or, where the Trustee is a corporate Trustee, the directors may appoint a director as a replacement director in the following special circumstances[6]:

1. Where a member dies, the legal personal representative may be appointed as a Trustee or director of the Fund's corporate Trustee but only from such time as the member dies until death benefits commence to be paid.

2. Where the member is under a legal disability, the legal personal representative may become a replacement Trustee on the member's behalf.

3. At any time a member's legal personal representative may be appointed as Trustee or director of the Fund's corporate Trustee, where the legal personal representative holds the member's enduring power of attorney. It is important to understand that

6 Section 17A(3) SISA

a person with an enduring power of attorney cannot force their way onto a board of directors or Trustee. Any such appointment must be specifically catered for in the memorandum and articles of association of any corporate Trustee, or in the trust deed of the Fund, where the Trustees of the Fund are individuals. Ensure that the power of attorney is an enduring power and not a general power of attorney.

4. If a child under the age of 18 is a member and does not have a legal personal representative, then the child's parent or guardian may be appointed as a Trustee.

5. The Commissioner of Taxation may appoint an acting Trustee under s134 of SISA where the Commissioner has removed or suspended the Trustee in order to address one or more compliance problems with the Fund. Let's hope this does not happen to you or anyone you know.

c) Appointment problems

First and foremost, the above replacement Trustees can only be appointed where the Fund's trust deed specifically authorises the appointment. This is also the case where a corporate Trustee is the Trustee of the Fund — the company's constitution must allow an appointment of a director in the above special circumstance.

In addition, if the deed allows the Trustees to appoint a new Trustee or if the Trustee company constitution authorises the appointment of a new director, it does not necessarily mean that the appointment is automatic. For example, imagine where we have a Family SMSF with one elderly parent who becomes legally incapacitated with dementia and his second spouse and two children from his first marriage are also members of the Fund. The family's SMSF trust deed allows the incapacitated parent to resign as Trustee, however, with no automatic appointment of the other parent as Trustee, the remaining Trustees will need to vote on whether the incapacitated member's spouse can be a replacement Trustee. If the Fund has one vote per Trustee, then the children may block the spouse becoming the replacement Trustee, and in fact, can remove the member with dementia as a member and may even remove the second spouse as member of the Fund.

Even then, unless special voting provisions have been written into the deed to cover a Trustee acting on behalf of two members, the non-in-capacitated member and the two children will have one vote each. Both parents would be out-voted by the children despite their small superannuation interests in the Fund.

STRATEGY **Get a Good SMSF Deed**

A good SMSF trust deed must have an automatic power of appointment for replacement and additional Trustees — likewise with a special purpose SMSF corporate Trustee. Quite apart from these provisions, the trust deeds and special purpose corporate Trustees that I have written, also ensure that the only Trustee or director of the Fund's corporate Trustee, can vote on the deceased or incapacitated member's behalf is the member's legal personal represen-tative, acting as a replacement.

For providers of the deeds and specialist SMSF documentation that I have authored in line with the strategies contained in "The Guru's Guide to SMSFs" and my mentorship programs go to www.Ilovesmsf. com

4.6 **Australian and Foreign SMSFs**

Only a resident regulated superannuation Fund can be a complying SMSF and get the wide range of tax concessions available to Trustees and members of the Fund. A resident regulated superannuation fund is only an "Australian superannuation fund for the purposes of the ITAA 1997."

The income tax laws states that a superannuation fund is an Australian superannuation fund[7] at a time, and for the income year in which that time occurs, if:

1. the Fund was established in Australia, or any asset of the Fund is situated in Australia at that time. This condition will apply to all SMSFs as they are uniquely limited to Australia.

2. at that time, the central management and control of the Fund is ordinarily in Australia and the law states that[8] "to avoid doubt, the central management and control of a superannuation Fund is ordinarily in Australia at a time even if that central management and control is temporarily outside Australia for a period of not more than 2 years."

STRATEGY **How to meet central management and control requirements when a non-resident**

An executive on temporary secondment may depart Australia and become a non-resident and maintain central management if the secondment is not permanent and to be safe – the investments and investment strategy of the Fund is conducted when the Trustee is back in Australia. If the secondment is permanent, then the Trustee can create a replacement Trustee who holds the Trustee's enduring power of attorney. This is not a bad solution and fits in with the exceptions for SMSF Trustees above – however, note that the replacement Trustee will control the Fund – do you want that? Another solution is to create a small super Fund which is run by a professional Australian Trustee – it is not a SMSF but known as a small APRA Fund. It enables investment choice but solves this central management and control issue. At that time the Fund, in terms of member contributions, has either:

---

7 Section 295-95(2) of the ITAA 1997. For a literal reading of s 295-95(2) it appears that to be an Australian superannuation fund, the conditions in subsection (2) need to be met only at a particular time for the superannuation fund to be considered an Australian superannuation Fund for the year of income. This has been confirmed in the Commissioner's SMSF ruling - Taxation Ruling – TR 2008/9 on the meaning of 'Australian superannuation fund' in subsection 295-95(2) of the ITAA 1997.
8 Section 295-95(4).

i) not received any contributions on behalf of a non-resident member during the current year of income; or

ii) contributions have been made on behalf of a non-resident member but at that time at least 50% of the total market value of the Fund's assets attributable to superannuation interests held by contributing members, is attributable to superannuation interests held by contributing members, who are Australian residents.

If the only members of the Fund are pension members, who do not contribute, then only ii) above is important.

4.7 SMSF Strategy — Member and Trustee moving Overseas

Trustees Note: This is where we start to get into the heavy stuff. So for Trustees who are not going to live overseas feel free to skip this section but know that it is here.

Adviser Question: We are just confirming our discussion at your SMSF training course about being able to appoint a person as a member's enduring power of attorney to act as Trustee of a Fund. This is while the member is overseas, to satisfy the central management and control requirements where the two members/Trustees of a SMSF are moving overseas, and have no intention of returning to Australia for three to four years.

Grant's Strategy Response

The Commissioner's ruling on Australian superannuation funds, TR 2008/9, provides a detailed analysis of what is central management and control in the context of a superannuation Fund. It borrows heavily from key taxation cases on central management and control, including *Egyptian Delta Land and Investment Company Ltd v Todd* [1929] AC 1, *Koitaki Para Rubber Estates Ltd v FCT* (1941) 64 CLR 241; (1941) 6 ATD 82, *Esquire Nominees Ltd v FC of T (Esquire Nominees)* (1973) 129 CLR 177; 72 ATC 4076; (1972) 3 ATR 105.

At para 100–102 of TR 2008/9, the Commissioner considers what actions are crucial to central management and control. He states as follows:

"Like companies, determining the central management and control of a superannuation Fund involves a focus on the who, when and where of the strategic and high level decision making of the Fund.

In the context of the operations of a superannuation Fund, the strategic and high level decision making of the Fund includes the performance of the following duties and activities:

- *formulating the investment strategy for the Fund*

- *reviewing and updating or altering the investment strategy of the Fund as well as monitoring and reviewing the performance of the Fund's investments*

- *if the Fund has reserves — the formulation of a strategy for their prudential management, and*

- *determining how the assets of the Fund are used to Fund member benefits, for example the decision to segregate certain Fund assets to support superannuation income stream benefits.*

In the majority of cases, the other principal areas of operation of a superannuation Fund, such as the acceptance of contributions, the actual investment of the Fund's assets, the fulfillment of administrative duties and the preservation, payment and portability of benefits are not of a strategic or high level nature to constitute central management and control. Rather these activities form part of the day-to-day or productive side of the operations of a superannuation Fund."

Key examples from the Commissioner's ruling relevant and strategically useful to this particular client case study is as follows:

"Example 5(a) — person other than Trustee exercising central management and control whilst the Trustees are overseas

Henry and Eleanor are the Trustees of their SMSF, the 'Plantagenet Family Superannuation Fund' which was established in Australia. The members of the Plantagenet Family Superannuation Fund are Henry and Eleanor.

On 29 September 2009, Henry and Eleanor travel to France to take up management of Eleanor's family business interests in Europe. They do not have an expected return date although they do intend to return to Australia at some point in the future. They take their children with them to France, and they move into Eleanor's family home. The children are enrolled in local schools in France. Henry and Eleanor return to Australia permanently on 22 September 2011.

Prior to moving overseas, Henry and Eleanor arrange for Richard to perform the duties and activities that constitute the central management and control of the Fund. Such activities include reviewing and monitoring the performance of the Fund's investments, re-balancing the investment portfolio and altering the Fund's investment strategy. During Henry and Eleanor's absence from Australia, Richard undertakes these activities without reference to Henry and Eleanor. Furthermore, Henry and Eleanor did not participate in any of these high level decision making activities whilst overseas.

In these circumstances, the central management and control of the Plantagenet Family Superannuation Fund continues to be ordinarily in Australia (by virtue of Richard exercising the central management and control in Australia) within the meaning of paragraph 295-95(2)(b) of the ITAA 1997 at all times during Henry and Eleanor's absence from Australia. At no stage do Henry and Eleanor participate in the central management and control of the Fund during their absence from Australia."

STRATEGY The Guru's Enduring Power of Attorney
Strategy for Non-Residents

An alternative to the ATO strategy above is also provided by s17A of SISA that allows the Trustee of a SMSF, to appoint a person with a member's enduring power of attorney, as Trustee of the Fund. Provided the appointed person exercises central management and control of the Fund in Australia, while acting as the member's replacement Trustee, then central management and control should be held to ordinarily reside in Australia. Importantly the member overseas may not indirectly control the replacement Trustee.

In and Out of Australia

"ATO Ruling: Example 6 — central management and control of the Fund is 'ordinarily' in Australia

Simon and his wife Donna are the Trustees and members of their SMSF which was established in Australia. They have an established home in Australia but also decide to establish a second home in an overseas country. The couple and their family spend approximately 6 months at the overseas home and the rest of the year at the Australian home. The majority of Trustee meetings are held in Australia at which the high level decisions in respect of the Fund are made. The central management and control of the Fund is only occasionally exercised in the overseas country.

In this situation, the central management and control of the Fund is regularly, usually or customarily exercised in Australia and is only being casually or intermittently exercised overseas. Therefore, the central management and control of the Fund is 'ordinarily' in Australia within the meaning of paragraph 295-95(2)(b) of the ITAA 1997 at all times."

Grant's Comment

This is an important declaration by the Commissioner and may be used in conjunction with The Commissioner's example 5(a) above. If the non-resident members want to have a say in the key decision-making of the Fund, they should not impede or infringe upon the person appointed with central management and control powers but may have their say on the Fund's investment strategy when they travel back to Australia. This is a crucial time for decision-making and investment strategy updates for the Fund.

4.8 Taxation of a Foreign SMSF – an Absolute Disaster

Adviser question

The Commissioner has ruled that one of our clients has become a foreign superannuation Fund under the ITAA 1997. What does this mean in terms of taxation of the Trustee of the Fund?

Grant's Strategic Response

First off I would challenge the ATO ruling because your client may be in big trouble. Let's start to work away through the technical side of the Commissioner's ruling to see if the Fund is a foreign superannuation Fund.

Section 995-1(1) of ITAA 1997 provides the following definition for a foreign superannuation Fund:

Foreign superannuation Fund means:

(a) a superannuation Fund is a **foreign superannuation Fund** at a time if the Fund is not an Australian superannuation Fund at that time; and

(b) a superannuation Fund is a **foreign superannuation Fund** for an income year if the Fund is not an Australian superannuation Fund for the income year.

The definition of an Australian superannuation Fund is found at s 295-95(2) and has been considered in detail above. As the Commissioner has ruled that the Fund is a foreign superannuation Fund then it is to be taxed as a non-complying superannuation Fund at a rate of 45% on the Fund's taxable income — s 26(2) of the *Income Tax Rates Act 1986*.

Division 295 of Pt 3-30 of ITAA 1997, makes important modifications for the taxation of non-complying superannuation Funds, including:

(1) **Capital gains tax not the primary code** - section 295-85 provides that where any asset is sold by the Trustee of a *complying superannuation Fund*, with the exclusion of currency gains and gains made on the disposal of a security, capital gains tax is to apply before the other provisions of the ITAA 1997. For example, this would mean that a Trustee of a complying superannuation Fund that engages in property development would obtain a 33.33% discount on any realised capital gain. A foreign superannuation Fund is taxed as an ordinary taxpayer and capital gains tax is not the primary code in relation to the disposal of an asset by the Trustee.

(2) **Deductions relating to obtaining contributions** - section 295-95(1) of ITAA 1997 provides that the Trustee of a foreign superannuation Fund cannot claim a deduction in relation to expenses incurred in obtaining contributions. As such part of any audit/administration fees that relate to obtaining contributions is non-deductible.

(3) **Contributions to a foreign superannuation Fund** - section 295-160, item 2 provides that a foreign superannuation Fund is to bring to account contributions made by another person (such as an employer or spouse) into the Fund where the member is a resident of Australia only, but is to exclude a temporary resident.

(4) **Non-exemption for pension assets** - section 295-385 and s 295-390 provide an exemption for complying superannuation Funds for income and capital gains earned in relation to pension assets held by the Trustee of a superannuation Fund. A foreign superannuation Fund is not exempt on earnings or gains from its current segregated or any pension assets.

(5) **Deductions for insurance premiums** - only complying super-annuation Funds can claim a deduction for premiums paid to a life insurance company for the provision of life insurance.

Switching from a foreign superannuation Fund to an Australian SMSF

Section 295-330 of the ITAA 1997 provides that where a foreign super-annuation Fund becomes a complying SMSF, the Trustee of the Fund is required to bring to account as assessable income, the market value of the assets in the income year when the Fund changed to a complying superannuation Fund. This income is to be included in the following year's income tax return.

Summary

Don't become a non-complying SMSF under any circumstances and in particular steer clear of being a foreign super Fund. I suggest that your client gets good tax counsel to negotiate with the Commissioner of Taxation. If you are seeking a specialist in this area of tax negotiations go to TGA Legal – www.tgalegal.com.au

CHAPTER FIVE

The New SMSF – A Strategic Revolution

"The current super laws provide the tools to create an ideal SMSF — a Fund that provides the desired lifestyle income for a member at any time, while creating a tax effective environment to pass on wealth to the next generation."

5.1 Introduction to SMSF Version 2.0

By now you should have recognised that my focus with a SMSF is always on strategy which you would have seen from the earlier chapters in *The Guru's Guide to SMSFs*. If you have your own SMSF, then no doubt you have a strong goal on where you want to head. From all my work with Trustees, it is generally to maximise a secure, safe and consistent income stream in retirement and, if possible, pass as much on at death.

To date, establishing and maintaining a SMSF has been a simple, in fact very simple, four step process:

(1) Set up the SMSF;

(2) Contribute;

(3) Invest; and

(4) Pay a pension.

Now when a member got to the pension stage of the Fund – apart from changing investment strategies, that member's pension account paid until the member ran out of Funds or died. It was a real set and forget Fund which meant that "SMSFs for Beginners" could be written in a few pages and there would hardly be a need for a comprehensive book like *The Guru's Guide to SMSFs*. It is also limited as to the differences between a retail or industry super fund compared to a SMSF.

5.2 No More Set and Forget –Thanks Treasurer Morrison

Thanks to Treasurer Scott Morrison in the 2016 Budget, things have changed quite dramatically for many current and future SMSFs. At first glance I wondered, like so many others, why they were attacking SMSFs but it dawned on me that SMSFs do not add to the Budget. They actually cost the Government money in the form of refunds on imputation credits. And with the Budgets these days in perennial deficits, expect more and more gouging into SMSF tax benefits.

Unfortunately, this brings a lot more complexity and increases the need for careful, calculated strategic advice. The changes that have been implemented appear small but they really change the composition and direction of SMSFs – so much so that I am calling them SMSF Version 2.0. Let's look at the changes and what the new SMSF Version 2.0 looks like now.

5.3 SMSF with Pension accounts of more than $1.6 million

From July 2017, any member of a SMSF or superannuation fund will only be able to set up a pension account with $1.6M. This is referred to as the member's Transfer Balance Cap (TBC). In the case where the Trustee of the fund is a company, any excess should remain in the accumulation account or can be withdrawn as a lump sum payment. Where the Trustee of the fund is an individual, any excess will be required to be withdrawn from super as it is not being used for the purposes of the payment of old age pensions (as defined in s19 of the SISA 93).

However, if a member commences a pension with more than their TBC, the Commissioner of Taxation will notify them that they need to commute the excess amount. A commutation is the conversion of a pension to a lump sum. For example, if a member commenced a pension with $2M on 1 December 2017 the Commissioner will notify the member to reduce their balance to $1.6M by withdrawing $400,000 from the pension account as a lump sum – known as a commutation.

The lump sum withdrawal can be by way of a roll back of the excess part of the pension to the accumulation account for the member of the SMSF (if the Trustee is a company) or withdrawn as a lump sum. Apart from tax penalties, if the excess pension is not commuted within the time frame provided by the Commissioner, then there is a loss of the Fund's tax exemption.

Pension Members pre-July 2017 treated unfairly?
Pension members who have balances over the $1.6M TBC at 30 June 2017 were forced to reduce their pension account balances to their TBC. If not then the Commissioner will force a commutation of the excess.

However, for TBC pensions (those that are TBC tested and approved), post June 2017 we know that future growth is not tested for TBC again. This means that on the one hand a TBC pension of $1.6M that commenced in July 2017 and grows, thanks to good investments and minimum income withdrawals to $4M in December 2019 will not breach their TBC again. But a pension member that started with $1.6M in 2014 and grew to $4M in July 2017, with the exact same investment and income strategy, will have an excess of $2.4M to commute. For the life of me this seems unfair but the law is the law.

Dealing with a Pension over TBC of $1.6M

The question is what should a pension member with assets over $1.6M do if they are over that balance at 30 June 2017? From the ATO statistics, there are tens of thousands of SMSF members impacted.

Let's look at Gary Smith, aged 64 who has $2M in his account based pension on 1 July 2017. This means he has an excess of $400,000 – so far so good. Gary decides to commute the $400K, that is, turn it into a lump sum and transfer, or what I call roll back the pension to the accumulation side of his Fund. This is one of the allowed commutation strategies, in addition, to the withdrawal of the excess from super Fund completely.

It is important that we look at the consequences of the roll back to the accumulation account. These are discussed below.

1. The Bad:

- *Loss of tax exempt status:* Income and capital gains used to support a private pension, no matter what amount or size, are all exempt from tax. However income and capital gains (which are entitled to a 33 1/3% discount if the asset is held for more than a year) in a member's accumulation account are subject to tax at a rate of 15%.

- *No more non-concessional contributions:* Where a member of a super fund has a total superannuation balance of $1.6M, which includes the value of their pension and accumulation accounts in any super fund including a SMSF, they are not able to make a non-concessional contribution.

- *Loss of Segregation of Pension Assets:* Remember my Dad's story about transferring his Computershare stocks from the accumulation side of the fund to the pension side? Because he was running a segregated investment strategy for the pension when the shares were sold, it was tax free. But for any member that has reached a total super balance of $1.6M in aggregate over their superannuation accounts and they have a pension account, then the Trustee of the Fund cannot segregate pension assets. They have to use a proportional exemption which can make a significant difference, particularly for larger funds with sizable accumulation and pension accounts.

2. The Good:

- *No drawdown:* One of the requirements of a pension is that a minimum amount must be drawn down from the pension account each year. For a pension member under age 65, the minimum is 4% so for Gary that would have been $80,000 if his pension balance was $2M on 1 July 2016.

So what should Gary do? Considering the above points, Gary should transfer the $400k back into his accumulation account. Once rolled back, there is no requirement for him to draw down on this amount although any income and capital gains will be taxed within the Fund. Importantly if Gary withdraws a lump sum from his accumulation account, it will be tax free in his hands as lump sums and pensions for a member of a SMSF are tax free once they are over age 60.

From 1 July 2017, Gary will be required to draw down 4% x $1.6M = $64K for the 2017-2018 income year. as his continuing pension. There are a couple of other things to note for Gary. Firstly, as noted above Gary will not be able to make any further contributions into superannuation as he has reached his $1.6M total superannuation balance. Secondly, and I think strategically, if his pension account balance grows to $2.1M by 1 July 2018, good on Gary as it will not be tested again.

STRATEGY   **SMSF Version 2.0**

If Gary's pension account balance provides him with enough income to live on each and every year, then what is the purpose of his accumulation account?

This question has never been asked before because the old rules simply required the set and forget pension. So Gary would draw upon the pension as required, at the very least the minimum, and if anything was left over when he passed away it would be distributed according to any binding nomination or at the Trustee's discretion as we saw in Katz's case.

But thanks to the Morrison changes - the excess accumulation account, which may never be drawn upon in Gary's life, should be held over for Estate Planning purposes – to pass onto his spouse, children, financial dependants or legal estate for distribution by his Executor. So now we have a SMSF which is purpose built for separate retirement income and estate planning strategies – SMSF Version 2.0.

5.4 SMSF Accounts currently in Accumulation

To reiterate, under current law a member of a superannuation fund will not be able to commence a pension account with a balance of more than $1.6M. Like Gary above, if a SMSF member commences a pension, or one or more pensions, with total account balances of no more than $1.6M, then any increase in the pension balance through investment earnings is not tested again. Any amount greater than the $1.6M will be left in the member's accumulation account and subject to the 15% tax but with no drawdown requirements.

5.5 What does it mean for SMSF Excess Accumulation members?

Up until 2017, subject to the contribution and borrowing laws, the smarter SMSF members sought to maximise the amount of assets in their Fund, particularly the closer they were to retirement. This saw, for example, people transferring buildings they owned into their SMSF, using a mix of contributions and borrowings so that income received on the building was ultimately tax free when it became part of the member's pension. This is a great strategy but for expensive commercial real estate – it now creates a problem. Do we want the excess inside of the Fund in an accumulation account or perhaps in a Family Trust so that there is a joint venture with the member's SMSF? Only modelling and a strategic adviser can solve that problem and long term it will have, amongst others, the following impacts:

- Ongoing tax in the Fund in the accumulation account versus using tax streaming and splitting rules within a trust for distributions to other members of a family;

- Estate planning as any sale or transfer in-specie of the property on the death of the member (if necessary) will be subject to tax as a disposal by the Trustee of the Fund on the accumulation side of the Fund compared to no disposal in a Family Trust;

- If the proceeds on death are taxable components within the Fund then they are taxed at 17.5% in the hands of a non tax dependant – an adult child.

💡 **Grant's Tip**

As can be seen, there is a lot going on with the introduction of the TBC. Tax and superannuation planning requires ongoing reviews and for many, a solid restructuring. The previous desire to put as much as possible in the tax advantaged superannuation environment (in particular for high income earners and those with high value assets which could be transferred into a SMSF) is now lessened and far more complicated. The use of a Family Trust may now become more advantageous - with good advice!

This also applies for Gary. Is he better off transferring the excess $400,000 back into the accumulation side of his SMSF or perhaps take it out and direct it into a Family Trust? Again, good tax, estate planning and superannuation modelling and advice is crucial when dealing with SMSF Version 2.0

5.6 Some Important SMSF Strategic Issues

I love this sort of strategic work and as you can see there are no more set and forget strategies. This is great work for strategic SMSF advisers and also Trustees that can tailor the Fund to suit their family's circumstances. With the next generation of wealth coming through, and some with significant superannuation balances (courtesy of a lifetime of SG contributions), the TBC issue will be a strategic issue for decades to come. In fact, how will you be impacted?

So here are some high-level issues that I see at this stage:

1. Get a Good SMSF and Tax Adviser

By now you would have realised, whether a potential SMSF member, existing SMSF member or a professional working in this field, that strategy is fundamental to a great, long lasting and living SMSF. More importantly, the TBC rules, briefly discussed above, have made a significant impact on tax and superannuation strategy PLUS they have a big impact on Estate Planning. My word of advice – get a great SMSF and Tax adviser.

2. "Real time" Member Accounts

When establishing a pension, the Trustee of the Fund must ensure that they have accurate member accounts to deliver member pension account figures to the ATO, and ensuring that the member's TBC is not breached. It is a necessity that real time member accounts using online SMSF accounting systems with feeds into various investment databases become the norm for SMSF Trustees and not the exception.

3. Trust Deed and Compliance Documentation

We are about to look at the importance of the Trust Deed of the Fund and also its Governing Rules which include the documentation around commencing any pension, commuting any pension, making under-lying investments, creating a SMSF Will or Binding Death Benefit Nomination and so much more. We saw in Chapter 3 - the Death Benefit Flow Chart all of the key steps that a Trustee and more importantly, their adviser must implement for a successful death benefit payout. The sets of steps for Gary Smith with his $2M pension is just as complex and more vital, given the penalties that may apply.

O━━╤ **Key Point**

It is highly recommended that the Trust Deed for Gary's Fund be reviewed and probably, given the breadth of changes to the superannuation laws, be upgraded. For example, as we discussed in Chapter 3, the possible disaster if the Fund's trust deed only allowed the payment of pensions and not lump sums. What would Gary do on 1 July 2017 with the excess, and how would this restrictive term in the trust deed impact the strategies we have reviewed above?

4. Not just a SMSF anymore

I used to believe that a SMSF could be used for almost everything, except running a business or dealing with related parties. For many who listened to me, they structured, built and rebuilt their wealth into SMSFs and have benefited to a huge extent. However, the limitation of pension accounts to $1.6M for existing SMSF members as at 30 June 2017 and for the acquisition of future pensions, means that SMSFs are not what they once were.

SMSF Version 2.0 is a SMSF that has one or more of the following characteristics:

a) It is a Family SMSF with a strong eye on longevity and the passing of wealth from one generation to another;

b) There are specific SMSF estate plans in place and preferably using a SMSF Will which incorporates Binding Directions to the Trustee as well as directions to build Testamentary Trusts for both dependants, non-dependants and others;

c) For small and medium businesses, SMSFs are an essential tool in the armoury of the business owner and their accountants. But by far, it is not the be all and end all. It has to be used with Family Trusts and companies.

d) The structure is flexible and enabling in terms of changes to the laws relating to companies, SMSFs or Family Trusts.

CHAPTER SIX

Setting up a SMSF from the Get Go

"A great deal of thought needs to go into a SMSF. Not only if it is right for a member or their family, but what are the long term aspirations and purposes of the Fund. They can be easy to set up but getting them right the first time will save a lot – a lot of trouble down the track."

6.1 **Introduction**

One of my most popular videos on YouTube is "How to Set up a SMSF" and although it goes for only two minutes, it covers the key steps necessary to establish a SMSF. It has more than 31,000 views. This chapter is designed to flesh out that video in detail and ensuring we build SMSF Version 2.0 from scratch and preferably, a Family SMSF.

 **SMSF Adviser Guide:** For accountants, financial planners, auditors and other SMSF professionals, I have included a comprehensive chart on the steps to setting up a SMSF for a client – ten of them with various sub-steps (27 in all) at the end of this chapter. It is vital to follow them in order and ensure that you have a good trust deed that builds SMSF Version 2.0 for your client.

6.2 **The Steps to Establishing a SMSF**

If you already have a SMSF then there is no need to go through these steps – or is there? In fact, I would advise you to go through each of these and check that when you set up your SMSF, all of these steps were completed. Failure to complete one of the steps, for example the Fund's investment strategy, can result in serious issues as we will see later in the chapter.

If you are looking to set up a SMSF, heed my advice and either:

a) **Get Professional Help** – the whole process can be completed in a short amount of time so that you carry your momentum for setting up a Fund into the investment process, which is the best part of a SMSF.

b) **Get a Good Online Automation SMSF Set Up Service** – there are a number of on-line providers that can help you set up a Fund but, as I have said on a number of occasions, it is better to get things sorted strategically from the get go – so seek professional help. Better still, make sure that they are using one of my latest SMSF deeds. I do not recommended going it alone.

The Steps to Set up a SMSF

Step One: Get a Trustee for the Fund – Corporate or Individuals Trustees? See my views on this issue later.

Step Two: *Get a strategic SMSF Trust Deed* – upgrade it regularly and if possible make it one that I have written. Personally, I advise annual upgrades given the constant changes. Most accountants can provide that as an inclusion in their service – it is cheaper and safer.

Step Three: Appoint an Accountant or Administrator, plus an Auditor, to complete the Fund's tax and compliance returns to lodge with the ATO. Register for an Australian Business Number and a Tax File Number.

Step Four: Accept Members to the Fund – consider whether you want to restrict future membership to bloodline.

Step Five: Establish a Bank Account or Cash Management Account.

Step Six: Establish an Investment Strategy for the Fund. This has to be done before any monies get transferred into the SMSF.

Step Seven: Accept Contributions and Roll Overs into the Fund on behalf of Members. See my comment below – this is easier said than done in many cases. Any existing insurances should be considered prior to completing this step (and in most cases, I would always recommended the use of a specialised adviser in this area).

Step Eight: Make Investments in the name of the Trustee of the Fund – the exciting part of the equation.

Step Nine: Put in place a Binding Death Benefit Nomination or SMSF Will regarding member benefit distributions in the event of death.

We saw the problem in the Katz case about legal challenge - so make sure this is completed very quickly after set up. Again, consider the use of life insurance in the Fund to provide meaningful death benefits to your spouse and children in the event that you pass away, or in the unlikely case that you and your partner pass away at the same time. The taxation laws provide great tax incentives for Trustees to provide life, total and permanent disability as well as sickness and accident insurance in the Fund.

Be Smart: Getting your Super Money to your SMSF

It is a lot of fun and liberating to set up your SMSF and finally take control and invest your super. But there is a big snag - you have to get your existing super out of your current retail or industry fund and into your new SMSF. It is not surprising that your existing super fund manager, who are making investment fees every day you stay with them, are extremely tardy when releasing or rolling over your super. So my advice is be aggressive. Ring them daily to see when your super will be rolled over. There was a case - *Dunstone v Irving* [2000] VSC 488 where the Trustee of the Fund did not release a member's superannuation monies even though they had completed all forms correctly. As this was a breach of the Fund's trust deed, the member was able to recover damages for loss of investment earnings.

All nine steps above are crucial for a well-run Fund and more importantly, are necessary to meet the Fund's legal compliance requirements under SISA. Many of these important issues will be covered in other chapters of the *The Guru's Guide to SMSFs* but it is vital, crucial and absolutely important, to establish a strategic foundation for your SMSF being:

1) The SMSF Trust Deed (see paragraph 6.3 below)

2) The Right SMSF Trustee (see paragraph 6.5 below).

6.3 The SMSF Trust Deed – the Strategy Platform

"Why bother about a SMSF strategy when most SMSFs have a trust deed that pre-dates the July 2017 changes and as such won't let an adviser do even the most basic strategies? Perhaps if advisers and their clients could actually read and understand their SMSF trust deed, instead of getting confused with 100 word sentences, they may realise how few strategy options that they really have. A good deed should be a good read."

The trust deed of a SMSF is its strategic engine. It is the foundation for everything we do with the SMSF and a poor trust deed will let you down - each and every time. There are a lot of cases that prove this – so my advice is *pick a good one and know it well*.

But like motor vehicles there are many types of trust deeds — believe it or not there are more than 100 different types of SMSF trust deeds available. Strategically, the quality of offerings within this range of trust deeds can be compared to that in a range of motor vehicles from a fully-featured Aston Martin, to a twenty-year-old Holden Commodore. However, unlike motor vehicles where there can be thousands, if not hundreds of thousands of difference in price, the cost of most SMSF trust deeds fall within a small price range of each other, usually $200 - $400. The standard SMSF trust deed should cost no more than $500, irrespective of strategic quality.

It would come as a shock to most SMSF Trustees that a comprehensive strategic SMSF trust deed written specifically for the recent Morrison changes, may cost the same or even less than a trust deed that was written ten years ago (and which had been given cursory changes over time by a non-specialist SMSF lawyer). These newer trust deeds must allow specific tailoring to a family's unique circumstances by way of a wide range of in-built strategic options such as SMSF Wills, SMSF Life Wills and borrowing rules.

Apart from strategy there is also the big question of compliance. Trust deed compliance is one area that is generally overlooked by accountants, SMSF Trustees, financial planners and less experienced SMSF advisers. In that regard, s 55(1) of SISA provides that the Trustee of a superannuation fund and any other person who is professionally involved with the Fund, including the Fund's accountant, financial planner and auditor, must not contravene *any* rule contained in the trust deed or any other governing rules of the Fund.

Check the Deed along the Way

Simply, every action from receiving a contribution, allocating income to a member's account, acquiring or disposing of an asset, paying a pension and paying a death benefit plus any proposed strategy or investment strategy, must be checked against the Fund's trust deed and governing rules for compliance purposes. If the trust deed and governing rules are breached, even in a minor way, the SMSF may become a non-complying SMSF under s 42A(1) of SISA which costs a lot in penalty taxes.

To see this in practice, look no further than the *Dunstone v Irving* case which cost the Trustee over $300,000 in damages because they did not release a member's money when it was duly authorised under the deed! No kidding.

More importantly, for any person working with a SMSF Trustee, the cost of not having an up to date trust deed or reviewing the deed to see if an action or strategy can be undertaken can prove significant. If the Trustee suffers any loss they can recover damages against the adviser under s 55(3) of SISA.

STRATEGY Can a Trustee recover Investment Losses?

Years ago, when I was professionally advising, I looked into the case of a financial planner who recommended the Trustee of a SMSF to invest in an international managed fund for investment diversification purposes in accordance with the Fund's investment strategy under s 52B(2)(f) of SISA. The auditor, an experienced specialist SMSF auditor, reviewed the Fund's trust deed and ascertained that the Trustee of the Fund was authorised under the deed to only invest in Australian based assets. Since the time of the investment, the international managed funds had fallen in value significantly. The Trustee of the Fund was able to dispose of their international investment and recover, in full, all losses from the financial planner AND their dealer group as a consequence of the financial planner breaching the Fund's trust deed. Importantly, liability under s55(3) cannot be mitigated except where the investment is made in accordance with the Fund's trust deed and investment strategy.

6.4 The Three Must Know SMSF Trust Deed Rules

1) The trust deed rules cannot be broken

As noted above, the rules of the trust deed are paramount and cannot be broken — s 55(1) of SISA. Breach of the trust deed and governing rules of the Fund may result in the Fund becoming a non-complying SMSF. This also enables members of the Fund and the Trustee to sue for any loss occasioned as a consequence of the breach by one of the Fund's advisers, or by members if the Trustee breaches the provisions of the deed.

Section 55(1) has led to important strategies including the development of the SMSF Will. This is a legal document planning for the disposal of a member's superannuation benefits in the event of the member's death.

The SMSF Will is an attachment to the trust deed of the Fund thereby becoming part of the governing rules of the Fund. Once accepted by the Trustee as binding, then the member is afforded protection that their wishes for their superannuation benefits will be carried out. If the member dies and the remaining Trustee breaches the binding SMSF Will that has become part of the Fund's governing rules, s 202 of SISA may result in the Trustee, if convicted of an offence, subject to a maximum term of imprisonment for a period no longer than five years.

2) The SMSF is a trust and trust law applies

A SMSF is a trust which is essentially a legal structure that provides rules that are designed to look after beneficiaries, or in the case of a SMSF – its members. The first step is to appoint a Trustee who has to abide by the rules and the relevant Trustee laws in each Australian state. Once the Trustee is appointed a person settles property in the trust on behalf of the beneficiaries – for SMSFs that is a contribution. At law there has to be property in order for there to be a trust.

Given that a trust, and hence a SMSF is a complex legal structure it is important for a lawyer to have prepared a SMSF trust deed for a client, as well as any upgrade to the trust deed where the Trustee seeks to change the rules of the Fund (generally the old rules are replaced in their entirety with the new rules). As an aside I highly recommend that Trustees set in place an annual deed upgrade cycle to ensure that it covers latest changes and strategies. It is not an expensive process to complete annual upgrades rather than change every few years or not at all. But mark my words – do not leave upgrades too long!

In terms of legal protection for the SMSF trust, apart from SISA, there is a vast array of rules in the laws of equity that apply in relation to the Trustee's actions for investments in the Fund and dealing with beneficiaries (members) interests. In addition, all states of Australia have a Trustee Act, which regulates the actions of a Trustee. The laws of equity and the various state Trustee Acts require the Trustee to abide by the rules of the trust deed.

3) SISA compliance extends beyond the Trust Deed to the Governing Rules

Section 10(1) of SISA provides that the governing rules of a superannuation fund includes "all rules contained in the trust deed, any other document, legislation or any unwritten rules governing the establishment or operation of the Fund". As noted above, s 55(1) of SISA ensures that the broad set of governing rules cannot be breached by the Trustee, accountant, financial planner or lawyer to the Fund, without providing a member with recourse against the person concerned, or the Fund becomes non-complying.

Apart from the trust deed, a strategic SMSF trust deed should ensure the following strategies are incorporated into the governing rules of the Fund, thereby being afforded with the protection of SISA:

- Pension Roll Back;

- In Specie Commutations – paying assets not just cash;

- Entering into joint ventures[9];

- SMSF Will;

- Segregated Investment Strategies;

- Reserves of a SMSF including a pension reserve and an investment reserve;

- SMSF Borrowing;

- SMSF Living Will; and

- Creating continuing pensions and auto-reversionary pensions.

6.5 Getting the Right SMSF Trustee

The strategic decision of who or what entity is going to be the Trustee of the Fund, is linked to the SMSF trust deed. By way of background, for a superannuation fund to be a SMSF, all members of the Fund must be Trustees or directors of the corporate Trustee of the Fund. There are some exceptions to the rule, if the trust deed allows and we have already looked at these.

---

9 The Commissioner of Taxation has advised that he will be considering the use of joint ventures between SMSFs and related entities. Although not outlawed there are several areas which need to be applied such as the sole purpose test, the arm's length rules, in-house assets test and the contribution rules when considering any related party transaction.

Importantly from a strategic perspective, getting the right Trustee is crucial as the Trustee holds all the power and, also the responsibilities of the Fund. Essentially there are two options:

1. the members themselves individually as Trustees; or

2. a company as a corporate Trustee – where all the directors of the company are the members of the SMSF, may be established.

Although there is a small initial expense to create a company to act as Trustee (generally no more than $700) there are significant taxation, practical and financial benefits in choosing to do so. These include:

1) Longevity for future generations

It is a requirement under equity law that a trust is to last no more than 80 years. This rule, known as the "rule against perpetuities" was designed to prevent family assets being locked into a trust forever and not being subject to death duties or being brought into the capital gains tax net on the death of the appointor or beneficiaries of the trust. Although a SMSF is a trust, s 343 of SISA provides that the rule against perpetuities does not apply to trusts established as superannuation funds including a SMSF. Strategically this means that "a SMSF lasts forever".

If the Fund lasts forever, by virtue of the SISA, it is also important for the Trustee to have the capacity to last forever. The only entity that makes the grade is a company which lasts until wound up or deregistered. Current and future members may come and go as directors but the company remains constant as the Trustee.

2) Concessional taxation guaranteed for a Trustee Company

The most significant strategic change in the new pension limit rules, is the ability to run the pension side as an all encompassing income generator, with an accumulation account for lump sum payment and estate planning purposes - aka SMSF Version 2.0. This means that if necessary they may draw money as a lump sum from the accumulation side – for example to pay a Refundable Accommodation Deposit – RAD - for an Aged Care place.

However, s 19 of SISA provides that ONLY SMSFs with corporate Trustees can pay lump sums as well as pensions. If a SMSF has individual Trustees, the sole or primary purpose of the Fund must be to pay old age pensions — otherwise the Fund and its members will lose their concessional taxation status. Unfortunately, lump sums and estate planning benefits do not fit within these tight individual Trustee guidelines. A SMSF with individual Trustees seeking to run a modern day SMSF with accumulation (and also pension) accounts for a retiree member, as well as having extensive SMSF estate planning, needs to change Trusteeship to a corporate Trustee or limit superannuation benefits to primarily pensions only.

3) Administration simplicity — Trustees come and go

Members move in and out of the Fund, as a consequence of marriage, divorce, death, disability or bankruptcy. A requirement under the superannuation laws and by the Commissioner of Taxation is that the SMSF Trustee must hold all of its assets in the names of the Trustee. Where a member leaves the Fund or a new member joins the Fund and the Trusteeship is by way of individual Trustees, it is incumbent upon the Trustee to notify all share and unit holder registries, land title offices and other asset registries that there has been a change in Trustee. After a divorce or death or adding a new member, this can be a sizeable and very time consuming administrative task, and can also be costly. Strategically a corporate Trustee remains constant even though the underlying director/members may change on occasion.

4) Litigation protection

Trustees are potentially confronted with being sued should an event occur to an asset of the Fund. For example, the Trustee of a Fund may own a residential investment property and, as a result of an accident or for some other reason, a tenant or visitor may sue the Trustee under owner's liability. If a corporate Trustee is in place, the directors – who are members - are personally protected, but not so for individual Trustees.

As with SMSF Trust Deeds, not all companies are suitable to act as a SMSF corporate Trustee. A corporate Trustee of a SMSF must be built specifically for a SMSF in order to ensure that the Trustee can be focused on SMSF strategy rather than the ordinary business and shareholder principles found in most proprietary limited and shelf companies.

There is also a legal and financial reason to put in place a special purpose corporate Trustee for a SMSF. In 2003 the Government introduced legislation, the Corporations (Review Fees) Regulations 2003, that provided for a "special purpose company" which acted as Trustee of a SMSF. The benefit of being a special purpose SMSF Trustee company is that the annual ASIC fees are $47 compared with the normal $249 for a proprietary company (as at time of print).

In order to be classified as a special purpose SMSF corporate Trustee, r 3 of CRFR provides that the following two conditions must be met:

(i) the constitution of the company prohibits distribution of the company's income or property to its members, and

(ii) the sole purpose of the company is to act as the Trustee of a regulated superannuation fund.

Generally, a special purpose Corporate Trustee Constitution will have been built to cover all SMSF strategies. This means that the company should act exclusively as a Trustee of a SMSF, not to be the Trustee of a family trust or to run a business. For members with an existing dormant or unwanted company, an upgrade to the company constitution to convert the company to a special purpose corporate Trustee is a simple and inexpensive exercise.

STRATEGY 6.6 SMSF Strategy Alert - Keeping SMSF Control with Children in the Fund

Adviser Question — Control of a Family SMSF

We have recently taken on board a client with a sizable SMSF following a talk that you gave to SMSF Trustees in our area. In discussing the multi-generational nature of a superannuation fund, our new SMSF clients, both in their 60s with account balances in excess of $1M, want to bring their two children into their family SMSF. Their son is aged 40 and currently has $75,000 with an industry-based superannuation fund and their daughter is aged 35 with $35,000 in a retail superannuation fund. We are looking at rolling these superannuation benefits into their parents' Fund as soon as possible. The main advantages in adding their two children as members was to save them administration fees (these are to be deducted solely from the parent member's accounts) and, also provide reasonable life, total and permanent (TPD) and salary continuance insurance cover in the Fund — ideas they picked up at your SMSF estate planning seminar.

However, on reviewing their deed, which was last upgraded by their accountant in September 2006, we found that each Trustee of the Fund has one vote at any Trustee meeting. What does this mean in terms of mum and dad's control of the Fund if we accept the two children as members?

Grant's Strategy Response

A SMSF is a multi-generational Fund and it makes sense strategically to involve children in Fund membership as soon as possible. For some this may be at an early age (there is no age limit on membership under the Superannuation Laws) or it may be when the child first begins receiving super. As noted above the two main reasons for children becoming part of the Fund is to save on retail and industry based superannuation fund fees as well as providing insurance cover in the event that they die or become incapacitated. There are a number of strategic reasons but these are significant advantages.

However, before rolling over the children's superannuation benefits, an upgrade of the deed to a deed with *proportional voting* needs to be undertaken. Although the SMSF trust deed has been upgraded recently, it is dangerous to provide each Trustee with one vote, irrespective of the size of their superannuation account balance. Why should a member with more than $1 million in their account balance have the same voting power and control as someone with $75,000 or for that matter only $100 in superannuation benefits. If there is a corporate Trustee, then a proportional voting rule should be put in place for directors in a directors' meeting dependent upon the account balance of the member the director represents (if the company provides as such).

The serious problems that may arise with the one Trustee/one vote rule are:

1) Investment powers lie with the Trustee

Each member is a Trustee with one vote. The children (with small superannuation account balances) have the same power and control of the Fund as their parents. Initially this may not be a problem but if they voted in unison it could potentially throw the Trusteeship into a stalemate where the children voted against their parents. For example, the two older Trustees may have invested the Fund's assets into shares and cash to ensure liquidity for pension purposes once they retire. However, the children may decide that a particular property, subject to a limited recourse borrowing arrangement, is better suited for the Fund. If the parents, as Trustees wish to sell any shares due to a correction in the market, the younger Trustees could block the move unless the proceeds are put into property.

2) The Trustee controls what may happen on the Death of a Member

At some point in time, one of the older Trustees may pass away, leaving their spouse and children as remaining Trustee/members of the Fund. Unless a SMSF Will is used, the remaining Trustees will decide what to do with a deceased parent's superannuation benefit. At any meeting after the death of the member, the majority of Trustees will decide where, when, how and who any death benefits of the deceased member is to be transferred to. At that meeting the son and daughter will have a majority voting interest as opposed to the remaining parent Trustee. This means that the daughter and son, if there has not been a binding nomination or a SMSF Will put in place, may pay the parent's super-annuation death benefits to themselves and not take into account any wishes the parent had to pay a pension or lump sum to their spouse. This is similar to the facts in *Katz v Grossman* [2005] NSWSC 934 (*Katz's case*).

In Katz's case, the father of two adult children passed away and left the proceeds of his Family SMSF to be dealt with by the Trustee. His daughter was a member and Trustee of the family SMSF, and his son who was not a member or a Trustee. The member father left $1 million in superannuation benefits with a non-binding direction to the Trustee of the Fund that all superannuation assets of the father were to be split between the two children equally. On the father/member's death, the remaining Trustee — his daughter, did not pay regard to his nomination and paid all of the deceased member's benefits to herself.

The son took an action in the Supreme Court that their father had not validly appointed his sister a Trustee in the first instance thereby seeking to invalidate any action she sought to take as Trustee. Justice Smart held that, upon review of the Fund trust deed and the documentation produced, that she had been validly appointed. As such, any action she took was valid, including the payment of the deceased member's superannuation benefits to herself.

3) Once Legal Capacity goes, the Trustees control the Fund and fate of the Member

As with death there is a strong chance that one of the parents may lose their mental capacity and thus legal capacity. With the current SMSF trust deed in question the children would have the power to control the Fund. This could cause a number of financial problems for the parent members if the children/Trustees convert say a pension account for the mentally incapacitated member, to an accumulation account, with the aim of preserving capital for estate planning purposes rather than paying out sufficient income to obtain the best medical attention. As in Kratz's case, it is their prerogative to convert pensions to lump sums and carry out any action authorised under the Fund's trust deed.

STRATEGY **Do you have a SMSF Living Will?**

The SMSF Trust Deeds that I have authored[10] have an in-built SMSF Living Will enabling a member to instruct the Trustee of the Fund on how, when and how much of their superannuation benefits are to be paid in the event of legal incapacity. This also includes requiring the Trustee to create segregated assets of the Fund for the purpose of meeting the conditions of a SMSF Living Will, which may include appointing a SMSF investment strategy professional to choose, look after and maintain those segregated assets.

In the situation considered above, the upgrade of the Fund's trust deed to a well-constructed, strategic trust deed, quite apart from providing the members access to a SMSF Will and a SMSF Living Will, would ensure that the members of the Fund, the parents in this case, who have the highest account balances and thus the most to lose, control the Fund. In that regard, the trust deed provides that at any Trustee meeting, each Trustee is given one vote per dollar balance in the superannuation accounts. However, the Trustees may determine at a valid Trustee meeting, an alternative voting method of the Trustee for the purpose of that specific Trustee meeting, a matter to be decided at that meeting or for future meetings.

As noted above where a corporate Trustee has been appointed, the company constitution should also provide a control mechanism where each director, at a validly constituted director's meeting, has votes based on the superannuation account balances of the members they represent (including themselves). Importantly, a shelf company or traditional Pty Ltd company will not provide for proportional voting power but a one vote/one director rule. A great SMSF specialist company constitution will be built with the proportional voting rule in mind, as

---

10 The list of SMSF Trust Deeds that I have written can be found on the I Love SMSF website – www.ilovesmsf.com or by emailing support@ilovesmsf.com

well as a number of other strategies that may apply to member/Trustee company directors.

6.7 The Advisers Guide to Setting up a SMSF

**FLOWCHART TO COMMENCING A SMSF AND
THE FIRST YEAR'S COMPLIANCE REQUIREMENTS**

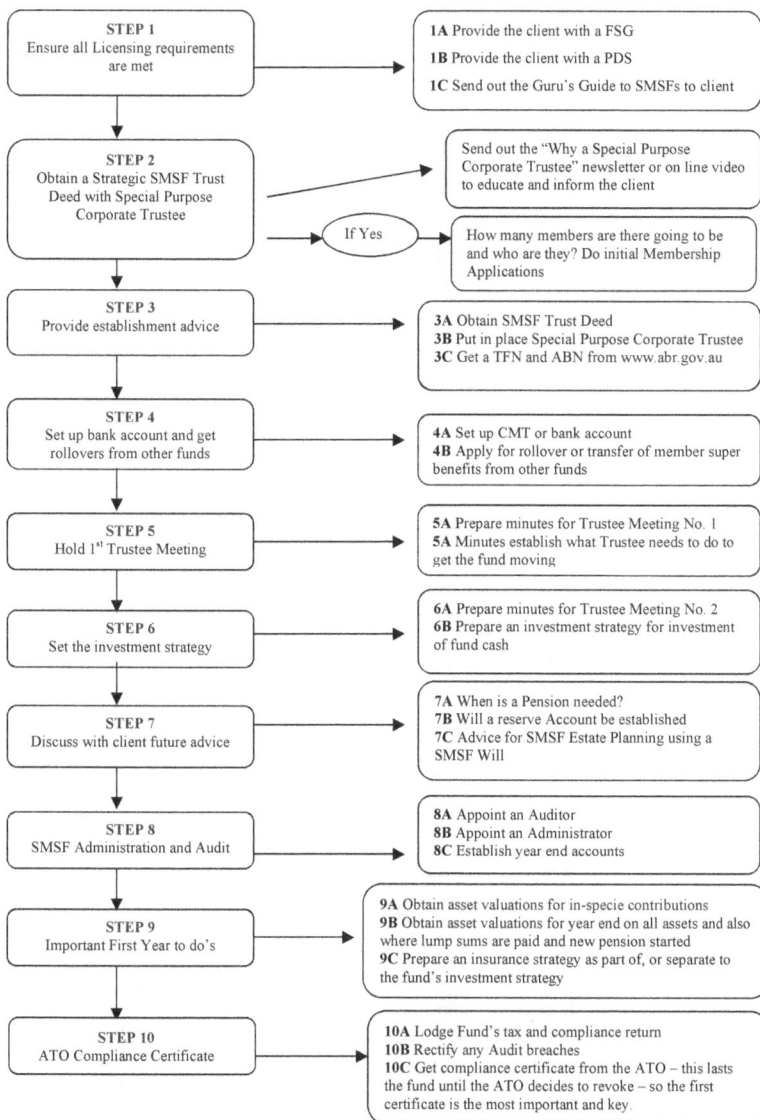

STEP 1 Ensure all Licensing requirements are met	1A Provide the client with a FSG 1B Provide the client with a PDS 1C Send out the Guru's Guide to SMSFs to client
STEP 2 Obtain a Strategic SMSF Trust Deed with Special Purpose Corporate Trustee	Send out the "Why a Special Purpose Corporate Trustee" newsletter or on line video to educate and inform the client *If Yes* → How many members are there going to be and who are they? Do initial Membership Applications
STEP 3 Provide establishment advice	3A Obtain SMSF Trust Deed 3B Put in place Special Purpose Corporate Trustee 3C Get a TFN and ABN from www.abr.gov.au
STEP 4 Set up bank account and get rollovers from other funds	4A Set up CMT or bank account 4B Apply for rollover or transfer of member super benefits from other funds
STEP 5 Hold 1st Trustee Meeting	5A Prepare minutes for Trustee Meeting No. 1 5A Minutes establish what Trustee needs to do to get the fund moving
STEP 6 Set the investment strategy	6A Prepare minutes for Trustee Meeting No. 2 6B Prepare an investment strategy for investment of fund cash
STEP 7 Discuss with client future advice	7A When is a Pension needed? 7B Will a reserve Account be established 7C Advice for SMSF Estate Planning using a SMSF Will
STEP 8 SMSF Administration and Audit	8A Appoint an Auditor 8B Appoint an Administrator 8C Establish year end accounts
STEP 9 Important First Year to do's	9A Obtain asset valuations for in-specie contributions 9B Obtain asset valuations for year end on all assets and also where lump sums are paid and new pension started 9C Prepare an insurance strategy as part of, or separate to the fund's investment strategy
STEP 10 ATO Compliance Certificate	10A Lodge Fund's tax and compliance return 10B Rectify any Audit breaches 10C Get compliance certificate from the ATO – this lasts the fund until the ATO decides to revoke – so the first certificate is the most important and key.

The Good and Bad Side of SMSF Bankruptcy

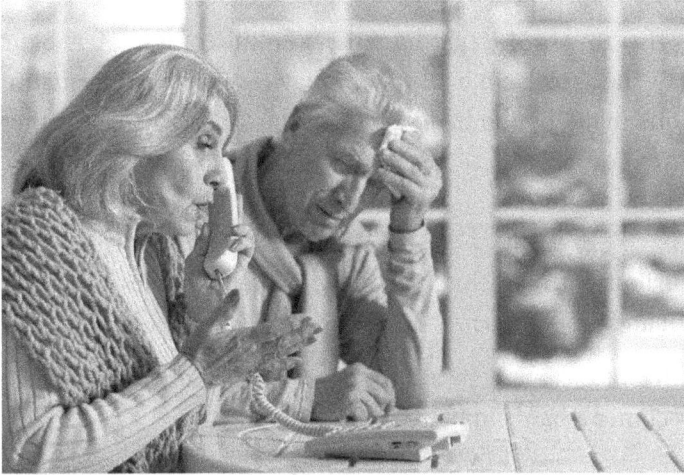

"You will hear a lot of accountants and lawyers talk about protecting your assets in the event of bankruptcy. The classic vehicle recommended is the Family Trust but Courts are starting to look into those. The SMSF has in-built legislative protection. A great asset protection vehicle not well known."

7.0 Introduction

There is both a good side and a bad side of a member of a SMSF going bankrupt – apart from the stress of it all. The good side is the Trustee in bankruptcy has limited access to the superannuation interests of the member of the Fund. The bad side is that a person cannot act as a Trustee of a superannuation fund, including a SMSF, where they are a bankrupt.

7.1 Protection of Superannuation — the Bankruptcy Act 1961

The Bankruptcy Act 1961 (BA 1961) provides protection in relation to a member's superannuation benefits in a superannuation fund as follows:

1) Contributions into the Fund

Under the BA 1961 regarding the administration of a bankrupt's property, the Trustee in bankruptcy may recover superannuation contributions made by the bankrupt or a third party to defeat the bankrupt's creditors.

There are two types of recoverable contributions:

(a) contributions made by a person who later becomes a bankrupt (see s 128B); and

(b) contributions made by a third party for the benefit of a person who later becomes a bankrupt (see s 128C).

Generally, s 128B of the BA 1961 provides that a contribution is recoverable where it would have formed part of the bankrupt's property, and the main purpose of making the contribution was to prevent it from being divisible among creditors. In determining the main purpose of making the contribution, consideration should be given to:

(i) whether the person is or was about to become insolvent at the time of making the contribution. Insolvency is presumed in s 128B(5) where a person has not kept their books and accounts up to date to reflect their true financial position or where the book and accounts have been lost, and

(ii) *the pattern and history of the person making the contribution.*

Section 128C mirrors this section in relation to employers, family companies and family trusts that make contributions under an arrangement with the bankrupt with the main purpose to prevent the contribution from being divisible among creditors.

2) Superannuation Interests in the SMSF

Section 116 of the BA 1961 provides that all property of a bankrupt is divisible among the bankrupt's creditors. Subsection (2) provides a number of exclusions, including "(iii) the interest of the bankrupt in a regulated superannuation fund (within the meaning of the SISA)".

This means that there is unlimited protection for a bankrupt in terms of their superannuation interests in the Fund, subject to the recoverable contributions rules considered above.

3) Superannuation Benefit Payments

Section 116(2) provides a further superannuation exclusion:

"(iv) a payment to the bankrupt from such a Fund received on or after the date of the bankruptcy, if the payment is not a pension within the meaning of the SISA."

This means lump sums, irrespective of their size, are protected from creditors whereas income streams are property divisible amongst creditors.

💡 **Grant's Tip for Bankrupts**

My advice - if you have been declared bankrupt, make sure you only run an accumulation account and not a pension account. You may be lucky that the Commissioner will allow you to remain as Trustee. Otherwise, the bankrupt members benefits will need to be rolled out to a retail or industry fund. Or, the Trustee may resign and the SMSF become a small APRA fund.

7.2 Disqualified persons and Trusteeship

Section 121(1) of the SISA provides that a person must not intentionally act as a Trustee where they are a disqualified person. A disqualified person is defined in s120 to be a person who is bankrupt or a company where a director is bankrupt. The penalty for a breach of s121(1) is two years' imprisonment. However, the disqualified person may apply to the Commissioner of Taxation to become or remain as Trustee of the Fund or director of the Fund's company Trustee.

STRATEGY 7.3 **SMSF Strategy Alert**

Adviser Question – Soon to be Bankrupt Member

We have a query from one of our Funds in relation to the best options and outcomes for a member/Trustee of a SMSF where there are currently actions being taken against one of the members of the Fund, which may result in the creditors forcing the member into bankruptcy. The Fund's trust deed has been upgraded to a recent deed you have written.

We believe that the simplest and most effective option, while any action is being taken, would be to have the member roll their benefits out of the SMSF into a commercial Fund until everything has been settled before rolling their benefits back into the Fund. Apart from this, what are the likely implications if the member wishes to remain a member of the Fund even though they are forced into bankruptcy?

Grant's Strategy Response

A person may not act as a Trustee of a superannuation fund, including a SMSF, where they are bankrupt — s121 of SISA. They are also required to tell the Commissioner in writing immediately when they become a bankrupt or a disqualified person — s121(3).

From an adviser's perspective, an offence under s121 is an offence of strict liability, carrying a potential two-year jail term if found guilty. *Where an adviser to a bankrupt Trustee "aids and abets", by way of knowing or ignorance, the bankrupt to remain as Trustee of a superannuation Fund while disqualified, the Criminal Code Act 1995 applies such that the adviser will be subject to the same offence and potential penalty.*

Given the extreme danger of bankrupt Trustees, a good trust deed will remove the Trustee/member of the Fund where they are a disqualified person. However, the Fund remains a SMSF for six months, so if a member becomes bankrupt there is six months to sort the removal of the member as member and Trustee.

The two options are to roll over the member's benefits to an industry-based or retail superannuation fund in the interim or appoint an approved Trustee.

CHAPTER EIGHT

Contributions

8.0   The Big Opportunity and the Huge Nightmare

8.1   What is a Contribution?

8.2   What is NOT a Contribution?

8.3   Cash or In-Specie Contributions

8.4   The Joy of Real Life SMSFs – A Big Contributions Case Study

8.5   SISR Contribution Rules

8.6   Tax Laws — The Deductibility of Contributions

8.7   Splitting Concessional Contributions with a Spouse

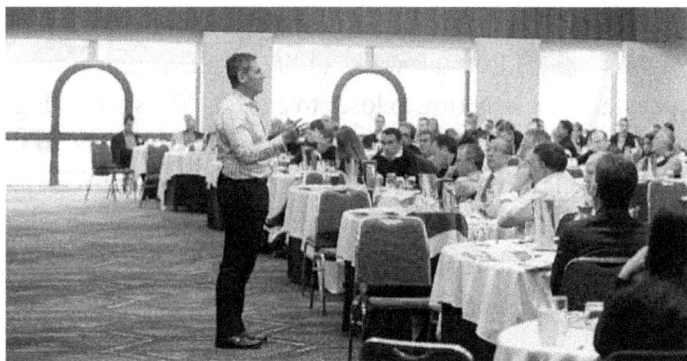

"Australia is the envy of the retiree world with tax-free lump sums and pensions. However, the limits on contributions, contributions caps and contributions taxes means a lot of strategy work for Australian SMSF advisers both here and with expatriate retirees coming to Australia. The going is getting tougher every day!"

8.0 **The Big Opportunity and the Huge Nightmare**

There are sizable tax, wealth accumulation and estate planning benefits in running SMSF Version 2.0 and with over $700 billion in SMSF assets, the Government is losing tax dollars each and every day as smart investors seek to squirrel as much away as they can in superannuation. SMSF tax is a golden egg for high net worth retirees with:

- tax free lump sum and pensions post age 60;

- tax exempt pension earnings within the Fund on balance transfers of $1.6M; and

- 15% tax on earning held in a Fund's accumulation accounts.

The Government knows this and has continuously made it harder and harder to contribute large amounts of money and assets into superannuation.

8.1 **What is a Contribution?**

a) Introduction

Since the advent of tax free super post age 60 there has been a great push for Australians from all walks of life to put as much as they can into super – particularly those closer to age 60. The succeeding Prime Ministers from 2007 have ruled out making any changes to tax free super post age 60 (too many votes to lose) and have targeted contributions. For example, in 2006 the amount an employer could contribute as a deductible contribution – now known as a concessional contribution, to a superannuation fund was:

Salary Sacrifice[11] Aged Based Limits – 2006

Age Band	$
Under Age 35	$15,260
Age 35-50	$42,385
Over age 50	$105,113

And in those days there were no contribution caps!

Now we have a concessional contribution limit for all super members of only $25,000. Seriously! It is okay for the politicians on their government funded superannuation schemes who don't have to worry about the caps, but for those people who are genuinely looking to be self-sufficient in retirement, this limit is way too low. And the amount allowed assumes that there will be consistency throughout the life of a member. In reality though, most families are having children in their late 20's and early 30's, such that meaningful retirement contributions do not arise until post age 45 – catch ups. Way too late.

STRATEGY The Bonus of Concessional Contribution Catch ups

To the Government's credit, there is a five year catch up rule which will allow individuals to make additional concessional superannuation contributions in a financial year by utilising unused concessional contribution cap amounts from up to five previous financial years, providing their total superannuation balance just before the start of the financial year was below $500,000.

b) The meaning of a Contribution

There are no legal cases or authority on what is a contribution for superannuation purposes. This means that as advisers and Trustees, we are best to apply the Commissioner of Taxation's ruling on contribu-

---

11 The term "salary sacrifice" is where an employee enters into an arrangement with their employer to contribute some or even all of their salary, wages, bonuses or commissions into superannuation for their benefit. These contributions are concessional contributions and although deductible may result in the employee breaching their concessional contribution caps. One warning, the ability to salary sacrifice must be in the employee's employment contract or the Commissioner may treat any purported salary sacrifice as an after-tax or non-concessional contribution.

tions – TR 2010/1 – *all 61 pages of it*. For Trustees it is not light reading so stick to using the Guru's Guide for your contribution knowledge but for advisers -TR 2010/1 is mandatory reading as there are a lot of traps, pitfalls and strategies hidden in its depths. And let's face it, if the Commissioner signs off on what is in the ruling – that is good enough for me and you.

c) Tax Ruling TR 2010/1

In TR 2010/1, the Commissioner states "a contribution is anything of value that increases the capital of a superannuation fund provided by a person whose purpose is to benefit one or more particular members of the Fund or all of the members in general."

The Commissioner provides examples of when an increase in the capital of the Fund will be a contribution including:

- transferring funds to the superannuation provider;
- rolling over a superannuation benefit from another superannuation fund;
- transferring an existing asset to the superannuation provider (an *in specie* contribution);
- creating rights in the superannuation provider (also an *in specie* contribution); or
- increasing the value of an existing asset held by the superannuation provider.

The capital of a superannuation fund can also be increased indirectly by:

- paying an amount to a third party for the benefit of the superannuation provider;
- forgiving a debt owed by the superannuation provider; or
- shifting value to an asset owned by the superannuation provider.

🔑 **Grant's Strategic Advice**

Given the penalties for exceeding the contributions cap limits (which we will look at shortly), it is vital for Trustees and certainly crucial for accountants to know what is and what is not a contribution. But remember – this is the Commissioner's view and there will come a time when all things "contributions" will be tested in Court. But as the Commissioner of Taxation is the Regulator – our friend and foe – we are best following his lead on this matter.

d) Commissioner's Contributions Examples

The Commissioner provides the following examples of contributions *out of the ordinary* from his Ruling TR 2010/1:

Example 1 - contribution made by paying a Fund's expense

Jane has a self-managed superannuation fund of which she is the sole member. During the 2010-11 income year, Jane arranged accounting and audit services to ensure the Fund met its income tax and regulatory obligations for the year ended 30 June 2010. Jane paid the accounting and audit fees for the Fund from her own money. Jane did not reimburse her outlay from Fund monies.

By satisfying a liability of the Fund, Jane has indirectly increased the capital of the Fund. Jane's purpose in paying the liability of the Fund without reimbursement was to increase the benefits she would ultimately receive from the Fund. Therefore, Jane made a contribution to the Fund when she paid the accounting and audit fees.

Example 2 - no contribution made by a free service

Jasmine has a self-managed superannuation fund of which she is the sole member. She is a chartered accountant and has significant experience in general accounting, taxation and superannuation matters. Jasmine prepares the accounts and income tax and regulatory return for her self-managed superannuation fund each year without remuneration.

By ensuring the Fund does not incur a liability in having the Fund accounts prepared, Jasmine does not increase the capital of the Fund and there is no contribution.

Example 3 - contribution made by forgiving liability

Gus and Pina are the only members of a self-managed superannuation fund. They are the shareholders of a company through which they operate a successful advisory business which provides accounting, taxation and superannuation services. An employee of their company prepares the Fund's accounts. The company invoices Gus and Pina as Trustees of the Fund for the services provided by the company, but Gus and Pina as shareholders of the company forgive the invoiced liability.

By forgiving the liability, Gus and Pina have increased the capital of the Fund. Therefore, they have made a contribution equal to the forgiven amount.

8.2 What is NOT a Contribution?

In terms of *what is not a contribution* – which importantly means that it is not caught up in the contributions laws and rules:

1. A payment made by an Insurance company under a policy on the life on an insured member. The payment increases the capital of the Fund however there is no purpose to benefit any specific person by way of contribution.

2. The Trustee enters into a borrowing arrangement to acquire Bob's land above using a commercial bank and paying a deposit to Bob of 20% of the value of the property as required by the bank. The loan by the bank is not a contribution. There are also strict rules for related party lending where Bob could provide the loan – which again is not a contribution but as noted, the rules for related party lending are strict and must be adhered to.

3. The allocation of an amount from a Fund Reserve account. The Trustee of the Fund, where the trust deed allows, may transfer earnings or insurance payouts to a reserve for future allocations to a member. When a reserve amount is allocated this is not a contribution as it does not increase the assets of the Fund – it is already in the Fund. HOWEVER, it is counted towards the concessional or non-concessional contribution caps – depending upon its character and subject to some exceptions in the reserving rules[12].

8.3 Cash or In-Specie Contributions

Strategically, SMSFs are different from other superannuation funds in many ways. One of the most prominent differences is the ability of a member or related entity to the member, such as a family trust or family company, being able to make in-specie contributions into the Fund. An "in-specie" contribution is a contribution by way of property and also in kind. For example, the Commissioner has ruled that where an employer pays the deductible expenses on behalf of the Trustee of the Fund that this is to be treated as a contribution by the employer — TR 2010/1.

One of the stumbling blocks in making an "in-specie" contribution is s 66(1) of SISA, which prevents the Trustee of a regulated superannuation fund – a SMSF - from acquiring a member or related party's asset. There are some exceptions to s 66(1) and these will be discussed in detail in the chapter on SIS Compliance and SMSF Investments. In summary, the following assets owned by a member or related party of the Trustee of a SMSF may be transferred or contributed "in-specie" into the Fund:[13]

---

12 Reserves and in particular the use of Reserves in a SMSF have long been a mystery for advisers and also Trustees. There are some unique benefits to using reserves in specific cases but as an allocation from a reserve to a member's account is a concessional contribution – they can prove expensive if used in the wrong hands.

13 Great care should be had in transferring any asset to a SMSF by way of sale or in-specie contribution. The penalty for a breach of s 66(1), if found guilty of an offence, is a maximum of one year's

- Investments listed on the Australian Stock Exchange and other recognised exchanges including overseas stock exchanges such as the New York, London, Hong Kong and Paris stock exchanges. Investments would include shares, debentures, warrants, listed property trusts, CDO's — essentially anything that is listed on an approved stock exchange.

- Term and other deposits with an approved deposit institution such as a bank.

- Investments in a widely-held unit trust including most managed funds and, in certain instances, syndicated property trusts with more than 20 unitholders holding 75% or more of the capital and income units of the trust.

- Business real property — this includes both freehold and leasehold property wholly and exclusively used in one or more businesses. For the Commissioner's view on what is business real property, reference should be had to the comprehensive ruling on the subject — **SMSFR 2009/1.**

- Shares in a company or units in a unit trust that meets the conditions of r 13.22C of SISR.

8.4 The Joy of Real Life SMSFs – A Big Contributions Case Study

STRATEGY 1) The GP SMSF has bought a property and the Trustee – George Panagiotidis, who is also a builder, extends the property to include a granny flat and outdoor area, paying for all materials at a cost of $25,000 and no cost for his team of builders to complete. Normally he would charge $15,000 for the job. But upon completion his best Greek

---

imprisonment and the Fund. In addition the Fund may be treated as a non-complying superannuation fund — *Lock v Commissioner of Taxation* [2003] FCA 309 (9 April 2003)

mate, a real estate agent, thinks it has added $100,000 to the value of the property.

2) In the SMSF, George has completed three of these developments in the last five years with properties owned by the Fund. His accountant was not aware of what was going on nor was the auditor, but the total increase in the asset values in the Fund over the last five years has been $800,000 – the market value of the property has been going crazy, so it is hard to work out what amount of the increase relates to the renovations and improvements. What do you think it is?

3) George and his wife Anna are members of the Fund with his father – a retired builder, Antonio. George has $1.1M in the Fund and Anna has $500,000 while his father, Antonio, who is 78 years old and taking a pension, has $650,000. These Fund values are based on the historical cost of the properties in the Fund from five years ago.

4) George has an office from where he works that he owns freehold with Anna and it is valued at $800,000. They each own 50%. George and Anna have not made any non-concessional cash or property contributions in the past five years and his accountant has told him that it would be a great idea to transfer the property into the Fund and then lease it back to his business. George agrees and the property is due to be transferred on 1 April 2018 when they have decided to draw up a commercial lease. To date George's business has only been paying sporadic rent.

5) There is a $350,000 capital gain on the property which the Accountant is going to claim as tax exempt under the small business concession rules – given it is a business asset and has been held for 15 years or more and is to be used for his retirement purposes.

This case study is not unlike a lot that I deal with on a day to day basis and there is a lot going on. All I can say is that George and his accountant will have hell to pay if the Commissioner of Taxation audits his

Fund and the ATO find out what has been going on. Can you see any problems from what you have learned in "The Guru's Guide to SMSFs" to date?

Do something for me. Come back and look at this case study when you have completed *The Guru's Guide to SMSFs* and see what problems you can see. Or alternatively print or photocopy the case study and keep on referring to its facts when you learn new areas of SMSF strategy and law.

If I was mentoring you, I would tell you that we need to read the laws, understand them and then apply the laws to George's cast study. With the big changes to the superannuation contribution laws which limit the making of a non-concessional (after tax contribution) into a Fund if a member's total superannuation benefits are greater than $1.6M, there is a lot of work to be completed here. This includes when a contribution was made, how much and is it spread across all members and in what proportions, as this will impact on Antonio's pension – is it rolled back and recommenced? And isn't it illegal to make a contribution post age 75? What is George's real balance and does the contribution of the business property breach the laws? What amount of the contribution is to be included in the various members accounts – particularly as it is held 50/50 by George and Anna? So many questions and I could go on. I will be looking at this case study in future SMSF strategy sessions so ensure you are registered to receive all of my latest updates (you can register at www.ilovesmsf.com or by emailing support@ilovesmsf.com)

8.5 SISR Contribution Rules

Part 7 of the SIS Regulations 1994 (SISR) allow the Trustee, subject to the rules of the Fund, to accept contributions on behalf of a member, as shown in the table following:

a) Contributions under Part 7 of the SISR

Age	Rules for Contributing
Under age 65	No conditions
Age 65-69	The contributions are made under an industrial agreement or the member is engaged in part time gainful employment being 40 hours of gainful employment or self-employment over a 30-day period during the contribution income year, and the contributions are made by a member or their employer.
Age 70–74	The contributions are made under an industrial agreement or the member is engaged in part time gainful employment being 40 hours of gainful employment or self employment over a 30-day period during the contribution income year, and the contributions are made by a member or their employer.
After Age 75	Contributions may be accepted by the Trustee after these times if in the Trustee's opinion they relate back to an earlier contribution time or the contributions are made under an industrial agreement — SISR 7.04(6) or are SGC contributions

STRATEGY **Strategy Alert: Contributions Rules Exceptions**

Contributions may be accepted by the Trustee after these times, if in the Trustee's opinion, they relate back to an earlier contribution time or the contributions are made under an industrial agreement — SISR 7.04(6). For example, John Jones has retired at age 64 and desires to make a non-concessional contribution but is waiting on the sale of an investment property. The sale does not eventuate until post-age 65 when he no longer meets the condition of making a personal contribution. However, as long as the Trustee has been notified in accordance with SISR 7.04(6), the Trustee may accept the contribution without John having to meet any part time gainful employment test.

b) Lesser Known Contribution Rules

There are some important but lesser known contribution rules that a Trustee may or may not fall into:

- **Spouse Contributions** - Contributions may also be made for a spouse[14] who is under age 65 at the time of making the contribution. The age of the spouse contributor is immaterial. Any contribution on behalf of the spouse is a non-concessional contribution.

- **Government co-contribution** - A contribution that meets the co-contribution guidelines has been made by the member to a complying superannuation fund by the Government. The ATO states the following in relation to co-contributions – "if you're a low- or middle-income earner and make personal (after-tax) contributions to your super fund, the Government also makes a contribution (called a co-contribution) up to a maximum amount of $500. The amount of government co-contribution you receive depends on your income and how much you contribute. In addition, to be eligible for a co-contribution:

  » you must have a Total Superannuation Balance less than the general transfer balance cap for that year

  » the contribution you made to your super fund must not exceed your non-concessional contributions cap for that year."

- **No TFN** - The Trustee must not accept any contributions in relation to a member if a TFN has not been provided to the Trustee — SISR 7.04(2). These contributions must be refunded within a period of 30 days.

- **Child Contribution** – a contribution may be made by a parent, grandparent or employer on behalf of a child under the age of 18.

---

14 Spouse includes two people in a same sex relationship provided they are living together.

8.6 Tax Laws — The Deductibility of Contributions

The benefit of superannuation as a "savings system" is the ability to shift profits, salary and wages into a super fund as a tax deductible contribution. Ideally, this would be made into a SMSF without any tax being levied on the transfer (of what would ordinarily be assessable income of the transferor). These contributions, because they are deductible to the transferor are called "concessional contributions" and the Trustee will need to bring them to account in the Fund's assessable income.

STRATEGY **1) Strategy Alert – Reducing Contributions Tax**

It is important to note here that a SMSF is not like an industry or retail super fund where the tax on contributions (which we will look at later) – often referred to as a 15% contributions tax - is deducted at source when a concessional contribution is made. For example, if a $5,000 salary sacrifice contribution is made to an industry super fund then more often than not, only $4,250 will be added to the members account. The Trustee of the industry or retail super fund deducts $750 and carries it to a tax provision reserve. In contrast, the Trustee of a SMSF does not take anything out and the whole $5,000 is credited to the member's account and tax will be paid when it is paid.

Bonus Strategy: If the Trustee of the Fund invests the $5,000 in a company that has Early Stage Innovation Company status, where the $5,000 receives a 20% tax offset, then NO contributions tax will be paid. Does that make sense? Is that strategically smart?

2) Timing of Contributions and Deductions

In terms of when a contribution is deductible to a member or employer, the Commissioner's contributions ruling TR 2010/1 states:

"The time at which a contribution is made will determine the period for which the person making the contribution may be eligible to claim a deduction. Sub-sections 290-60(3) and 290-150(3) of ITAA 1997 prescribe that a contribution made in an income year is deductible in that income year. When a contribution is made, is also relevant to the operation of the excess contributions taxes. Further, a contribution that is included in the assessable income of a superannuation Fund is normally included in the income year in which it is received.

i) General rule – a contribution is made when received by the Fund

A superannuation contribution is made when the capital of the Fund is increased. As explained, the contribution may be made when an amount is received, or ownership of an asset is obtained, or the fund otherwise obtains the benefit of an amount.

- **Property - TR 2010/6 - Example 6 - when in specie contribution of real property are made**

Bob owns land on which retail premises have been constructed. Those premises include the site from which Bob runs his pharmacy business. Bob decides to contribute the land (being business real property) to his self-managed superannuation fund. The Fund has a corporate Trustee, CarPharm Pty Ltd, of which Bob and his wife Janet are directors. The directors of CarPharm Pty Ltd resolve to accept the contribution of the land on 1 June 2009. After obtaining advice from their solicitor, Bob, as owner of the land, and Bob and Janet, as directors of the corporate Trustee of the Fund, complete the necessary land transfer forms and take possession of those forms and the relevant title deeds on Monday, 29 June 2009 to hold in their capacity as directors of the corporate Trustee. Therefore, as at that date, Bob and Janet hold all the documents in registrable form necessary to obtain registration of title to the land in their capacity as directors of the Trustee of the Fund. Janet lodges them with the registrar of land titles on 2 July 2009. CarPharm Pty Ltd is registered as owner of the land on 9 July 2009. In these circumstances, Bob's contribution will be made on 29 June 2009.

- **Contributions of monies**

A contribution of funds as cash or an electronic funds transfer, is made when the amount is received by the superannuation provider or credited to the relevant account. This was upheld in the Courts in *Liwszyc v Commissioner of Taxation* [2014] FCA 112. A contribution made by money order, cheque or promissory note is made when the order, cheque or note is received by the Trustee of the Fund.

3) Personal contributions

Section 290-150 of the ITAA 1997 provides that personal contributions made by a member of a superannuation fund are deductible provided the following five conditions are met:

(i) the Fund is a complying regulated superannuation fund;

(ii) the contribution is made no later than 28 days after the member's 75th birthday;

(iii) the member provides the Trustee with a s 290-170 notice of their intent to claim a tax deduction for the contribution and how much is sought to be claimed;

(iv) the member has not split the concessional contribution with their spouse prior to giving the Trustee a s 290-170 notice; and

(v) if the member is under 18 they must have derived income from a business or as an employee.

Note:

There is no limit under the taxation laws on the amount of deductions that may be claimed as a personal tax-deductible contribution provided the above conditions are met. However, any excess concessional contribution made over the caps - $25,000 from 1 July 2017 will be included in the member's taxable income in the year in which they are made and assessed at the member's marginal tax rate less 15%.

Grant's Strategic Note

Prior to 1 July 2017, an employee could only make a personal deductible contribution where 10% or less of the member's assessable income and reportable fringe benefits come from employment activities (including directorships). This rule has now gone.

STRATEGY **Strategy Alert: Grandparent Contributions**

Although concessional contributions are not often made for children - for a grandparent that has a Family Trust and is able to stream assessable income to a grandchild, this may be worth it as the child, under the age of 18, is genuinely employed and could deduct the personal contribution. However, the contribution must go into the child's bank account and then into super at their behest. Good luck with that one!

4) Employer Contributions

Section 290-60 of ITAA 1997 provides that superannuation contributions on behalf of an employee are deductible provided the following six conditions are met:

(i) For a SMSF the Trustee of the Fund had reasonable grounds to believe that there had not been a breach of SISA, the SISR or that the Fund was a foreign superannuation fund or unregulated superannuation Fund.[15]

(ii) The contribution is not a rollover or transfer from a foreign superannuation fund.

(iii) The contribution is made no later than 28 days after the member's 75th birthday.

(iv) The contribution is made on behalf of an employee as defined under s 12 of the *Superannuation Guarantee (Administration) Act 1992* (SGA 1992), including directors that are paid for their services.[16]

(v) The employee must be either engaged in producing assessable income for the employer or, if the employer is engaged in business, the employee is a resident of Australia.

---

15 This is a tall order for the SMSF Trustee and puts the onus on the Fund's SMSF adviser and auditor to ensure that there is no breach of any rule or regulation in SISA or SISR, including undertaking a transaction or doing anything in breach of the rules of the trust deed.

16 In order for a director to be considered an "employee" and thereby enabling the company or family trust (where the member is a director of the corporate Trustee of the family trust) to claim a deduction, the director must be paid or expected to be paid for services.

(vi) A deduction is available in limited circumstance where the person was a former employee.

Strategy Note: There is no limit on the amount of deductions that may be claimed as an employer deductible contribution provided the above conditions are met but the employee will need to wear the excess concessional contributions consequences.

8.7 Splitting Concessional Contributions with a Spouse

Division 6.7 of SISR provides the regulations and mechanisms that allow members of a superannuation fund to split both deductible employer and deductible member contributions made into superannuation with their spouse. A spouse is defined in s10 of SISA to include any person, same sex included, that although not legally married to the person, lives with the person on a genuine domestic basis in a relationship as a couple.

In terms of contributions splitting:

- Contributions may be split after year end, and at any time up to the end of the following year. For example, employer contributions made in the period 1 July 2016 – 30 June 2017, may be split by the recipient member at any time up to and including 30 June 2018.

- The trust deed of the Fund must allow the splitting of contributions as it is not mandatory for the Trustee of a superannuation fund to offer splitting to members.

- A transfer may not be made to a spouse who is already retired. Retirement in this regard means they are aged 55 and the Trustee of the Fund is satisfied that they will never work at least part time again.

- Where a concessional contribution is made by an employer or a person seeking to claim a tax deduction then only 85% of the contribution may be split. This is based on the underlying assumption that the Trustee of the Fund will be required to bring to account the contribution as assessable income of the Fund. Tax payable on Fund taxable income is 15%.

- Non-concessional contributions may not be split with a spouse.

CHAPTER NINE

Excess Contributions Rules

"The Excess Contribution Rules have added an immense, and can I say intense, layer of complexity to the superannuation and taxation laws. There is simply no easy way to cut through it. BUT if you do and you are working in fast rising investment markets, and you know your stuff about the benefits of tax deferral, then going over the caps can prove promising. However, this is not for the faint hearted and only the best SMSF specialist advisers will be able to see the woods for the trees."

9.0 The New Contribution Strategies

There have been so many variations and changes to the Excess Contribution rules that it is a tough task to keep up with them all. The 1 July 2017 changes have added complexity to the contribution rules, with a lot of detail and exacting. There are many advantages of going into excess concessional, and in some cases, excess non-concessional contributions, but before you do, make sure you understand and apply the principles in this chapter. This is the hardest chapter of the *The Guru's Guide to SMSFs*.

9.1 Why the Excess Contribution Rules?

Superannuation and SMSFs are provided with extremely generous tax concessions, which is necessary if the Government wants people to be self-funded in retirement. However, to limit the amount the tax costs Peter Costello introduced the concept of excessive contributions tax. Originally this was a heavy tax penalty, when a member went above their concessional contribution limits and/or their non-concessional limits. This created significant problems where unintended contributions cap breaches occurred, through having multiple employer contributions, timing of contributions at year end being inadvertently made and just plain accidental oversight, causing thousands of people to begin receiving excess contributions taxes and penalties. Day after day, case after case the negative feedback was significant – even the Leader of the Opposition Bill Shorten was caught.

In 2013, the Government introduced new laws where excess concessional contributions were to be taxed at the member's marginal tax rate less 15% (for deemed contributions tax) plus an accrued charge for the monies being in a concessional tax environment for a period. For excess non-concessional contributions - those that are essentially non-deductible - they can either be withdrawn or are taxed at a heavy rate of 45%. Clearly the withdrawal method is the best option

– provided the withdrawal is completed within the time limits allowed. Let's see what are concessional and non-concessional contributions and the caps currently in place and to be in place from 1 July 2017.

9.2 Contributions Caps

Type of contribution	Threshold to 1 July 2017	Post 1 July 2017	Other Rules
Concessional	$30,000*	$25,000	*For any member over age 50 during an income year – for the year ending 30 June 2017, a higher $35,000 cap applies
Non-concessional	$180,000	$100,000	A three-year bring-for-ward rule applies to a member under age 65.

* The concessional contribution threshold is to be indexed to average weekly ordinary time earnings but rounded down to the nearest $5,000.

9.3 What is a Concessional Contribution?

Section 291-25 of the ITAA 1997 includes as a concessional contribution:

a) contributions assessable to the Trustee of the Fund pursuant to section 295-160. These include contributions made on behalf of another person. Generally, this section provides that all contributions made on behalf of another person - with the exceptions of spouse, child and government co-contributions - are to be included in the Fund's assessable income. This would include a contribution from a family trust into the Fund on behalf of a member of the Fund; and

b) personal tax-deductible contributions.

Excluded from the concessional contribution rules are:

- transfers from a foreign superannuation fund where the member has elected to transfer the tax liability to the Trustee of the Fund[17];

- spouse contributions – not splittable contributions, as these are recorded on behalf of the member who the contribution is for – not the spouse to whom they are split;

- government co-contributions;

- child contributions; and

- contributions made by the Trustee of a superannuation fund.

A concessional contribution also includes an allocation from a reserve under section 291-25(3), although there are some exceptions contained in regulation 291-170.04 of the Income Tax Regulations 1997 (ITR). Reserves are a wonderful art form in themselves and will be briefly described in this book, but simply, they are assets or monies - set aside by the Trustee of a Fund for specific purposes - that do not belong to members until allocated by the Trustee as such.

9.4 What is a non-concessional contribution?

Section 292-90 of ITAA 1997 includes as non-concessional contributions the following amounts:

- excess concessional contributions[18];

- contributions made to a Fund that are not included in the Fund's assessable income, such as spouse contributions; and

---

17 This relates to foreign super funds and is an art itself. We have looked at what is a foreign super fund in Chapter 4 and here we are considering the transfer of monies from a foreign super fund into a SMSF. For the most part foreign retirement and pension funds do not allow these transfers without taxation. However, in the UK, a member may transfer an amount from a UK pension fund to a Qualifying Recognized Overseas Pension Scheme ("QROP"). The rules were changed in April 2016 to make it harder but a number of SMSF specialists have managed to transfer amounts to an Australian SMSF successfully.

18 Be ultra-wary of this non-concessional contribution. As we will see, in some cases going over the concessional contribution cap is a good strategy but be careful how it impacts the non-concessional contributions of a member.

- allocations from a reserve account in limited circumstances. In the majority of cases, an allocation from a reserve will be a concessional contribution.

However, non-concessional contributions have specific exclusions including:

- an amount representing the CGT excluded amount under the small business concessions as well as amounts that would have been excluded if the CGT small business concessions applied (including pre-CGT business assets). However, there is a lifetime limit in terms of the exemption from the non-concessional contributions. For the 2017-2018 year the CGT Cap is $1,445,000. This is indexed each year and the amount can be found on the ATO website – like most caps and other superannuation thresholds[19];

- an award under a structured personal injury settlement. Although there is no lifetime $ limit there are strict guidelines that need to be met in terms of the type of settlement that the exemption covers — section 292-95;

- government co-contributions; and

- rollover superannuation benefits.

O━━┳┓ **Key Point**

The CGT small business and personal injury exemptions from non-concessional contributions are worthy of a chapter on their own, given their complexity, importance and interaction with elements of many other laws. For any adviser, Trustee or member seeking to take advantage of these exemptions - it is highly advised that a specialist SMSF adviser be employed to devise the best strategic opportunity.

9.5 **Excess Contributions Taxes — the New Rules**

I am a great fan of the current excess contributions regime that was introduced in 2013. As noted earlier, harsh penalties have been relaxed so that excess concessional contributions are now taxed at a member's marginal tax rate. This measure eliminated the many contribution and tax penalty issues faced by tens of thousands of Australians who inadvertently exceeded their contributions caps.

The Contributions Caps are tough – be careful both Adviser and Trustee

I have to admit that this section dealing with contributions, caps, release authorities and all things to do with excess concessional and non-concessional contributions was by far the hardest part of the book. This area of the law is complex but also littered with great strategies along with big technical hurdles.

1) **Excess concessional contributions taxed at marginal rates**

Instead of being subject to penalty taxes (a blessing), excess concessional contributions are now taxed at a member's marginal tax rate – less 15%.[20] However, and this is important, as the tax on excess contributions is collected later than normal income or PAYG tax, there is in-built into the system an excess concessional contributions charge (ECCC is set at the bank bill rate + 3%). The ECCC starts at the commencement of the year in which the excess concessional contribution was made even though it may have been made in the last day of the income year.

We will discuss the superannuation preservation laws in a later chapter. However, in short, a member's superannuation benefits are usually

---

20   The Tax Laws Amendment (Fairer Taxation Of Excess Concessional Contributions) Act 2013 and Superannuation (Excess Concessional Contributions Charge) Act 2013 have replaced the Excess Concessional Contributions Tax with effect from 1 July 2013. The reduction of 15% is on the assumption that the Fund has paid 15% contributions tax on all concessional contributions made to the Fund – s291-15 ITAA 1997

accessed at the time of retirement. An exception to the rule is where the member has made an excess concessional contribution (ECC). These may be withdrawn by the member upon making an election to the ATO to withdraw up to 85% of their ECC – see s 96-5(1) of the Taxation Administration Act 1953 (TAA 1953).

Case Study: Greg Jones – Employee with SMSF

Greg Jones is a 45 year old manager of a company on a $150,000 salary package. For the year ending 30 June 2018 Greg Jones makes a concessional contribution of $50,000 by way of salary sacrifice into the Jones SMSF. This means that Greg's assessable income for the year is $100,000.

For the year ending 30 June 2018 Greg's concessional contribution cap is $25,000. This means that his excess concessional contribution (ECC) is $25,000 which must be added back to his assessable income. Greg is on a marginal tax rate of 39% (including Medicare and NDIS charges) but when we reduce that tax rate by 15% (the deemed contributions tax) - he will have to pay tax on $25,000 (ECC) x 24% = $6,000.

In addition, Greg will need to pay a ECCC on the $6,000 from 1 July 2018 until the date of the assessment by the Commissioner of an ECC. This could be anytime from November 2018 to May 2019 if Greg is on a tax agent's lodgement list and can lodge his personal and Fund tax returns later than normal statutory lodgement dates.

After receiving his assessment, Greg may elect to release any amount up to 85% of his ECC of $25,000 = $21,250. The Trustee must notify the Commissioner of Taxation within 7 days of receiving the election to release.

Greg will receive a personal tax offset of the amount withdrawn to be used against tax payable – say the $6,000 plus the ECCC.

STRATEGY **Some Strategic Ideas to consider**

Considering the scenario of Greg Jones in the example above, based on a remuneration package of $150,000, his employer's 9.5% superannuation guarantee charge is $14,250 less $2,137 in potential contribuitons tax. Greg wants to contribute an additional $35,750 as a salary sacrifice contribution – which is credited to his account without PAYG or immediate payment of contributions tax. Here are some strategic ideas for Greg:

1. Go the Cash and don't Salary Sacrifice: Instead of salary sacrificing the $35,750 Greg could pay PAYG tax of $13,942 leaving him with $21,808 to invest.

2. Invest in Early Stage Innovation Companies: We will see later that an investment by the Trustee of a Fund in an ESIC investment (a start-up company that meets ESIC guidelines) sees the Trustee receiving a 20% non-refundable tax offset on the amount invested. In addition, if the shares in the company are sold or transferred within ten years of acquisition there is no capital gains tax.

Is there a strategy here for Greg? He has salary sacrificed his wages for a contribution of $50,000 (including SGC) into the Fund which has gone into his member's account in the Jones SMSF. The Trustee of the Fund can invest the $50,000 into a portfolio of ESIC investments. At the end of the income year, the Trustee is required to include the $50,000 concessional contribution in the Fund's assessable income. If there are no deductions then a 15% tax will be applied on the concessional contribution (is it is taxable income). This is $7,500. However, we know that an ESIC investment has a 20% tax offset – which is $10,000. This means the Trustee will not have to pay contributions tax and even has some tax offset remaining for other tax liabilities of the Fund (except for excess contributions taxes as they form part of the member's assessable income not the Fund's).

As we learned above Greg will have to pay $6,000 tax for the ECC plus an additional amount for the ECCC. If Greg had funds personally available, he could pay this directly or withdraw some cash from the Fund to pay the Commissioner's assessment amount. Of course, Greg could withdraw up to $21,500, being 85% of the ECC if he wants – which is not recommended.

The end result? Greg has $50,000 working hard in his SMSF ($6,000 +ECCC less if he wants to pay the ECC and ECCC) and if the Trustee receives a dividend or sells the shares inside of ten years – it is tax free.

3. Invest in Dividend Paying Stocks

Greg again salary sacrifices $50,000 but the Trustee invests in dividend paying stocks. If the Trustee's timing is right then the monies may be invested prior to any dividend payments. Let's say the Trustee invests in Best Bank shares that pay a 5% fully franked dividend.

What does that mean tax wise? There is not much change in the $50,000 being included in the Fund's assessable income. If the Trustee receives $2,500 in fully franked dividends then the Trustee will need to include $1,071 in franking credits as well; total tax payable is 15% x $53,571 = $8,036. But the Trustee has a franking credit of $1,071 so total tax payable by the Fund is $6,965. Greg will have to pay the $6,000 in ECC tax and the additional ECCC. Altogether in the Fund, if Greg withdraws the $6,000 ECC, and the $6,965 Trustee tax payable is deducted from his member account balance – Greg has overall net wealth of $37,000.

9.6 Excess Non-Concessional Contributions Rules

1) Overview

Like concessional contributions, prior to 2013 excess non-concessional contributions (NCC) were taxed at the top marginal tax rate of 47%. Given non-concessional superannuation contributions come from income that had already previously been taxed, this could have taken the overall tax rate up to a staggering 93%.

In the 2014 Budget, the Government made the following announce-ment, to apply retrospectively – "For any excess contributions made after 1 July 2013, breaching the non-concessional cap, the Government will allow individuals to withdraw those excess contributions and associated earnings. If an individual chooses this option, no excess contributions tax will be payable and any related earnings will be taxed at the individual's marginal tax rate. Individuals who leave their excess contributions in the fund will continue to be taxed on these contribu-tions at the top marginal rate."

Generally, the rules are designed to:

- provide an escape to the excess non-concessional contributions tax of 45% by allowing a withdrawal of excess non-concessional contributions; and

- provide the member with an election to withdraw the excess concessional contributions tax within 60 days upon receiving an assessment from the Commissioner – much the same as the ECC above but this is paid directly to the member. However, an earnings rate of the General Intereste Charge (GIC) is applied to the non-concessional amount withdrawn from the first day of the year the contribution is made to the time of withdrawal. The applied earnings rate is added to the member's assessable income for the year in which the contribution is made.

Let's look at Greg's spouse, Janet Jones. She has made a NCC into the Jones SMSF for the 2018 income year of $100,000 but forgot that she had previously contributed up to her maximum NCC using the three-year rule. As Janet has an excess, she will receive a notice from the Commissioner to withdraw the excess or pay 47% excess NCC tax on the amount. Janet chooses to withdraw the excess NCC and will also have to include in her assessable income for the 2018 income year an earnings amount of the GIC on the $100,000 up to the date of the assessment. This is taxed at her marginal tax rates.

9.7 **Extra Contributions Tax for High Income Earners**

From 2012, an additional 15% tax has been applied to certain super contributions to reduce the concessional tax treatment of those contributions made for high income individuals (Division 293 ITAA 97). The high-income threshold was originally $300,000 but for the 2017-2018 income year and onwards it has been reduced to $250,000.

Concessional contributions are added to an individual's income with division 293 tax of 15% on the excess over the threshold, or on the super contributions, whichever is less.

⬤━🔨 Key Point

Division 293 tax is not payable on excess concessional contributions that have been taxed under Division 292 (or refunded under section 292–467).

9.8 **SMSF Trust Deed Impact**

By now, whether you are an accountant, adviser, financial planner or SMSF Trustee you should have realised the absolute importance of a modern, strategic and importantly up to date trust deed. This applies to contributions and it is highly recommended that all deeds be upgraded for the 1 July 2017 changes and that the deed in question have the following in relation to contributions:

(i) the trustee being able to receive in-specie and in-kind contributions that meet the superannuation laws and in particular s 66(1) and the SMSF borrowing rules in s 67(4A) - *An in-kind contribution* comes from the Commissioner's contributions ruling – 2010/1 where a person, employer or member paying for a fund's expenses is considered of having made a contribution to the fund for the benefit of members of the fund. However, the trust deed must have a rule that allows this otherwise it may be characterised as an illegal loan;

(ii) the trustee being able to repay contributions within 30 days if they exceed the non-concessional contribution and concessional contribution caps — r 7.04(4) of SISR;

(iii) the creation of a contributions reserve under r 7.08 of SISR allowing employer and other contributions to be warehoused for a short period, particularly at year end – a very popular strategy for SMSFs;

(iv) the trustee refunding contributions where a tax file number has not been quoted by the member of the fund;

(v) the trustee being able to transfer out specific assets in satisfaction of a return of contributions; and

(vi) the trustee being able to receive in-specie contributions.

CHAPTER TEN

SMSF Contribution and Investment Strategies

10.0 Let's bring it altogether

This chapter is where we put things together – reading, understanding and applying the law – the basic requirement for anyone providing advice on a SMSF.

For many SMSF specialists and others advising on SMSFs, these are just some of the many adviser questions I get on a weekly basis and there is no easy answer – read the law, understand the law and apply it. For Trustees, read the case studies as there may be something in the facts that resonate with you – it might be the desire to contribute a property into a Fund, make contributions on behalf of your children enabling them to access the First Home Buyers Super Saver scheme or keeping your super to your bloodline. My strategic responses may get a little technical but see if you can get on top of it – this is your SMSF and you have it for life, so use it to all its wonderful advantages.

10.1 Personal contributions

Adviser question — Personal contributions, exceeding the concessional contributions cap and meeting the expenses of a Fund's life policy

Could you please clarify a couple of minor points in relation to contributions?

1) We have a client who is aged 58 on 1 September 2017 and has a remuneration package of $85,000. They wish to elect to salary sacrifice 100% of their remuneration as an employer superannuation contribution in the 2017-2018 income year — is the employee then still able to make a personal deductible contribution for the year of up to $15,000?

2) A client is personally paying for a life insurance policy premium $5,000 owned by their SMSF. They are under age 65 and do not work. Does the payment of the premium amount to a contribution? Is it deductible? Will it form part of their concessional contributions for the year?

The Guru's Strategic Response

Background

From 1 July 2017 s 290-150 of ITAA 1997 provides that personal contributions are deductible where:

- the Fund is a complying superannuation Fund; and

- the member provides the Trustee with a s 290-170 notice of their intent to claim a tax deduction for the contribution.

There are no limits on the amount of deduction that may be claimed as a personal deductible contribution, as long as the above conditions are met. However, where the contribution, which is a concessional contribution, exceeds the $25,000 limit, the excess amount of $75,000 is to be added back to the client's assessable income.

In response to question 1) above, the problem is that the client will receive a $15,000 personal tax deduction to offset personal assessable income but the deduction a person claims can only reduce their taxable income to nil. It cannot add to or create a loss. As the member is already in a nil taxable income position, it cannot put the client into a loss when the excess concessional contribution is added back. When the $75,000 is added back to the taxpayer member's assessable income for excess contributions tax purposes, it will be taxed at the member's marginal tax rate less 15%.

Although the concessional contributions cap comes into play, consideration must be given to what happens if the concessional contribution cap is exceeded. What are the advantages and disadvantages of this strategy?

SMSF Strategy — Exceeding the concessional contributions cap

There may be cases where it is beneficial for a member to exceed their concessional contributions cap like in the following situations:

1) The member is on the top marginal tax rate with a large capital gain, distribution or has significant taxable income during the income year.

Making a personal deductible contribution can be used to offset any personal assessable income. There is an excess concessional contributions tax cost in the Fund. The deductible amount is also to be included in the Fund's assessable income. However, the assessable income amount may be reduced with deductible expenses in the Fund, such as life insurance premiums with taxes, also reduced by imputation credits. As such the cost of making an excessive concessional contribution may be less than the member's marginal tax rate. Importantly any concessional contribution in excess of the cap is to be included as a non-concessional contribution — s 292-90(1)(b) of ITAA 1997.

2) There is a timing advantage in the payment of the Fund's tax — either the Fund gets a tax deduction for use of the payment (life insurance) or the Fund has tax offsets.

Grant's Key Point

The key disadvantage for a member making excess concessional contributions is their inclusion as part of the taxable component of a member's accumulation superannuation interest. Any non-concessional contribution forms part of the tax-free component except if they are excess concessional contributions. This makes a big difference when it comes to passing superannuation benefits to non-dependants.

Life insurance policy

The payment of deductible expenses by an employer on behalf of the Trustee of a SMSF was considered in tax ruling MT2004/2. The Commissioner stated in that ruling that, as long as the Trustee of the superannuation fund recognised the expense incurred by the employer as a contribution, then "the payment to the third party is treated for all tax purposes as though the employer or eligible person had made the payment directly to the Fund and the Fund had separately paid an equal amount to the third party."

In a similar vein, the payment of the premium by the member personally in respect of the Fund's life policy would be a contribution made to the Fund by the member, provided the Trustee of the Fund recognised it as such. However, for it to be a deductible expense of the member, the member would have to give the Trustee a s 290-170 notice of their intent to claim a tax deduction for the contribution.

Once a tax deduction is claimed by way of a s 290-170 notice, the Trustee of the Fund will include it in the Fund's assessable income and report the contribution to the Commissioner to be taken into account for concessional contributions tax purposes.

10.2 Child Deductible Contributions

Trustee Question - Child Deductible Contributions

My accountant has suggested that my 16 year old daughter, who gets a significant assessable trust distribution each year, make a maximum deductible contribution. Is this possible under the superannuation laws? She currently genuinely works in our business doing social media marketing and posting to our Facebook page.

The Guru's Strategic Response

This is a great tax and superannuation planning question. However, it needs to be considered with a simple three-step strategy process:

1) Does SISR allow the strategy?

2) Does ITAA allow the proposed transaction?

3) Does the Fund's trust deed allow the transaction?

Let's consider each of these elements in turn.

1) SISR

Reg 7.04 of SISR provides that the Trustee of a regulated superannuation fund may accept contributions for any person under age 65. So as far as your daughter goes she and you as her employer can make a contribution on her behalf. In fact, a contribution can be made by any person on behalf of anyone under age 65, even a one week old infant.

2) ITAA 1997

In terms of the tax consequence of a minor – a person under the age of 18 - making a personal deductible contribution into a SMSF, s 290-165 of the ITAA provides the following age-related conditions:

If you were under the age of 18 at the end of the income year in which you made the contribution, you must have derived income in the income year:

(a) from the carrying on of a business; or

(b) attributable to activities covered by s 290-160(1).

In that regard s 290-160(1) of ITAA 1997 provides that the allowable activities, include the:

(i) holding an office or appointment;

(ii) performing functions or duties;

(iii) engaging in work;

(iv) doing acts or things, and

...(b) the activities result in you being treated as an employee for the purposes of the *Superannuation Guarantee (Administration) Act 1992 (SGC Act)*.

For a minor, who is a contributor to a superannuation fund, to claim a personal deductible contribution they will need to show:

1) they are in business — unlikely for most minors;

2) they are employed as evidenced by an employment agreement or

documents. This could include employment from McDonalds, a newspaper run or being employed in this instance presumably by the Family Trust. As an aside, an employer must make a contribution on all employee's behalf under the SGC Act, unless salary and wages being less than $450 per month, or if *the minor is employed for less than 30 hours per month* — see s 27(2) and 28 of the SGC Act.

So, both you as an employer and your daughter can make deductible contributions on her behalf. However, there are concessional contribution caps of $25,000 to comply with. Importantly there are *no limits for concessional contributions* but where the concessional contributions cap is exceeded, any excess concessional contributions are added back to your daughter's assessable income. This means that both she and her employer – your family entity - can contribute on her behalf. Plus, with her low marginal tax rate the add back of excess concessional contributions will be tax effective. You just have to watch the excess concessional contributions charge (ECCC).

In terms of taxation of the Trustee of the Fund in relation to the employer contribution, s 295-160 of SISA includes a contribution made on behalf of another person, as assessable income of the Fund. S 295-170(1)(b) exempts from assessable income a contribution on behalf of a member under the age of 18 unless it is by that person's employer – which is the case in point. This means that a contribution by a grandparent will be non-deductible to the grandparent, non-assessable to the Fund and also a tax-free component.

3) SMSF Trust Deed

In terms of contributions, the trust deed membership clause must provide that any person can be a member of the Fund if they become Trustees or directors of the Fund's corporate Trustee, unless a Replacement Trustee can be appointed under the rules of the Fund in accordance with s 17A of SISA. All of the deeds that I have authored have such clauses but check the deed that you are using to ensure that this is the case as some have age limits. In addition, when making contributions into the Fund, the trust deed should allow the Trustee to accept "any authorised contribution on behalf of a member, including a child member".

For Trusteeship assuming your deed is correct, your daughter may become a member of your SMSF. However, as her parent you will act as her Replacement Trustee and act on her behalf. As a current Trustee, there is no need to add to your existing appointment, simply agree to the fact that you carry her membership with your Trusteeship. If you have a corporate Trustee then you are already appointed as a director of the Fund's corporate Trustee and need to act on her behalf.

4) The Final Word – Accountants Statement of Advice

The above is just general advice, as I am not aware of your particular circumstances and would expect that your accountant is on top of your tax and financial affairs. Apart from this, generally when an accountant provides advice on contributions being made into a SMSF they provide a Statement of Advice on this issue. Check that the above advice correlates to the advice that has been provided.

10.3 Re-contributions into a SMSF for Estate Planning Purposes

SMSF Strategy Adviser Question — Re-contributions into a SMSF for Estate Planning Purposes

If a 60 plus year-old client wants to withdraw a lump sum from their Fund and re-contribute it back into the Fund up to age 65 - for the purpose of increasing the tax-free component in their accumulation account (to benefit their adult children on death), do you actually have to remove the money from the Fund or can you just do a journal entry debiting lump sum payment and crediting non-concessional contribution?

The Guru's Strategic Response

A superannuation benefit is described in s 307-5 of the ITAA 1997 as:

Table — Superannuation Benefits require a Payment

Superannuation benefit type	Superannuation member benefit	Superannuation death benefit
Superannuation Fund payment	A payment to you from a superannuation Fund because you are a Fund member.	A payment to you from a superannuation Fund, after another person's death, because the other person was a Fund member.

There are two considerations to this strategy. Firstly, does a journal entry of a payment and subsequent contribution make the strategy work and, secondly, can a re-contribution strategy be used to increase the member's tax-free component?

In relation to these two issues the Commissioner has previously addressed both of these issues:

1) Lump sum payments and contributions via journal entry.

2) Recontributing into superannuation.

1) Lump sum payments and contributions via journal entry

In ATO ID 2006/132 the Commissioner considered the case of where a member of the Fund had died and a lump sum death benefit payment, which had been contributed by the spouse back into the Fund was made. This is the so-called re-contribution strategy. The Commissioner held that a journal entry is not a payment under the former s 27A(1) of the *Income Tax Assessment Act 1936* (ITAA 1936) for the purposes of the definition of eligible termination payment (ETP) and thus the re-contribution was not valid. As can be seen from the table the current laws in section 307-5 of ITAA 97 also requires a payment to be made to the member of the Fund, for it to be a superannuation benefit.

The Commissioner's reasoning is as follows:

"To meet the definition of an ETP, the majority of the paragraphs of the definition require that a **payment be made**. It needs to be established whether the journal entries transferring the monies from the deceased member's account to the taxpayer's account represent a payment from a superannuation Fund for purposes of section 27A(1) of the ITAA 1936. The term 'payment' is not defined in the ITAA 1936. Therefore, it is necessary to consider the common law meaning of the term. [21]

For the majority of cases that consider whether a journal entry is a payment, refer to the principle stated in *Re Harmony and Montague Tin & Copper Mining* (Spargo's case) (1873) LR 8 LR Ch App 407. In *Spargo's* case it was held that a payment will occur where two parties both have a present liability or legal obligation to the other (mutual liabilities or mutual obligations) and they make an agreement and set off the liabilities against each other using a book entry.

Based on the principle in *Spargo's case,* a journal entry will only constitute a payment if there are mutual liabilities between the taxpayer and the SMSF and there is an agreement between those parties to set-off the liabilities. There is no mutual liability in this case as the taxpayer does not have a liability to the SMSF (*Case 18/97*).

Therefore, a journal entry is not sufficient to establish that the SMSF has made a payment to the taxpayer under the provisions of subsection 27A(1) of the ITAA 1936."

2) Recontributing into Superannuation

It has been and continues to be a popular strategy for members of a superannuation fund to withdraw their superannuation benefits and recontribute this back into their Fund. The idea is to take a lump sum out tax-free post age 60 and recontribute back into the Fund as a non-concessional contribution. This makes it a tax-free component for

---

21 Where any term is not defined in the Superannuation Laws, the common law or the ordinary usages of that term must be considered. For example the term "dependant" includes specific definitions however its ordinary meaning — that of financial dependant remains to be determined under the common law.

the purposes of future death benefit payments.

The issue was hotly debated until the Commissioner issued a Media Release on 4 August 2004 — MR 2004/058. In terms of re-contributions specifically, the Commissioner stated:

"The Tax Office today confirmed that commonly-used superannuation strategies will not attract the anti-avoidance provisions in the tax law. Tax Commissioner Michael Carmody said he wanted to provide clarity for people on the treatment of a range of superannuation practices.

"We have examined a number of straightforward strategies and confirm that they will not attract the general anti-avoidance provisions."

"Under the law, there is a certain amount of flexibility and choice about when and how people draw on their super savings."

"The strategies and variations we have examined so far are arrangements to maximise an individual's retirement benefits and are allowable under law."

New SMSF Strategy rules

From 1 July 2017 the Pension Transfer Balance Limit for a retired member of a Fund is $1,600,000. The Trustee of a Fund cannot accept any more superannuation benefits into the member's pension account once the pension transfer balance limit is exceeded. This means that in a two-member SMSF – a Mum and Dad Fund, the superannuation balances should be equalised in order to maximise a couple's tax-exempt pension balances. It does not make sense for one of the members to have $2M in accumulation and building for a pension and the other only $800,000. In this case the re-contribution strategy above should be used – however, using cash, not journal entries.

In addition, a member of a Fund making a non-concessional contribution or a spouse seeking to make a spouse contribution is limited under the new rules where the member on whose behalf the contribution is made, has a total superannuation balance in excess of $1,600,000.

STRATEGY **Promissory Note Strategy**

In the Commissioner's ruling on contributions TR2010/1, he discusses the use of a promissory note as being akin to a cash contribution. However, there are certain terms and conditions in relation to the use of a promissory note and you are well advised to discuss this with a specialist SMSF lawyer.

10.4 CGT small business rules

Advanced SMSF Strategy Adviser question — CGT small business rules and the non-concessional component

We have a client that is looking at transferring their factory into their SMSF in late 2017. They have just had the factory valued at $1,200,000. The client – Joe is 65 and his wife - Sally is 61. The factory is in their joint names and their business trades via a family company. They are semi-retired and their son and daughter run the business. They have not sold the business to the son and daughter as they want to retain control for as long as possible. At this stage, they own all the shares and are the only directors. They work in the business for about 20 hours per week and receive a car allowance and $80,000 salary.

The business is not being sold but can they make an in-specie contribution of the factory of $600k each? The capital gain on the factory is currently $600,000, or $300,000 each.

The factory has been owned for 10 years but they have been in business 25 years. Do they get the retirement concession for CGT on transfer of the factory as effectively being sold?

They have had a SMSF for fifteen years and his balance is $1.2M all in accumulation with a $600,000 tax free component and hers is $1M with $400,000 tax free component. Will this take us over the allowable contribution limits?

The Guru's Strategic Response

Introduction

Over the years it has become a popular strategy to contribute business real property into a SMSF. In fact there is more than $50 billion of business real property in SMSFs. From a compliance perspective, the Trustee is able to acquire the asset under the exemption in s 66(2) of SISA and any lease back to the business is not caught by the in-house assets test in s 84(1) of SISA. This means it ticks all the right boxes for SISA compliance and there are great tax benefits – the real driver of the strategy, which include:

- tax deductible rent paid to the SMSF by the Trustee of the Family Trust which will minimise taxable income distributions to beneficiaries;

- rents are not contributions for excess contributions cap purposes;

- rent provides good cash flow to fund an account based pension for the clients. Generally commercial yields can be up to 10% per annum;

- future capital gains and rents in the property will be tax-free if the asset forms part of the Fund's segregated current pension assets – subject to the total superannuation balance rules;

- if the asset is an active asset of the business, the small business CGT concessions may result in the contribution/transfer to the Fund, being CGT free.

The CGT small business rules

O—🔑 Grant's Key Point

The following is only a summary, and a detailed review of the small business concessions in Div 152 of the ITAA 1997 is required to ensure that all of the conditions for claiming a small business CGT concession are met. Before embarking on any CGT concession matter it is highly recommended to seek advice from a CGT expert and particularly a CGT expert who also has detailed knowledge of SMSFs, so that the CGT non-concessional contribution exemption in s 292-100 may be taken into account. This is key to the strategy.

As an incentive for small business owners to become self-funded retirees, a number of CGT exemptions and discounts are available when they dispose of their business or a business asset. Apart from the CGT small business concessions on the sale of any CGT asset, business or otherwise, an individual, family trust or partnership is entitled to a 50% CGT discount where the asset has been held for more than 12 months — s 102-5(1) of the ITAA 1997. This does not apply in relation to a family company-owned asset where there is no CGT discount. The Trustee of a regulated complying superannuation fund is entitled to a 33 1/3% discount.

Where the CGT small business concession rules apply to the disposal of a business asset by a taxpayer, the available concessions include:

(i) Subdivision 152-B: 15 year exemption. If the taxpayer has held the asset for 15 years, there is no capital gain realised on the disposal of the asset. Importantly capital losses are not set off against the tax-free gain.

(ii) Subdivision 152-C: 50% exemption. There is an additional 50% discount available under section 152-205.

(iii) Subdivision 152-D: The CGT retirement exemption applies up to a lifetime limit of $500,000 under section 152-310. The taxpayer may choose to apply the CGT retirement exemption before section 152-205. This is beneficial as the CGT retirement exemption is not a non-concessional contribution but sub-division 152-C is a non-concessional contribution.

Small Business Concession Requirements – the ATO view

To claim the small business concessions, the taxpayer must show firstly that they are a small business. In that regard the Commissioner notes that you will be a small business entity if you are an individual, partnership, company or trust that:

- is carrying on a business , and

- has an aggregated turnover of less than $2 million.

What is aggregated turnover?

Aggregated turnover is your annual turnover plus the annual turnovers of any business entities that are your affiliates or that are connected with you. The aggregation rules help you determine whether you need to include the annual turnover of another business entity (a relevant entity) when calculating your aggregated turnover. These rules aim to prevent businesses splitting their activities in order to inappropriately access the small business entity concessions.

Once the small business entity test is met, which we assume is the case in this instance, then the following three conditions are required — *these are summaries only of the significant conditions, further conditions do apply*:

(a) The business owner must have net assets of $6 million or less. Net assets include assets owned by the business owner, their spouse, children and any entities connected with them such as family trusts and companies where the business owner controls the entity. However, assets such as personal use assets, superannuation fund benefits or life insurance policies are not to be taken into account in determining whether the taxpayer has breached the $6 million threshold.

(b) The asset disposed of must be an active asset — this would include property used by the business, such as goodwill and real property. S 152-40 includes as an active asset an asset that is held by a person but used as part of a business of an entity connected with them such as a family trust. For more detail on passively held assets – such as property held by a person and then used in a business that is an entity connected with the person, go to the ATO website and search for the detailed analysis and examples under CGT retirement concessions.

(c) If the relevant asset is a share in a company or unit in a unit trust, the taxpayer or their spouse must be a significant individual in relation to the entity — they must hold 20% or more of the capital and voting power either directly or indirectly.

Application to the case study

I have assumed that the clients in question are able to meet the above conditions in relation to a small business entity and being under the $6M threshold. Provided the SMSF trust deed allows, the property may be contributed into the Fund as an in-specie contribution. This would require a formal transfer of the property from joint names to the name of the Trustee of the Fund. As there is a disposal, it will result in stamp duty and a capital gain. Interestingly in Victoria and to some extent in WA and SA, if the trust deed and transactions are structured properly, there will be no stamp duty on the transfer.

In terms of the CGT small business concessions, the property is held in joint names and used in a business run by a controlled entity — the family company. This would qualify the property as an active asset under s 152-40 of ITAA 1997.

Provided the net assets of the clients are less than $6 million, they will be able to utilise the various CGT concessions as follows – note the 15 year exemption is not available as the asset has only been held for ten years.

Table — Application of the CGT small business rules to each member

Asset disposal	Business property case 1	Business property case 2
Transfer Amount	$600,000	$60,000
Capital gain	$300,000	$300,000
Ordinary 50% discount	$150,000	$150,000
Subdivision 152-C discount	$75,000	$0
Subdivision 152-D CGT retirement exemption	$75,000	$150,000

Note: Being able to choose whether to apply Subdivision 152-C or 152-D first makes a difference in terms of the non-concessional contribution rules as can be seen below. It also reduces the lifetime limit of $500,000 of CGT retirement exemption.

10.5 Non-Concessional Contributions Cap

S 292-80 of ITAA 1997 provides that a taxpayer is liable to pay excess non-concessional contributions tax where the taxpayer has excess non-concessional contributions. The rate payable on the excess is 45% pursuant to the *Superannuation (Non-concessional Contributions Tax) Act 2006*.

S 292-85(2) provides that a taxpayer has excess non-concessional contributions where their non-concessional contributions exceed four times the limit set down for the concessional contributions cap (for the 2017–2018 income year, this is $25,000). For the 2017–2018 income year, the non-concessional contributions cap is $100,000. S 292-85(3) provides that, where the taxpayer is under age 65, the non-concessional contributions cap may be brought forward over a three year period such that a client may contribute $300,000 non-concessional contributions in an income year where they are under age 65 and do not have a prior year bring-forward contribution.

Importantly s 292-100 provides relief for taxpayers from the non-concessional contributions rules where they are making a contribution into superannuation as a result of the disposal of a CGT small business asset. The Explanatory Memorandum to Pt 3-30 of ITAA 1997 states, "this exemption recognises that many small business people invest in their business rather than make regular contributions into superannuation and later use the equity in their business to fund their retirement."

The CGT small business exemption for the non-concessional contributions cap is limited to a maximum lifetime limit per taxpayer of $1,445,000 for the 2017-2018 income years — s 292-105.

What contributions are allowed?

The contributions allowed under the CGT non-concessional exemption cap are:

- up to $500,000 of capital gains that are disregarded under the CGT exemption in Subdivision 152-D — CGT retirement exemption — s 292-100(7). This supports the underlying CGT exemption, which requires that capital gains that are disregarded under Subdivision 152-D, be contributed to superannuation if the person is under preservation age;

- capital proceeds from the disposal of assets that qualify for the CGT exemption in Subdivision 152-B — 15-year exemption — section 292-100(2); and

- capital proceeds from the disposal of assets that would have qualified for the CGT exemption in Subdivision 152-B but for:

  – the disposal of the asset resulting in no capital gain or a capital loss — s 292-100(2);

  – the asset being a pre-CGT asset — s 292-100(5); or

  – the asset being disposed of before the required 15-year holding period had elapsed because of the permanent incapacity of the person (which occurred after the asset was purchased) — s 292-100(3) and (6).

In terms of the contributions there is an important distinction between the CGT retirement exemption, where only the exempt capital gains fall within the CGT cap, and the 15-year rule, where the actual proceeds from the disposal which arose from the permanent incapacity fall within the cap. This is further explained in the following example sourced from the Explanatory Memorandum. Please be aware that the figures below relate to 2007 – the CGT non-concessional cap is $1,445,000 for 2017-2018.

Example – CGT retirement exemption v the 15-year exemption

Ruth, aged 59, sells an active asset used in her small business which she has owned continuously for over 15 years. The proceeds from the sale are $1.1 million. She qualifies for the CGT exemption in Subdivision 152-B and disregards the capital gain of $390,000 on this basis. Ruth would like to contribute the entire proceeds to her superannuation Fund.

Assuming Ruth has not previously made any contributions or used her CGT cap, she may elect to contribute $1 million under the cap exemption22 and have the remaining $100,000 count towards her non-concessional contributions cap. This would allow her to make an additional $50,000 worth of non-concessional contributions in the year without exceeding her annual cap.

Alternatively, as she is under 65, she may use the bring-forward rules to contribute $450,000 and only use her CGT cap for the remaining $650,000. This will leave Ruth with a CGT cap of $350,000 for use in future years. However, any further non-concessional contributions made in that year, and the following two years, will exceed her non-concessional contributions cap and result in an excess contributions tax liability.

---

22 The EM was produced in 2007 when the exemption was $1M. This has now grown to $1,445,000 for the 2017-2018 income year. And the bring forward rules are no longer $450,000 but $300,000 for the 2017-2018 year.

Note that if Ruth had her capital gain disregarded under the Subdivision 152-D exemption instead, she would have only been able to contribute the exempt capital gain and not the capital proceeds under the non-concessional contribution cap exemption.

Claiming the non-concessional contribution cap exemption

The CGT exemption from the non-concessional cap is not automatic and the taxpayer must ensure under section 292-100 to make the claim:

(a) The contribution must be made at no later than the day the person is required to lodge their income tax return for the year in question or 30 days from receipt of any capital proceeds.

(b) At the time of making the contribution the Trustee of the Fund must be notified in the approved form that the CGT small business non-concessional contribution is being made and more importantly the amount of non-concessional exemption claimed. This form can be found easily on the ATO website with a search.

(c) There are additional time limits where the monies are to be passed out from an entity such as a company or trust.

The Client Case Study

At the end of the day the clients will each be making a $600,000 in-specie contribution into their SMSF. For the year ending 30 June 2018 there are many ways it could play out and let's look at both Sally and Joe in turn from the case study above as the ages make a big difference.

The Best Solution for Sally

Upon transfer of the property into the Fund a contribution will be deemed to have been made for Sally. This is a potential $600,000 non-concessional contribution (NCC) – which means trouble given the NCC limits.

- As the in-specie transfer is a realisation for CGT purposes we find there is a capital gain of $300,000 for Sally's share of the property transfer but this is reduced by the 50% exemption to $150,000. Sally is best to claim the CGT retirement exemption for the remaining $150,000 as this is exempt from the non-concessional contribution rules. This is instead of claiming the 50% exemption under sub-division 152-C.

- Excluding the $150,000 as a NCC still creates a problem as Sally's remaining $450,000 exceeds her bring forward cap of $300,000. As such we still have to play with $150,000 and decide what to do with this amount. Of course, she could contribute but at some point the Commissioner will notify her to remove the excess NCC from the system or wear a 45% penalty tax.

- Apart from NCC and to help minimise NCC issues, although in a small way, Sally can claim a tax deduction for $25,000 and treat some of the transfer contribution as a concessional contribution leaving $125,000 in play. She can continue to do this each and every year up to the concessional contribution cap but cannot exceed the $25,000 as any excess concessional contribution is an NCC.

- As noted already the $125,000 will be treated as an excess non-concessional contribution and assessed as such by the Commissioner. There are some options that Sally faces:

  a. Don't contribute the $125,000 at this time, and leave part of the property out of the equation. This would see the Trustee of the Fund and Sally acting as joint owners or tenants in common with her $125,000 being her share of the property. Legally, documentary and administration wise this is a messy solution.

  b. Don't contribute the $125,000 and get the Fund to use its cash reserves to pay out the $125,000 to Sally for that part of the property. With this case, next year Sally can contribute a further $25,000 concessional contribution and so on, year after year provided she can contribute under SISA. Any excess money can be Sally's living money for the next couple of years.

c. Don't contribute the $125,000 and enter into a related party limited recourse borrowing arrangement – which will be discussed in the following chapters. Provided all the documentation is completed correctly and meets the Commissioner's guidelines then a loan will exist between Sally and the Fund with the Fund paying principal and interest payments to Sally over the period of the loan. Interest payments will be assessable to Sally but she is retired and on a low marginal tax rate. The Fund will get a tax deduction for the interest payments.

d. Ordinarily once her NCC cap kicks back in she would forgive $100,000 of the loan outstanding which will be treated as a NCC and within her cap. The problem that she will face is that once her Total Superannuation Balance exceeds the General Transfer Balance (GTB) of $1.6M she can no longer make non-concessional contributions. At the time of her contributions, Sally's Superannuation Balance is $1M plus $300k NCC from the transfer plus the $150K of CGT exempt – which takes her to $1.45K. So, at this stage she has some capacity but when she finishes her three-year NCC window we may find her balance exceeds the GTB from her making concessional contributions and investment growth in the intervening period. Of course, this will be reduced by any pension payments made from the Fund.

e. Once the in-specie contribution is made into the SMSF and let's go with the payment option – the Trustee of the SMSF paying Sally $125,000 cash, Sally should ask the Trustee to set up an accounts based pension with her $1.45M in superannuation balances. This will be credited against her Pension Transfer Balance Limit. The advantage of commencing it so soon is that once tested any future growth will not impact the $1.45M already tested for her Pension Transfer Balance. However, it is still counted in her Total

Superannuation Balance. Any future concessional contributions that Sally makes post the pension assessment can be used to Fund another pension up to the value of $150,000.

f. From an estate planning perspective, the best type of death benefit payment to be received by an adult child or grandchild is filled with tax-free component. An adult child, who is not a dependant for tax purposes, pays tax at a rate of 17.5% on any taxable component of a death benefit payment. Hence the desire to have tax-free component which is as its name suggests tax free to the recipient. The issue we have here is that if the $450,000 NCC and CGT exempt contribution is made, and these are tax-free components into Sally's existing accumulation Fund made up of $400,000 of tax-free component, then she will have $1.45M of accumulation Funds to commence a pension. This start up amount includes $850,000 of tax-free component. As pension is tested for tax-free/taxable percentage at the time of commencement it means any payment, whether pension or lump sum death benefit commutation will be 58.6% tax-free.

g. An alternative is for Sally to commence a pension with the current $1M in her Fund – which includes $400,000 of tax-free component so that her tax-free percentage for Pension No 1 will be only 40%. Once that is completed then a pension with the $450,000 of tax-free component can be swung straight into a 100% tax free Pension No 2. This provides flexibility and a smart desire to reduce the taxable component by ensuring that any pension payments above the minimum or commutations should be made from Pension No 1.

h. With a two-pronged investment strategy and a desire to draw upon Pension No 1, from an investment strategy perspective the property should be segregated into this Pension for its income potential. Pension No 2 should be invested for growth as this increases the tax-free component.

The Best Solution for Joe

The best solution for Joe has a similar nature as Sally except:

i) He is age 65 and so he cannot use the three-year rule and is locked into a $100,000 NCC this year in combination with a $25,000 concessional contribution. He can also obtain the $150,000 CGT exempt component.

ii) This means that, while Sally had $125,000 to cash out of the Fund, Joe has $600,000 - $275,000 which is $325,000. This could be paid to Joe, but given the quantum it is worthwhile considering using a related party limited recourse lending arrangement (LRBA) for this part of the property.

iii) With the LRBA once 1 July 2018 ticks over Joe can contribute another $125,000 provided:

   a. He meets the conditions for a person over age 65 being able to contribute to superannuation;

   b. That his Total Superannuation Balance does not exceed $1.6M as this would prevent a NCC being made. Of course, a concessional contribution can be made. In that regard he has $1.2M in the Fund and includes $275,000 as a contribution of NCC, concessional contribution and CGT exempt amount. This would leave only $125,000 left in the Superannuation Balance to wait for next year's contribution. This is where a reserve may come in handing for earnings in the Fund.

   c. From an estate planning perspective a similar methodology and planning as with Sally should ensure and likewise relevant investment strategies to leverage the two Pensions for Joe.

10.6 **Investment Objectives and Investment Strategy**

Before we get into the compliance laws under SISA, it is a good time to look at investments and the process of choosing and making investments in a SMSF. Investments are the naturally the next following step once the Fund is established and contributions and rollovers have been made to the Fund. However investments in a SMSF cannot be made at random and SISA requires, under s55B(2)(f), that all investments of the Fund are made according to the Fund's investment strategy – essentially the plan the Trustee is required to make before investing for the Fund.

In making the plan, the Commissioner of Taxation requires there to be an investment objective for the Fund and then a strategy to meet that objective. A typical objective in a large employer fund may be to increase the Fund return over a five-year period by the Consumer Price Index + 2%. Let's now look at SMSFs and investments.

The Trust Deed, SISA and Investments

Although the investment objective and investment strategy are quite different in their purpose and use, it is difficult to break them apart. The reason for this is that they are part of a process undertaken by the Trustee to deliver something to a member of the Fund, whether that member is:

- taking a pension;
- accumulating their benefits in the Fund for the purpose of taking a pension; or
- seeking to maximise the benefits that may be distributed to their dependants on their death.

The trust deed of the Fund should provide an indication for the Trustee and their SMSF adviser on investment objectives and investment strategies. Even if this is not the case, the SISA provides a set of important rules around these two areas.

Trust Deed v SISA

The investment strategy is one instance where the Act overrides the trust deed — to ensure that the Trustee undertakes investment planning in the Fund. Section 52B(2)(f) provides that the Trustee of a SMSF must formulate and give effect to an investment strategy that has regard to the whole of the circumstances of the Fund including, but not limited to, the following:

- the risk involved in making, holding and realising, as stated in the law, and the likely return from the Fund's investments having regard to its investment objectives and its expected cash flow requirements;

- the composition of the Fund's investments as a whole, including the extent to which the investments are diverse or involve the Fund in being exposed to risks from inadequate diversification;

- the liquidity of the Fund's investments having regard to its expected cash flow requirements; and

- the ability of the entity to discharge its existing and prospective liabilities.

10.7 ATO Guidelines for Investment Objectives and Investment Strategies

The ATO has released important guidelines for Trustees of a SMSF and their advisers in relation to investment objectives and investment strategies in the fact sheet *Investment Strategy and Investment Restrictions — SMSF*. They must be strictly adhered to or the Fund may become a non-complying SMSF. The key principles raised by the ATO concerning investment objectives and investment strategies are:

- the Trustees of a SMSF are solely responsible and directly accountable for the prudential management of their members' benefits. They can use an adviser, but in the end, it is their responsibility;

- as part of this prudential responsibility, the Trustees of a SMSF are required to prepare and implement an investment strategy for the superannuation Fund;

- the strategy must reflect the purpose and circumstances of the Fund and have particular regard to the membership profile, benefit structure, tax position and liquidity requirements of the Fund;

- an investment strategy should set out the investment objectives of the Fund and detail the investment methods the Trustees will adopt to achieve those objectives;

- it is the Trustees' duty to make, implement and document decisions about investing Fund assets and to carefully monitor the performance of those assets;

- the Trustees must ensure all investment decisions are made in accordance with the investment strategy; and

- breaches of the investment strategy requirement may result in the Trustees being fined or sued for loss or damages. In addition, the Fund could lose its complying status.

10.8 **Can an Accountant complete an Investment Strategy or must it be a licensed adviser?**

Choosing the Investments

STRATEGY Under the *Corporations Act 2001 (CA)*, in dealing with the choice of investments, the Trustee is able to make their own investment decisions, but if they need guidance, then they need to engage a person who is a licensed financial planner. There are no exceptions to this rule, meaning that an accountant, administrator or any other person cannot provide advice regarding investments in the Fund unless they are licensed and competent to do so. The financial planner needs to have the skills not only to provide investment advice to a client but, more importantly, to provide investment advice to the Trustee of a SMSF. As evident from the ATO's guidelines and s 52B(2)(f) itself, it is complex to successfully complete an investment strategy. A key requirement for any Trustee, accountant or auditor seeking advice from a licensed person for investment objectives and investment strategies is whether that person has met the nationally endorsed training standards for providing advice in SMSFs. These standards provide that an adviser have and maintain specific knowledge and skill requirements in relation to advising on SMSF investment strategies.

General Asset Advice

However an accountant with a limited licence under the CA 2001 can provide general advice around assets in the Fund such as shares, property, fixed interest or cash – just not specific advice on what type of investments the Trustee should make.

Documenting the Investment Strategy

As for documenting the investment strategy made by the Trustee of the Fund, an unlicensed accountant or administrator can complete this process as directed and completed in writing by the Fund Trustee.

10.9 The Five Steps to an Investment Strategy

Step 1: Investment objective

There are a number of investment objectives that the Trustee of the Fund can employ on behalf of the Fund or member of the Fund. In the superannuation industry in general, investment objectives are broad, sweeping statements that pay no reference to specific members of the Fund. For example, a common investment objective for a number of retail superannuation Funds is "to return on average better than CPI returns".

In relation to the ATO guidelines, this is not appropriate for a SMSF. Membership profile, benefit standards and taxation are just some of the issues that need to be faced by the Trustee and their SMSF adviser when building an investment objective.

A suggested investment objective for a SMSF and its Members may be:

"The investment objective to be put in place by the Trustee of the Fund is to maximise the retirement incomes for all Members as well as provide the best possible outcome in terms of death benefits for the Member's Dependants and their Legal Estate."

Step 2: Develop an investment strategy — build a portfolio

Once an objective has been chosen by the Trustee — whether the objective is, Fund, member or product-based (such as a pension) — the Trustee is then required under sec 52B(2)(f) to prepare an investment strategy to meet the specific investment objective. As discussed, the investment strategy must take into account the whole of the circumstances of the Fund, the member's benefit structure, risks involved in holding a specific investment or class of investments, and also the extent that there is risk in the Fund's diversification of assets.

An important part of the investment strategy process will be the building of a portfolio. The portfolio building, as well as Steps 3 and 4, may be undertaken by the Trustee, but need to be well documented. For the most part, a sound investment strategy is generally a detailed document, and Trustees may be well advised to have the process undertaken by a licensed SMSF investment adviser, skilled at building long-term investment strategies to Fund lifetime incomes in a SMSF.

ASX Portfolio Building Case Study

In terms of portfolio building in a SMSF, the Australian Stock Exchange (ASX) makes the following comments in its *Products* course.

"Most Trustees will be suited to an investment portfolio which provides a balance between the relative capital and income stability of fixed interest assets — such as corporate bonds — and the relative growth — with uncertainty of capital and income — offered by shares. As part of this balanced portfolio, other financial instruments such as property investments and commodities such as gold may be included to diversify the risk and return opportunities provided by the portfolio.

Balanced portfolios require ongoing management and rebalancing as economic conditions change, for example, low returns from fixed interest assets may be offset by higher growth opportunities from the share market or property assets or vice versa. Within each asset class, over time, individual sectors or regions may provide higher potential for returns than others and this may be reflected in changing composition of those components of the portfolio.

Shares are perhaps the most dynamic component of the balanced portfolio, as illustrated by the volatility of their individual prices. Volatility is a measure of the degree and frequency of price fluctuation. One of the desired outcomes of the construction of a balanced portfolio is the reduction of overall portfolio volatility with the simultaneous retention of the potential for growth."

In addition to a balanced portfolio, there are numerous other styles of portfolio that may be constructed by a specialist SMSF investment adviser to meet the specific needs of a member's investment objectives. This could range from a defensive portfolio made up primarily of fixed interest securities and cash to an aggressive portfolio consisting primarily of growth assets such as shares and property.

Step 3: Choose an investment style

Part of the strategy according to the ATO is "to detail the investment methods the Trustees will adopt to achieve the investment objectives". If the Trustee has decided upon a balanced portfolio for the Fund, the next step is to look at an asset class and then determine the type of investments that may fill that class.

ASX Equities Strategy

STRATEGY The following comments have also been provided by ASX Limited in its *Products* course, focusing on investment style in the equities component of a balanced portfolio.

"It is an observable reality that the volatility of a portfolio of shares is typically lower than the volatility of individual shares. Within the component of a portfolio which is allocated to shares, various investment styles may be employed, depending largely on the preferences of the Trustee. For example, risk averse Trustees may prefer a stable or low growth share portfolio, while younger Trustees with an appetite for higher growth and risk may prefer a share portfolio which targets stocks with potential for growth, or those which appear to offer good value — often because they are trading at prices which are below those which have previously prevailed but are considered to be `turnaround' stocks. An `intermediate' style of share portfolio involves a focus on stocks with high proven potential for yield which is often also a measure of economic strength and, hence, yield stocks will often hold their value better than growth stocks."

Step 4: Choose investment types

Step 4 is perhaps the easiest of the five steps. It is a matter of the SMSF investment adviser choosing the type of investment to use. If we reconsider the Fund's equity portfolio referred to by the ASX (see above) and use an intermediate/growth style, the task is how to fulfil this strategy.

For example, in relation to shares, there are a wide variety of choices including, among others:

• domestic equity Funds;

• international equity Funds;

• Australian listed equities;

• international listed equities;

• private equity;

- early stage innovation companies;

- listed exchange traded Funds;

- listed investment companies;

- hedge Funds;

- instalment warrants; and

- options and warrants.

Although this step may be the easiest, it can also prove to be Fundamental to the inherent investment returns of the strategy.

Step 5: Choose the investments

Once the type of investment is chosen under the specific asset allocation, the next step for the SMSF adviser is to choose specific investments. This is the most difficult part of the investment strategy. The adviser must spend time researching all the various options available, with a view to meeting the investment objectives for the client in the Fund.

10.10 Investing in Early Stage Innovation Companies

Trustee Question- I have heard that there are a number of tax concessions provided for Trustees of SMSFs to invest in start-up companies. I have come across one that says it has Early Stage Innovation Companies (ESIC) status. Can you also tell me about the risks in the investment?

The Guru's Strategic Response

First and foremost, I am not an investment expert. However I can say, many times I have made an investment, based on tax advantages rather than focused on the underlying benefits of the investment. Many SMSF members of the Australian SMSF Members Association also do likewise when they invest in Australian shares that pay fully franked dividends. These annual payments of company profits to shareholders come with tax credits which if not used are "refundable". For Trustees with a Fund wholly in tax exempt pension mode this means no tax in the Fund but a tax refund. Don't you like that?

From 1 July 2017 the Government introduced innovation guidelines for Early Stage Innovation Companies (ESIC). The details for investors in ESIC investments - found at www.innovation.gov.au is as follows:

"We have made changes to our tax system to incentivise investors to support innovative, high-growth potential start-ups."

What is new?

Tax incentives for eligible investors include:

- A 20% non-refundable carry-forward tax offset on investment, capped at $200,000 per investor, per year.

- A 10-year capital gains tax exemption for qualifying investments held for at least twelve months.

Who is eligible?

To be eligible for the incentives, an investor must meet the 'sophisticated investor' test under the Corporations Act 2001 or, if the investor does not meet this test, their total investment in qualifying companies must be $50,000 or less for that income year.

The incentives will be available for investments where the company is:

- early stage, determined against criteria related to expenditure, assessable income, stock exchange listing and incorporation; and

- involved in innovation, determined by allowing the company to self-assess against either a principles-based test or a points-based gateway test, or by receiving a determination from the Australian Tax Office.

How this works for SMSFs – Case Study

STRATEGY John Aldershot is 40 years of age and with his wife Janice they have the JJA Super Fund. It currently has $320,000 of accumulated member benefits and is invested in a residential property in Richmond, Victoria which is now paying for itself with positive assessable income (after deductible expenses) of $5,000.

John and Janice's employers contribute SGC on their behalf and they would like to top it up to the maximum concessional contributions limit of $25,000 each for the 2017 income year. John has a friend who helps raise money for start ups and has been offered the opportunity of putting money into a technology start up – Tech Company - that has met the requirements of ESIC.

So what happens for tax purposes for the JJA Super Fund?

a) The Trustee of the Fund commits to investing the $50,000 that John and Janice salary sacrifice into the Fund for the 2017 income year

b) The Trustee of the Fund will include the $50,000 as part of the Fund's assessable income pursuant to s290-160 of the ITAA 97 and pay tax of $7,500

c) As an ESIC qualified investment the Trustee receives a tax offset of $10,000 of which $7,500 can be applied to pay for the contributions tax on John and Janice's salary sacrifice contributions and the remainder can also be used to reduce tax payable on their Richmond rental property of $5,000 x 15% = $650. Plus, there is some tax offset left over which if not used is lost.

Let's say, and there is never any guarantee with start-ups, that the JJA Super Fund's investment in Tech Company lists on the ASX and in 2025 is worth $350,000. If the Trustee of the JJA Fund sells at that time, then there is no capital gains tax as it is within the ten-year window.

CHAPTER ELEVEN

Compliance with the Super Laws

11.0 The Commissioner of Taxation – Chris Jordan is looking over your SMSF!

11.1 Introduction – Compliance Rules

11.2 What actions will the Commissioner take for Non-Compliance?

11.3 The SMSF Auditor – the Important Compliance Piece

11.4 The SMSF Compliance Process

11.5 Tax Concessions and Complying SMSFs

11.6 Super Strategy Hint: Learn from the Commissioner

11.7 The Sole Purpose Test – It's not what it used to be

11.8 Acquisition of Assets from Members and Related Parties

11.9 Transactions to be at Arm's Length – section 109

11.0 The Commissioner of Taxation – Chris Jordan is looking over your SMSF!

"I once pulled a fortune cookie that said "the law sometimes sleeps but never forgets". And this has to be front of mind when doing anything with a SMSF. It might look great, fancy and have great results but if it fails the laws – watch out."

11.1 Introduction – Compliance Rules

By this stage of the *Guru's Guide to SMSFs*, you should know that I love SMSFs, and why? SMSFs are simply loaded with tax concessions. We have seen the benefits of contributing to a Fund in a tax effective manner and in upcoming chapters we will look at the favourable concessional tax rules applying to income and capital gains inside the Fund. And of course, there is tax-free lump sums and private pensions plus estate planning still coming – *all very exciting and enticing.*

But all of this comes at a cost. The Government is not going to let you have a great concessionally taxed investment vehicle, purpose built for retirement, and let you use it to buy your family home or an apartment for your children[23]. However, the laws do allow the Trustee of a SMSF to acquire an office, factory or farm and lease that back to a business owned by a member, Trustee or related party of the Fund.

---

23 In the 2018 Budget the Treasurer announced rules to apply from 1 July 2017 enabling a person to contribute pre-tax contributions, salary sacrifice over and above employer SGC and have these set aside for the purposes of using as a deposit on a first home. The maximum amount that can be saved in the First Home Super Saver scheme is $30,000 and any withdrawal from super is to be taxed at marginal tax rates but with a 30% tax offset.

O—🔑 Grant's Key Point

SMSF compliance rules can be fickle but the law is the law. And the ATO, the Fund auditor and any adviser to the Fund must be absolutely on top of compliance or they and the Trustees of the Fund will end up like the accountant in *Holloways* case we saw earlier in the *Guru's Guide to SMSFs*.

In this chapter, we will be looking at the major compliance laws – the rules and regulations a Trustee must understand and the penalties they face by way of a fine or the Fund being made non-compliant. At this time, there are a wide range of penalty fines the Commissioner of Taxation can apply to the Trustee of a Fund where there is a specific breach of a SMSF law. And, here's the fun part, many of these breaches are notified to him by the auditor of the Fund in the annual compliance return for the Fund. Talk about dobbing in.

11.2 **What actions will the Commissioner take for Non-Compliance?**

The ATO website describes the following courses of action that are available to the Commissioner to deal with SMSF Trustees who have not complied with the super laws:

- education direction;
- enforceable undertaking;
- rectification direction;
- administrative penalties;
- disqualification of a Trustee;
- civil and criminal penalties;

- allowing the SMSF to wind up;

- notice of non-compliance; and

- freezing an SMSF's assets.

I don't think we need to investigate all of these – let's just say the Commissioner has used them all and I sincerely hope that you are never involved in a negotiation with the ATO over which penalty to use – particularly the criminal one!

11.3 The SMSF Auditor – the Important Compliance Piece

STRATEGY We saw earlier that when we set up a SMSF, we must appoint an auditor to the Fund. Traditional company auditors check the financial wherewithal of a company ensuring that its profit and loss and balance sheet are exactly what it says it is to be. With a SMSF, the auditor is a compliance auditor and is there to check not only the financial status of the Fund but also that the Fund meets with its compliance rules – which are laid down by SISA and often interpreted by the Commissioner of Taxation.

One of the most important areas an auditor must check when dealing with a SMSF is that all transactions undertaken by the Trustee of a Fund are authorised and completed in the manner set down in the Fund's trust deed and governing rules. Generally, the SMSF auditor stands between the Trustee and the Commissioner of Taxation and is an important part of the compliance process. So make sure you get a knowledgeable auditor who knows their stuff and is able to add value to the compliance process. If you need help finding an appropriate auditor, email me at support@ilovesmsf.com for assistance.

11.4 The SMSF Compliance Process

In this chapter, we will consider the various compliance laws and in particular the laws relating to SMSF investments and member benefits, pick out some of the more interesting comments, strategies and examples from the Commissioner's guidelines and then consider some SMSF strategies on various compliance issues.

Note: All Commissioner's rulings, determinations and interpretive decisions can be found at www.ato.gov.au

11.5 Tax Concessions and Complying SMSFs

a) Maintaining Tax Concessions for the Fund

S 45 of SISA is the cornerstone provision of the superannuation laws and links the ITAA and SISA. If you breach s 45 there are no tax concessions, so compliance is mandatory. Now in order to be a complying super Fund, the Commissioner must provide to the Trustee, a notice of compliance each and every year. This is generally a given as the Commissioner does not measure compliance every year, but leaves it to the Trustee and more importantly, the auditor to notify of a non-compliance event. S 45(3) provides that the Commissioner can revoke the compliance certificate at any time meaning that a Trustee can never, ever really assume compliance unless they meet all of the conditions of s 42A of SISA – Complying SMSF.

b) What is a Complying SMSF?

S 42A of SISA is simple in its terms and dynamite in its effect. Generally, because all of the members of a SMSF are Trustees or represented by persons who hold their Enduring Power of Attorney, the SISA operates under the assumption that all Trustees and directors - if there is a Corporate Trustee - are knowingly responsible for the compliance of the Fund.

As such s 42A provides that where the Trustee of a Fund breaches any SISA compliance rules, which includes the provisions and rules in the Fund's trust deed, the Fund is primarily a non-complying SMSF. This means that when an auditor qualifies a SMSF or notifies the Commissioner of a breach of SISA or the Fund's trust deed, the Fund is a non-complying SMSF. However, the Trustee may apply to the Commissioner for his discretion in making the Fund a complying SMSF. To do so the Commissioner takes into account the seriousness of the offence, and the likely financial imposition for the members of the Fund and can grant compliance. But it is not guaranteed and really does depend on the severity of the offence. This zero-tolerance test puts all the power in the Commissioner's hands so tread lightly with what you do inside the Fund and don't push the limits.

c) The Tax Penalties of Non-Compliance

If the Commissioner hits the Trustee of the Fund with a non-compliance certificate, then if the Fund was a previously complying SMSF – s 295-325 of the ITAA 1997 applies to bring to account in the Fund's assessable income for the current year:

- the market value of the entire Fund's assets as at 30 June in the prior income year less any non-concessional contributions; and

- any assessable income for the current income year.

Any allowable deductions are taken from this with the resulting taxable income taxed at a rate of 45%. A quick example will highlight this nuclear option.

- *Example - Penalties for non-compliance*

The Trustees of the John Smith Family SMSF in December 2015 gave $50,000 to the member's daughter Theresa to buy an apartment in Sydney. They did it out of the goodness of their hearts as they couldn't stand to see her renting anymore. The Trustees and members – John and Janice Smith are both aged 52 and not able to access their superannuation under the preservation rules. There is no loan agreement, no proposed repayment schedule and this is not the first time that the Trustees have used the monies in the Fund for their own purposes. The Commissioner has reached the end of his tether and issues a non-compliance certificate for the 2015-2016 income year.

For the 2015-2016 income year the Fund's taxable income was $34,000 from the rent of another property and a small amount of interest income less allowable deductions. However, the accountant to the Fund and the Commissioner have agreed that the Fund's assets at 30 June 2015 was $954,000 which was a commercial property and cash. Under section 295-325 this is to be added back to the Fund's assessable income thereby increasing taxable income to $988,000. Are you getting a feeling how nasty non-compliance can be? And here is the money shot, the Commissioner issues an income tax assessment for the John Smith Family SMSF of $444,600.

When John finds out he can't believe his accountant did not tell him about the problem – despite the accountant showing him emails that told him when he first found out that the Fund was likely non-complying. John told the accountant that he does not have that cash and his accountant suggested the following:

1. The commercial property in the Fund cannot be financed as it is an existing asset of a Fund and not able to be lent against or this will amount to another breach. This means the Trustee of the Fund must sell the property and quickly.

2. A possibility is to get the money back from the daughter but that horse has already bolted and the $50,000 loan has turned into over $444,000 in tax payable and no doubt there will be penalties and interest charges to boot.

3. The members of the Fund can contribute the tax payable into the Fund but John tells the accountant they don't have that sort of money which can be used quickly.

John leaves the accountants office in a huff – locked into a course of events that could have so easily been avoided except for his recalcitrance.

Warning - Don't be like John!

d) Monetary Penalties for Non-Compliance

Apart from the tough non-compliance penalty above, the Commissioner can levy on the spot fines for breaches of various sections of SISA. These do not require the Commissioner to go through the Courts so it is usually the first course of action. The penalties are as follows (as time of print):

Section & Rule	Administrative Penalty
s.35B – failure to prepare Financial Statements	$2,100
s.65 – prohibition on lending or providing financial assistance to members & their relatives	$12,600
s.67 – prohibition on super fund borrowing, except as permitted, eg limited recourse borrowing arrangement	$12,600
s.84 – contravention of In-House Asset rules	$12,600
s.103(1) & (2) – failing to keep trustee minutes for at least 10 years	$2,100
s.103(2A) – failure to maintain a s.71E election, where applicable, in relation to a fund with an investment in a pre 11/8/99 related unit trust	$2,100
s.104 – failing to keep records of change of trustees for at least 10 years	$2,100
s.104A – failing to sign Trustee Declaration within 21 days of appointment and keeping for at least 10 years	$2,100
s.105 - failing to keep member reports for 10 years	$2,100
s.106 – failing to notify ATO of an event that has significant adverse effect on the fund's financial position	$12,600
s.106A – failing to notify ATO of change of status of SMSF, eg fund ceasing to be a SMSF	$4,200
s.124 – where an Investment Manager is appointed, failing to make the appointment in writing	$1,050
s.160 – failing to comply with ATO Education directive	$1,050
s.254(1) – Failing to provide the Regulator with information on the approved form within the prescribed time upon establishment of the fund	$1,050
s.347A(5) – Failing to complete a form with requested information provided by the Regulator as part of the Regulator's Statistical Program	$1,050

11.6 Super Strategy Hint: Learn from the Commissioner

STRATEGY I have been doing SMSF compliance and law for the past two decades, and many of my legal friends and I have had a lot of arguments over the meaning and interpretation of the various superannuation and taxation laws. As an adviser, we need to be able to read, understand and apply the law but that doesn't help when there are differing interpretations on an issue or the Fund's auditor doesn't sign off on a transaction. It can be hard to sway an auditors mind. Well as luck would have it, in 1999 the Commissioner of Taxation became the Regulator for SMSFs and that meant greater legal and technical resources being thrown into the ring. Over the last two decades he has been busy building a strong compliance legal team and importantly for all of us – whether adviser or Trustee – guidance notes, interpretative decisions and rulings have made life so much easier. Some of his rulings on specific subjects are huge and legally well thought out – in fact if you tried to get a barrister to write a legal opinion equivalent to the Commissioner's business real property or contributions ruling – it would cost $100,000 and they would not stand by it anyway. Given the above discussion of zero tolerance in terms of SMSF compliance the Commissioner's rulings are absolute gold.

Here is my big giveaway and please keep it secret. My best strategies from the past ten years have come from the Commissioner's rulings – see the Bed and Breakfast example in s 66 of SISA below. The beauty about the Commissioner's rulings and in very particular, his examples is that they provide the detailed analysis to his thinking and practical application. In fact, in many instances where I have been advising accountants who have had compliance issues with their auditor, I have had to refer the auditor to the relevant ATO ruling to clear up the matter. Which is one of the main problems – SMSF auditors are licensed by ASIC yet they are dealing with superannuation law regulated by the Commissioner of Taxation. Oh well – another layer of red tape to add to costs.

11.7 The Sole Purpose Test – It's not what it used to be

a) The Law

S 62(1) of SISA provides a strict test in terms of the benefits that can be provided to members of the Fund. So, the Trustee of the Fund cannot, for example buy a residential property with Fund monies and then proceed to live in the property rent free. This would be considered providing a benefit to a member, which does not fit in with the sole purpose test. It provides that the Fund is used solely for one or more of the three core purposes including the payment of retirement benefits, death benefits or benefits at age 65.

With the Morrison changes to apply from 1 July 2017, the sole purpose test becomes important for SMSF estate planning as it means that the Trustee of a SMSF may hold an accumulation Fund for a member, solely for the purpose of providing death benefits to the member's dependants or legal estate. In fact a member of a well-constructed SMSF, with sufficient financial resources outside of the SMSF to live off, is not required to draw upon their super in retirement, at age 65 or any other age, if they don't want to – all they need to do is leave their super in their accumulation account and not commence a pension account. Not many advisers, Trustees or people are aware of how to maximise this strategy – of course the children would be happy for it.

Apart from the three core purposes, the Trustee of the Fund can also use the Fund to provide certain side or ancillary benefits including incapacity benefits — such as temporary incapacity, salary continuance, accident coverage and total and permanent disablement benefits directly from a member's benefits in the Fund.

However, where the Trustee of the Fund seeks to provide benefits other than those regulated in s 62(1), the Commissioner may use one of the many non-compliance tools in his armoury to attack the issue.

b) ATO Guidance on using your SMSF now

We often have requests from auditors who want clarification about whether a particular SMSF investment complies with the super laws and in particular the sole purpose test. Along with specific acquisition and other related party rules, the Trustee should always consider whether the sole purpose rules might be breached.

For example, a Fund purchasing a freehold burial plot which can be resold at any time may not breach the sole purpose test. However, if instead, the Fund purchased a funeral plan which includes a burial plot to provide for a particular Fund member on the occasion of their death, this would be providing the member with financial assistance (to buy the plan) and also a present-day benefit to the member or their relatives, as Fund money has been used to purchase the plan and the plot.

The provision of present day benefits to Fund members or their relatives is a breach of the super laws as it is not in keeping with the sole purpose test. However, we now have a range of alternative compliance treatments available for Trustees who contravene the super laws.

These include directing Trustees to undertake education or to rectify contraventions and imposing financial penalties that Trustees have to pay out of their own pockets. For more serious matters, we can still disqualify Trustees or make the Fund non-complying, or both. Having a wide range of enforcement options helps us to regulate non-compliant Funds through appropriate education and other compliance action.

c) Commissioner's Sole Purpose Test Examples

The Commissioner's 32 page ruling on the sole purpose test SMSFR 2008/2 provides instructions and highlights some of the instances where a breach of the sole purpose test may occur. The Commissioner notes that "factors that would weigh in favour of a SMSF not being maintained in accordance with s 62 because of the provision of benefits not specified in s 62 include:

i. The Trustee negotiated for or sought out the benefit, even if the additional benefit is negotiated for, or sought out in the course of undertaking other activities that are consistent with s 62.

ii. The benefit has influenced the decision-making of the Trustee to favour one course of action over another.

iii. The benefit is provided by the SMSF to a member or another party at a cost or financial detriment to the SMSF.

iv. There is a pattern or preponderance of events that, when viewed in their entirety, amount to a material benefit being provided that is not specified under subsection 62(1)."

However, there are instances where an incidental benefit may be provided to the members of the Fund where: "the provision by an SMSF of benefits other than those specified in subsection 62(1) that are incidental, remote or insignificant does not of itself displace an assessment that the Trustee has not contravened the sole purpose test."

The incidental benefit rule is demonstrated in the following example taken from the Commissioner's ruling:

Example 1 — benefit inherent in investment: merely an incidental benefit

As part of a portfolio of property investments, an SMSF Trustee invests in a number of holiday apartments through a property syndicate. The investments are made through a widely held trust and the apartments are owned and managed by the trust. Income is pooled and allocated to investors on a pro-rata basis. No particular investor has a right to a specified holiday apartment.

All investors in the property syndicate pay normal market rates when staying at the apartments but, subject to availability on the day of arrival, may be able to upgrade their accommodation at no extra cost. Investors cannot dispose of this right.

Two members of the SMSF stay at the apartments and have their accommodation upgraded.

This benefit, represented by the upgrade right and its exercise, is incidental to the SMSF's investment in the holiday apartments. The Trustee does not contravene the sole purpose test in these circumstances.

The Trustee did not seek to obtain this benefit for the members and there is nothing to suggest that it influenced the Trustee's decision-making in making the investment. Further, it is an inherent feature of investing in the apartments available to all investors and is a relatively insignificant benefit.

Even if the Trustee makes a pattern of like property investments (for example, due to expertise the Trustee has in making property investments in certain holiday destinations) that each provide a similar benefit, this fact alone does not suggest a purpose of maintaining the SMSF in contravention of the sole purpose test.

In contrast to Example 1, Case 43 / 95 (the Swiss Chalet case) 95 ATC 374; (1995) 31 ATR 1067 is an example where there was a pattern of investing in assets that provided other benefits of a substantial nature to the members of the Fund. This was a significant factor the Administrative Appeals Tribunal considered when it found an ulterior purpose in relation to the maintenance of the Fund."

d) Penalties

Sole Purpose Penalty: The maximum civil penalty provision is 2,000 penalty units or $420,000 in addition to tax non-compliance. In *Deputy Commissioner of Taxation (Superannuation) v Ryan [2015] FCA 1037* the Federal Court of Australia decided that a combined fine of $40,000 was appropriate for Trustees of a Fund that had consistently dipped into their SMSF to Fund their lifestyle. The Commissioner may levy an on the spot fine of $12,600 should he not want to take the Trustee to court.

11.8 Acquisition of Assets from Members and Related Parties

a) The Law

The Trustee of the Fund must not acquire an asset from a member, employer-sponsor or related party of the Fund — s 66(1) of SISA. In terms of acquisition this may be by way of the direct or indirect purchase of an asset from a member or related party or where the member or related party makes an "in-specie" contribution into the Fund on behalf of a member. The Commissioner has released a ruling SMSFR 2010/1 on how s 66 applies to the Trustee of a SMSF.

b) Who is a Related Party?

S 10(1) of SISA provides that a related party is a member, employer-sponsor, or an associate of either, including:

i. any Trustee of the super Fund, if the Trustee is a company, all of the directors of the Trustee company;

ii. any relative of the member ranging from grandparents and first cousins through to lineal descendants and their spouses;

iii. a partnership where the member or employer-sponsor are partners. This includes the partners themselves, their spouses and their children;

iv. any company or trust controlled by a member of the Fund or employer sponsor including a company or trust where the member and any associated party of the member holds a controlling interest in the company or trust or the directors or Trustees are accustomed to act on the directions of the SMSF member. This is known as a "Related Trust".

Example

The John Smith Family SMSF (that we discussed earlier) decided to get out of the loan of the money to their daughter to buy the property she lives in, finance it with a SMSF Limited Recourse Borrowing Arrangement and then rent it out to her at commercial market value rent. Apart from this being wrong on many levels, the acquisition of the property from their daughter, a related party would breach s 66 of SISA. From what I know of the bank lending departments who put all SMSF loans under the microscope, they would not lend to a non-compliant SMSF.

c) Important Anti-Avoidance Measures

Section 66(3) has strong anti-avoidance measures as was evidenced in Lock v Commissioner of Taxation [2003] FCA 309 where Justice Goldberg struck down a complex arrangement using two trusts and a not-yet-formed SMSF to seek to defeat the operation of s 66(1). Justice Goldberg stated in terms of the application of the anti-avoidance rules:

"The end result of each scheme was that the applicants, as Trustees, did not acquire an asset from a member of the relevant Fund. The application of s 66(1) to each Fund was thereby avoided. But in each case the applicants, as Trustees, carried out part of the scheme, by subscribing for units in the Property Trust and the Willowbank Trust, with the intention during the respective year of income, that the scheme would result, or would be likely to result, in an acquisition of the type referred to in s 66(3)(a). This would be with the intention during the respective year of income that that acquisition would avoid the application of s 66(1). They intended not to contravene s 66(1) and they succeeded in that respect as by virtue of the scheme, the acquisition of the asset in the case of each Fund avoided the application of s 66(1)."

d) Important "Must Know" Exceptions to Section 66

The following assets are exceptions to s 66(1) including:

- Listed securities acquired at market value. This includes securities listed on the Australian Stock Exchange and other licensed markets authorised under the CA 2001 such as the London Stock Exchange or the New York Stock Exchange;

- Business real property, for a SMSF and superannuation Fund with fewer than five members – see Examples below on what is Business Real Property;

- In-house assets, provided the acquisition of such assets is at market value and does not result in the Fund exceeding the in-house assets test — see below. This also includes the exceptions to the in-house assets test such as investments in a widely-held unit trust, deposit with an approved depository institution or property held by the Trustee of the Fund and the related party as tenants in common. This includes both business and residential property that is an in-house asset of the Fund;

- Units in a unit trust or shares in a company that meet the conditions of reg 13.22C of SISR including that the Trustee of the unit trust or the company does not borrow, lease the property to a member or related party of the Fund unless the property is business real property and that there is no interest in another entity such as a shareholding or unit in a unit trust. For more on this special trust arrangement, which can be used for sophisticated strategies well outside this book, see the In-House Assets section below.

e) What is Business Real Property?

As business real property can be transferred into a SMSF (remember it must be at market value – whether as a contribution or purchase), there is a great deal of sweating on what is and is not business real property. And for this, thank goodness the Commissioner's 64-page ruling — SMSFR 2009/1 — provides some clarity. The key business real property conditions, according to the Commissioner are:

"Two basic conditions must be satisfied before an SMSF, or any other entity related to or dealing with an SMSF, can be said to hold business real property:

- the SMSF or the other entity must hold an eligible interest in real property; that is freehold, leasehold and assignable Crown interests in land; and

- the underlying land must satisfy the business use test in the definition, which requires the real property to be 'used wholly and exclusively in one or more businesses' carried on by any entity."

Commissioner's Examples on Business Real Property

Let's look at some of the interesting examples highlighted in the ATO Business Real Property ruling.

Example 1: Primary production business with private residence — case 1

The Harrison Vineyard is owned and managed by Peter and Denise Harrison who are members of the Harrison SMSF. The property has 10 hectares planted out with vines and on half a hectare of the property, they have build a private residence in which they live.

The vineyard has a grape supply agreement with a local winery for the next 5 years. This agreement forms the basis of a business of primary production that is being conducted on the property. The Harrison SMSF acquires the property from Peter and Denise at its market value. Peter and Denise then lease the property from the SMSF.

The property is business real property of both the Harrison SMSF after it acquires the property and of Peter and Denise at all times. At all relevant times, the Harrison SMSF and Peter and Denise hold either a freehold interest in the land or a leasehold interest in the land. The use of the private residence is permitted under the specific application of the 'wholly and exclusively' test in subsection 66(6). Therefore, the property is used wholly and exclusively in Peter and Denise's business at all times.

Therefore:

- the acquisition of property by the Harrison SMSF from Peter and Denise does not contravene the related party asset acquisition rule in section 66; and

- the freehold interest in the property is not an in-house asset of the Harrison SMSF under Part 8."

STRATEGY **The Guru's SMSF Strategy:** The example above provided by the Commissioner clarifies the important issue of transferring land that has grapes, wheat or other items that form part of a primary production business. The land with the grapes in this example is transferred and then leased back to the SMSF Trustees. The grapes are not severable from the land and become part and parcel of the business real property. In the past I have advised on many farms currently held in the names of members of a SMSF or their Family Trust being transferred into a SMSF by way of contribution, loan and purchase. This is a great tax, estate planning and commercial strategy but it does have a lot of pitfalls and should not be attempted with an uneducated adviser and definitely is not a DIY strategy.

Example 10: Residential property held in a property investment business

Mr Wood owns 20 residential units that are leased to long-term residents. Mr Wood manages and maintains the flats on a full-time basis living on the income generated from the leases. The units are not mortgaged. Mr Wood is approaching retirement and would like his SMSF to acquire some of the units rather than sell the units to a non-related party.

The scale of the operation together with the elements of repetition and purpose indicate that Mr Wood is carrying on a property investment business. Even though the tenants' use the properties for their own private or domestic purposes, this use remains incidental and relevant to Mr Wood's property investment business. Consequently, Mr Wood's interest in the property on which the units are built is business real property. Provided that the acquisition takes place at market value, the units may be acquired by the SMSF without contravening the related party asset acquisition rule in s 66.

Example 11: Motel with manager's residence

The Bruce family company owns and operates the Highway Motel. The company is a related party of the Bruce SMSF. The Trustee for the Bruce SMSF wants to purchase the motel. The Bruce family company employs Nadia as the manager of the motel. Nadia lives on site and is expected to make all decisions in relation to the day to day management of the motel.

The real property on which the motel is located is used in a business. The fact that the manager's residence is part of the motel is incidental and relevant to that business. Additionally, the use of the property by the guests for non-business purposes does not cause the business use test to be failed as this use is clearly an inherent part of the business.

The real property is therefore used wholly and exclusively in the motel business, making the company's interest in the land business real property. The proposed acquisition of the motel by the Bruce SMSF will not contravene the related party asset acquisition rule in s 66.

STRATEGY **The Guru's Best SMSF Strategy Examples**
As I said earlier, the Commissioner often surprises a SMSF advisory veteran like myself with some of his cases and examples by being a lot more lenient that I would ever have expected. Consider some of the following properties which may or may not be able to be transferred into a SMSF. And can I ask "Why would we do that anyway?" Well by now you should have grasped the benefits of warehousing as many assets as possible in super rather than outside – provided of course you have enough to live off outside a SMSF

Example 18: Bed and breakfast - case 2 - business

Dean Lamont owns a house with 5 bedrooms and 2 living areas. He uses one of the bedrooms himself. The other four bedrooms are let year-round as part of a bed and breakfast business. One living area is set aside for the exclusive use of guests. Breakfast is included in the room cost and other meals are available by arrangement.

Dean advertises his rooms with Worldwide B&B Internet bookings agency. Dean has a business plan, pays tax, and has three permanent part time employees. The business has operated since Dean acquired the house 17 years ago.

In this case, a business is being carried on. Dean's non-business use of the property is incidental and relevant to that business. Accordingly, the property is used wholly and exclusively in the business and is business real property.

Example 19: Strata titled hotel complex

Mr Chou owns a studio apartment in a strata titled hotel complex. The contract for purchase includes a requirement that the unit is leased for fifteen years to Xin Pty Ltd, hotel business, with rent paid to Mr Chou based on occupancy of the complex. The contract specifies that the freehold owner has no right to reside in the unit during the time it is leased to Xin Pty Ltd. Mr Chou wishes to sell the unit to his SMSF.

The real property is used wholly and exclusively in Xin Pty Ltd's hotel business and is business real property of Mr Chou for the purposes of acquisition. However, if Mr Chou or a related party of the SMSF intended to stay in the unit at any time, there may be in-house asset implications.

f) Penalties

Section 66 Penalty: The penalty provision for a breach is one year's imprisonment. In *Lock's case* the Court held that the Fund was a non-complying Fund and subject to penalty taxation.

11.9 Transactions to be at Arm's Length – section 109

a) The Law

S 109 of SISA provides that the Trustee must invest the moneys of the Fund in an arm's length manner. This does not preclude the Trustee dealing with closely associated parties, subject to the other provisions of SISA, it merely requires that the transaction stand up to commerciality. Where there is a relationship between the Trustee and the other party to the transaction, the Commissioner can be expected to pay close attention to the deal. Importantly, it is only those deals that favour an external party that the Commissioner will review.

For example, where a related party of a SMSF provides a "nil interest loan" the Commissioner has stated the following in a National Tax Liaison Group and also, various interpretive decisions that he has made on the subject:

"Further, as noted in ATO Interpretative Decision ATO ID 2010/162 - if such a borrowing is entered into between an SMSF Trustee and a lender that is a related party of the Fund, for example by refinancing the original loan, a fact that the borrowing is interest free does not cause a contravention of subsection 109 of the SISA."

So what transactions are to be caught by section 109? For that, the best guide in my opinion is to review the ATO guidelines for SMSF Auditors. This is an important look at the intricacies of auditing at this stage and the depth of compliance review that the Commissioner requires when considering whether a related party transaction is at arm's length.

b) Extreme Warning – Get the Documentation Right and in Place

The important fifth pillar of the compliance tree is documentation. Time and time again a Court action or a transaction falls down because the appropriate documentation between two parties is not effectively put in place. Let's look at a serious example from my history. I was called upon in a case to act as an expert witness where a transaction with a SMSF had gone sour and a client was suing the financial planner. On review of the documentation, I discovered that the Fund's trust deed, its fundamental set of governing rules, were not for a SMSF at all, but an old employer super fund and that the participating employer was no longer in existence – meaning that there was no employer fund anymore. So, if the purported SMSF was not a super fund what was it? Simply, it is a trust that does not distribute income which has nasty tax consequences for the Trustee, but more importantly it lets the financial planner off the hook, as the Trustee was bringing an action under the SISA – which only applies to superannuation funds.

So beware of the documentation – as can be seen from the following SMSF auditor guidelines produced by the Commissioner of Taxation in relation to s 109.

c) ATO Guideline - Audit of "Arm's Length Basis"

The auditor should satisfy him/herself that all the Fund's investment transactions have been made and maintained at arm's length. When assessing whether a transaction is on an arm's length basis, the auditor should consider the following:

1) Purchase or sale of assets

- the purchase/selling price was at a fair market value (valuation reports to be sighted where possible);
- money is actually paid - bank accounts statements to be sighted.

2) Lease arrangements

- written contract must be drawn up - to be sighted;
- the investment was entered into and maintained on commercial terms under the terms of the contract;
- lease payments and residual value to be at market value – commercial rates to be confirmed with local property market or industry;
- lease payments to be made - bank account statements to be sighted.

3) Loans

- written contract and repayment schedule must exist - to be sighted;

- conditions of loan to be on commercial rates including period of loan, repayments, security provided and interest rates – to be confirmed by market rates;

- repayments to be made - bank account statements to be sighted.

4) Investments in entities

- realisation of investments, shares issued, units allocated at market value;

- return on investments at commercial rates;

- return on investments to be paid (eg. trust distributions, dividends, etc) - bank account statements to be sighted.

5) Breaches of the Arm's Length Rule – Commissioner Guidelines

The investments by an SMSF must be made and maintained on a strict commercial basis and maintained at arm's length.

With the audit of a SMSF, the following aspects are found:

- The Fund has purchased a commercial property from a member/ Trustee of the Fund at market value for $1,000,000 and leases it back to the member for $2000 a year.

- There is no written lease agreement in place, however, the Minutes of Trustees meetings do include details of the arrangement. After the first year, the Fund has not received any money from the member and has decided as a favour to the member to write off the $2000 debt.

Action Required

a) As the commercial property purchased is 'business real property' as defined under s 66(5) of the SISA, there would be no contravention under s 66 of the SISA - the acquisition of assets from a related party.

b) As the property is classed as business real property, the lease between the Trustees of the Fund and the member, a related party of the Fund, would not be considered to be an in-house asset, if throughout the term of the lease the property remained business real property of the Fund within the meaning of sub-section 66(5) of the SISA.

c) As no formal written lease agreement exists between the Fund and the member, the auditor should insist that a formal lease be drawn-up and executed by both parties, with the lease rental being established at market rates.

d) Arm's length - The auditor should determine whether the rental of the property to determine if the $2,000 a year is a reasonable payment for the lease.

e) If the rental income is not considered to be in line with current market rates based upon rentals of similar properties in that locality, the auditor should inform the Trustees, in writing, that he considers that they contravened s 109 of the SISA since the lease arrangement was not at arm's length, as a consequence of the member receiving a favourable rental rate and because the debt had been written off as a favour to the member.

f) Even if the rental income is considered to be reasonable, the auditor will still need to write to the Trustees of the Fund advising that section 109 of the SISA has been contravened by writing off the debt as a favour to the member.

g) The auditor should request a report from the Trustees as to what action has or will be taken to rectify the contravention(s).

h) If the auditor is satisfied that the contravention(s) will or have been rectified, including the repayment of any loss of interest, the auditor should report the contravention in the audit report. Also, depending upon the seriousness and materiality of the contravention, the auditor should determine whether a qualification in the auditor's report is needed.

i) If the auditor does not receive a report from the Trustees or is not satisfied with the action or proposed action of the Trustees, the auditor must advise the ATO, in writing, outlining the details of the contravention and report the contravention in the audit report. Depending upon the seriousness and materiality of the contravention, the auditor will also need to determine whether a qualification is required.

d) Penalties

Section 109 Penalty:

The breach of section 109 is a civil penalty provision and may result in a $440,000 fine imposed by a court. However, the Commissioner may levy a $4,200 on the spot fine.

CHAPTER TWELVE

Dealing with Related Parties – the In-House Assets Test and Limited Recourse Borrowing Arrangements

"When I first started in SMSFs, never in a million years did I expect that the superannuation laws would allow the Trustee of a SMSF to borrow. Well it is here, tightly controlled and used with the right advice and in the right way can really turbo-charge super. But borrowing is risky – there is upside but so much downside. Look at what the GFC did to so many investors who had bought property off the plan."

12.1 Introduction

There is no doubt that SMSFs are making a big noise in Australia and all over the world. Did you know that in terms of pension systems, the Australian SMSF market is the third largest in the world with more than $700 Billion in funds? They are only behind the Japanese and Norwegian Government Pension Funds – can you imagine that?

In this chapter we will look at dealing with related parties such as relatives, business partners and companies that the member or Trustee control.

12.2 Lending to Members or Relatives

1) The Law

Section 65 of SISA 1993 provides that the Trustee of a superannuation fund must not lend to a member or relatives of a member of the fund *or provide financial assistance to members or relatives of members of the fund.* The Trustee may lend to related parties that are not members or relatives such as family trusts or companies. However, the in-house assets test — s 84(1) of SISA 93 or the sole purpose test provisions - may catch this loan. Remember the compliance chart – you might escape one thing and not another. Be careful and get a good adviser!

1) The Commissioner's Examples

The Commissioner has published a ruling on the provision of financial assistance in terms of section 65 — SMSFR 2008/1 and notes the following:

"The term 'financial assistance' is not defined in the SISA. It has no technical meaning and therefore takes its ordinary meaning having regard to the context in which it is appears. Financial assistance extends beyond the provision of loans (as covered by paragraph 65(1)(a)) and beyond other kinds of disposition of money or property.

Financial assistance can take the form of the giving of a guarantee, indemnity, security or charge or the taking on of an obligation, or any other arrangement that, on an objective assessment is in substance to provide financial assistance to a member or relative of a member using the resources of the SMSF.

In the Commissioner's view, a Trustee or investment manager of an SMSF contravenes the giving of financial assistance in section 65 by doing any of the following:

(i) giving a gift of an SMSF asset to a member or relative of a member;

(ii) selling an SMSF asset for less than its market value to a member or relative of a member;

(iii) purchasing an asset for greater than its market value from a member or relative of a member;

(iv) acquiring services in excess of what the SMSF requires from a member or relative of a member;

(v) paying an inflated price for services acquired from a member or relative of a member;

(vi) forgiving a debt owed to the SMSF by a member or relative of a member;

(vii) releasing a member or relative of a member from a financial obligation owed to the SMSF, including where the amount is not yet due and payable;

(viii) delaying recovery action for a debt owed to the SMSF by a member or relative of a member;

(ix) satisfying, or taking on, a financial obligation of a member or relative of a member;

(x) giving a guarantee or an indemnity for the benefit of a member or relative of a member; and

(xi) giving a security or charge over SMSF assets for the benefit of a member or relative of a member."

2) Penalties

Section 65 Penalty: Great care must be taken by the Trustee of a SMSF in any dealing with a member or relative. The penalty is an on the spot fine – without question – of $12,600, plus the fund may be made non-complying and the usual range of civil penalty orders under section 191, apply.

12.3 In House Assets Test – Section 84

1) The Law

Earlier in *The Gurus Guide to SMSFs* we looked at the sole purpose test. This test provides that the Trustee cannot provide a current benefit (advantage) to a member of the Fund unless it is a retirement, death or benefit payable after age 65. For example, the Trustee of the Fund could acquire a new Hyundai motor vehicle, with $40,000 of the Fund's assets, and then lease this to a member under an arm's length commercial lease arrangement. This is not a current benefit to the member as the member could access a similar deal from a bank or other commercial financing organisation. But no so fast. The in-house assets test provides that the Trustee must take into account, as an in-house asset any lease arrangement with a related party, such as a member. The value of the underlying property is to be determined and there will be a breach of the in-house assets if the total value of in-house assets, such as the Hyundai lease exceeds 5% of the market value of all the assets of the Fund.

2) What is an In-House Asset?

Section 71(1) of SISA 93 provides that "an in-house asset of a superannuation fund is an asset of the fund that is a loan to, or an investment in, a related party of the fund, an investment in a related trust of the fund, or an asset of the fund subject, to a lease or lease arrangement between a Trustee of the fund and a related party of the fund."

3) Related Trust

Section 66 and 84 fit snugly together and have similar terms. Related party is a key component under the in-house assets test and includes a "Related Trust".

The definition of a Related Trust is found in section 10(1) of the SISA 93 and means a trust where a member or employer sponsor holds:

> a) more than 50% of the rights to income and capital of the trust; or
>
> b) holds a right to appoint or remove the Trustees of the trust; or
>
> c) where the Trustee of the trust is accustomed or required to act according to the instructions, directions or wishes of the member or employer-sponsor.

Example

A typical scenario that would be caught under the Related Trust rules would be the investment by a SMSF in a unit trust where the Trustee owns 100% of the units in the unit trust. It would also include an investment by the Trustee of a Fund in a unit trust where the Trustee owns 5% of the units and the member owns 46% of the units personally. The unit trust is a Related Trust of the Fund because the member controls the unit trust in conjunction with the Fund. The minority investment by the Fund in the unit trust would be an in-house asset.

4) Leases are In-House Assets

The definition of in-house asset extends the reach of investments to a lease or lease arrangement with a member or employer-sponsor as we saw with the Hyundai motor vehicle example earlier.

A lease arrangement is defined in section 10(1) of the SISA 1993 to mean "any agreement, arrangement or understanding in the nature of a lease (other than a lease) between the Trustee of a superannuation fund and another person, under which the other person is to use, or control the use of, property owned by the fund."

Another great example taken from the explanatory memorandum provides "if a superannuation fund owns a beach house, and leased the beach house to a member for two months of the year, the full market value of the beach house would be included in the in-house assets ration of the fund during the two month period." This is, despite the fact, that the member may pay full commercial rent for the period of occupation.

Be Careful with Property Investments – don't deal with Related Parties unless Business Real Property

Trustees of SMSFs with investments in holiday homes, ski lodges, residential property and other property investments must be extremely vigilant in respect of members wishing to stay in the property, even if it is only for one night. As the in-house assets test is a day by day test and any stay by the member would require the Trustee to include the market value of the property as an in-house asset of the fund. If the market value exceeds the 5% rule then the Trustee is in breach of the in-house assets test.

5) Strong Anti-Avoidance Rules

The in-house assets test has anti-avoidance sections to catch most attempts by Trustees to circumvent the rules. Section 71(2) provides that where an arrangement has been entered into and a person is aware that as a result of the arrangement, a loan, investment or lease to a related party or a related trust is not caught by the in-house assets test then the asset is taken to be an in-house asset. Section 85 is another anti-avoidance rule and was used by the Court in Holloway's case.

In addition section 71(4) empowers the Commissioner to deem, by written notice, that any investment, loan or lease undertaken by the Trustee of the fund, to be an investment, loan or lease arrangement with a related party or an investment in a related trust. Section 71(4) is the most powerful anti-avoidance provision in the SISA 93.

6) Exceptions to the In-House Assets Rules

Section 71(1) provides exceptions to the in-house assets test. These include investments that are generally offered by commercial investment providers such as life insurance policies, managed funds, public sector bonds, term deposits and pooled super funds.

The main exception for in-house assets test purposes is business real property. This was discussed extensively when we looked at section 66(1) of SISA 93 – the Trustee acquiring related party assets. Business real property also extends beyond Torrens titles and extends to:

- any interest of the entity in Crown land other than a leasehold interest, being an interest that is capable of assignment or transfer. The extension to cover Crown land enables many rural properties on Crown land to be owned by a Fund and leased to a member or related company or family trust;

- property including residential property which is held as tenants in common as a partnership with a related party. However, this does not enable a member or related party to reside in the property – simply that a tenancy in common with a related party does not breach the in-house assets test; and

- an investment under the regulations that is deemed not to be an in-house asset. To that end the SISR 94 – Regulation 13.22C provides an exception for a specific type of related trust or company (wholly owned or exceeding the 50% rule) which can be owned by the SMSF Trustee and not breach the in-house assets test. The key conditions of the Reg13.22C trust/company are as follows:

  i) There is no borrowing in the Trust or the Company and note that this would extend to overdrafts and unpaid present entitlements or dividends.

  ii) There is no guarantee or charge over the assets of the Trust or Company.

iii) The assets of the Trust cannot include any investment in another entity such as a publicly listed share, managed fund, cash management trust, unit trust investment, etc. This limits the investments to property – residential, holiday, business or rural but excludes an investment in a property trust.

iv) The Trust or Company does not carry on a business at any time. If it starts as an investment trust or company and then through its activities grows into an trading business then SISR 13.22D would see it void its exemption and be caught under the in-house assets test.

v) There is no lease of any asset of the Trust or Company to a related party unless it is business real property.

There are a number of Interpretive Decisions issued by the Commissioner of Taxation on SIS Regulation 13.22C and 13.22D – with the latter the events and circumstances that may result in the Trustee or Company losing its exemption under SIS Regulation 13.22C.

STRATEGY **Acquiring SIS Regulation 13.22C Assets**

We have already reviewed the limitation of section 66(1) of SISA in terms of transferring related party assets into a SMSF. The exceptions for a transfer also include assets that meet the criteria of SIS Regulation 13.22C.

As such a member of a SMSF or related party may hold units in a SISR 13.22C trust. The units held by the member may be transferred by way of sale, contribution or loan to the Trustee of the Fund and not breach section 66(1). However, a number of other compliance issues need to be taken into account depending on how the transfer is specifically structured.

The Guru's Special Unit Trust/Company SMSF Strategy

STRATEGY A Related Trust is an in-house asset. The only exception is the SISR 1994 13.22C trust discussed above. But what if the Trustee of the Fund invests in a unit trust or company and does not control it?

Let's say you have a SMSF and it acquires 50% of the units in the Land Development Unit Trust (LDUT). There is a corporate Trustee of the LDUT of which you are a director. My SMSF has the remaining 50% of the units in LDUT and I am also a director of the corporate Trustee. We also have an independent chairperson. This is a very popular strategy for SMSF Trustees to enter into wide ranging investment and potentially business acquisitions where the investment is not a Related Trust or Company.

However, points to watch out for:

a) Any unlisted unit trust investment is commercially risky so the Trustee of the Fund must be extremely careful and this must be reflected in the Fund's investment strategy;

b) Your Fund cannot acquire any of my units or the 50% rule is breached so there needs to be an exit strategy that does not breach the SISA 93 in case there is a falling out between the parties;

c) Give the potential problems it is crucial to do a unitholders or shareholders agreement dealing with what happens when there is a death, divorce or dementia of the members and Trustees of the Funds;

d) Everything must be at arm's length. Don't forget all other provisions of the SISA 93 must be adhered to;

e) It is strongly recommended that a specialist SMSF lawyer be engaged to guide parties through the transaction and investment.

7) In House Assets Test Penalties

When it comes to penalties the in-house assets test is different. There are two sections where a Trustee may breach the laws and have penalties imposed under section 84.

Firstly section 83 provides that there is a breach of the in-house asset test if the Trustee of the Fund acquires an asset that exceeds the 5% market value asset rule. Let's go back to our earlier Hyundai example where it is leased to a member of the Fund. At the time of purchase the Hyundai was $40,000 and the total market value assets of the Fund was $1M. The acquisition of the Hyundai is not a breach of section 83 as it is only 4%.

On the other hand, section 82 looks at where the Trustee of the Fund has in-house assets already in the Fund and have exceeded the 5% rule at years end. Back to the Hyundai. If the Trustee of the Fund pays out $400,000 in benefits to members of the Fund then the total assets at the end of the year are $600,000. At the end of the year the Hyundai motor vehicle has a red book market value of $34,000. This is 7% of the value of the assets of the Fund. As such the Trustee must put in place a plan to dispose of any excess in-house assets by the end of the following income year. As the motor vehicle is a single asset, the Trustee will need to sell it by the end of the following year. If they don't then there is a breach of section 82 and section 84 applies. Section 84 provides for a fine of $12,600.

12.4 SMSF Borrowing

1) Introduction

Section 67 of SISA 93 prevents a Trustee of a SMSF from borrowing money except on a short- term basis to meet a securities settlement or to pay out a member's benefits. The criteria for these exemptions can be found in section 67 and we will not be looking at them in detail.

2) Exempt Limited Recourse Borrowing Arrangements

Apart from the short-term lending exemptions, a broader borrowing exemption can be found in section 67A. The Commissioner of Taxation has released an extensive ruling on limited recourse borrowing arrangements - SMSFR 2012/1 which will be drawn upon in this discussion.

Section 67A provides that a Trustee of a Fund may borrow monies, known as a Limited Recourse Borrowing Arrangement (LRBA) where the following conditions are met:

i) Condition One: Borrowing must be for a Single Acquirable Asset

The Trustee of the Fund may borrow for the purpose of acquiring a single acquirable asset. A popular strategy is the acquisition by the Trustee of a residential property under a LRBA. This property cannot be used by a member, the Trustee or related party. The residential property is a single acquirable asset.

A share or unit in a unit trust is a single acquirable asset but if more than one is acquired in a single transaction then they will be treated as a single acquirable asset where they form part of a collection. A collection is where the share or unit or other asset that forms part of the collection has the same characteristics such as voting power, payouts, class, etc. If the asset is not part of a collection then a separate borrowing must be undertaken for each share or unit. This is expensive and a lot of paperwork.

Let's consider the following example on what is a single acquirable asset from the Commissioner's ruling - SMSFR 2012/1. Many more can be found in this ruling.

Commissioner's Example - Property over more than one Title

A Trustee of an SMSF wants to enter into an LRBA to acquire a factory which is constructed across three titles. The existence of the factory adds considerably to the value of the land and thus is a significant part of the value of the asset. The factory is therefore relevant as a unifying physical object.

The factory and the land comprised of the three titles, is a single acquirable asset and can be acquired under a single LRBA. However, if the factory was derelict and thus not of significant value relative to the land this asset could not be acquired under a LRBA as the factory is not relevant as a unifying physical object and thus the assets are the three titles.

ii) Condition Two: The Borrowing can be refinanced

The borrowing may be for the purpose of the acquisition of the single acquirable asset or importantly, enabling a refinancing of an existing borrowing arrangement. The refinancing arrangement must meet the conditions of section 67A. In that regard refinancing can include the transfer of a current commercial arrangement to a related party lender, provided the loan is documented and under the same terms and conditions. And also vice-versa – taking a related party LRBA to a bank or building society.

iii) Condition Three: The borrowing only includes incidental costs plus current and future repairs

The borrowing may cover the acquisition price, any legal or other fees in relation to the acquisition such as stamp duties plus repairs. There is no limitation on repairs and thus current or future repairs of the asset would be appropriate. This may see a SMSF loan including the provision of future draw-downs to cover repairs. *BUT repairs may not include an improvement to an LRBA asset.*

The difference between a repair and an improvement is extensively covered in SMSFR 2012/1:

Commissioner's Example – Repair v Improvement

• *Residential Property Repair*

A fire damages part of the kitchen (cooktop, benches, walls and ceiling). Restoration (replacement) of the damaged part of the kitchen with modern equivalent materials or appliances would constitute repair or restoration of a part of the entire asset being the house and land.

If superior materials or appliances are used it is a question of degree as to whether the changes significantly improve the state or function of the asset as a whole. For example, the addition of a dishwasher would not amount to an improvement, even if a dishwasher was not previously part of the kitchen, on the basis that this is a minor or trifling improvement to the state or function of the asset as a whole.

• *Residential Property Improvement*

If the house was extended to increase the size of the kitchen this would be an improvement. If, as well as restoring the damaged part of the internal kitchen (a repair), a new external kitchen was added to the entertainment area of the house the external kitchen would be an improvement.

Funding an Improvement under a LRBA

STRATEGY Section 67A does not allow a Trustee of a SMSF to borrow to fund an improvement. This means that any improvement must be completed by the Trustee of the Fund from the assets or monies of the Fund. An external party, such as a member, may also fund the improvement. The problem with this is the market value of the improvement on the property, not just the actual costs is to be treated as a contribution. If there is no cash in the fund then consider contributing cash into the fund by a member or on behalf of a member to improve the property. As an aside ensure the investment strategy of the Fund and also the trust deed allows the improvement to take place.

iii) Condition Four: Legal Asset Title to be held on Bare Trust

The Trustee of the SMSF is borrowing but the legal title of the borrowing asset must be held under a trust arrangement. This is to provide protection for the Trustee of the Fund and limits recourse for any loan shortfall against the asset only not other Fund's assets. The trust is a bare trust and referred to by the Commissioner as a Holding Trust.

The Commissioner's Q&A on LRBA Trust arrangements – www.ato.gov.au

Q: Does the super law specify the type of trust that must be used as the holding trust in a limited recourse borrowing arrangement?

A: No. The law specifies only that the SMSF Trustee must have a beneficial interest in the asset being held in the holding trust and the right to acquire legal ownership of that asset after making one or more payments. In addition, for the special in-house asset rule to apply the asset must be the only property of the holding trust.

More complex trusts are unlikely to satisfy the requirement that the SMSF Trustee has the necessary interest in a particular asset of the holding trust. For example, a discretionary trust could not be used, nor could the SMSF Trustee be one of a number of unit holders in a unit trust.

v) Condition Five: Lender has access only to LRBA asset for recourse

The Explanatory Memorandum to the introduction of the LRBA laws in 2010 noted the following in terms of recourse by the lender or guarantor in the event of a default of the LRBA by the Trustee of the SMSF:

"Paragraph 67A(1)(d) will ensure that the rights of the lender or any other person against the RSF Trustee are limited to rights relating to the acquirable asset. No guarantee arrangement can be enforceable against the RSF Trustee other than the rights relating to the acquirable asset.

Paragraph 67A(1)(f) will ensure that the acquirable asset cannot be subject to any other charge than that associated with the direct borrowing arrangement.

With the exception of the asset that is the subject of the borrowing arrangement, the assets of the superannuation fund cannot be given as security for a borrowing without breaching regulation 13.14 of the Superannuation Industry (Supervision) Regulations 1994."

For example the Trustee of the Smith SMSF borrows $250,000 from a bank to acquire an $500,000 office property. The borrowing is by way of LRBA that conforms with section 67A of SISA 93. The main member of the Fund is retrenched and the Trustee cannot repay any borrowings. The Bank forecloses on the property and fire sales the property for $400,000. After outstanding fees, repayments and costs the Trustee of the Smith SMSF receives $150,000.

If the property had declined in value and the proceeds from the sale were only $200,000, the Bank would be precluded from suing the Trustee of the Smith SMSF for the outstanding loan amounts.

vi) Related Party LRBA – Allowed or Not?

Section 67A does not prevent a related party loan. This is acknowledged in the Commissioner's guidelines on related party loans:

Q: Is a SMSF allowed to borrow from a related party?

A: The law does not prohibit the lender from being a related party. However, SMSFs must continue to comply with other legislative requirements. For example, the SMSF must satisfy the sole purpose test and comply with existing investment restrictions, such as those applying to in-house assets and prohibitions on acquiring certain assets from a related party of the fund.

Q: Does interest on a borrowing from a related party need to be at commercial rates?

A Trustee of a SMSF or its investment manager must ensure that all investments are conducted on an arm's length basis or, if the parties are not at arm's length, that the terms of the investment are no more favourable to the other party than they would be if the parties were dealing at arm's length.

This means that an SMSF Trustee or investment manager cannot allow a related party lender to charge the fund more than an arm's length rate of interest under the arrangement.

The SMSF Trustee must be able to demonstrate that the SMSF was not paying in excess of an arm's length rate of interest to a related party. *The calculation of a rate that represents an arm's length rate of interest needs to be based on reasonably objective and supportable data – for example, the rates charged by arm's length financial institutions for a similar borrowing.*

Paying a member or relative of a member an excessive rate of interest would also contravene the prohibition on SMSF Trustees giving financial assistance to members or their relatives using the resources of the SMSF.

vii) Discounted and Zero Interest Loans

The issue of loans at less than market value interest rates, created considerable discussion at the time of introduction of the LRBA. Particularly as a zero interest loan with no repayments until the end of the term had the same effect as a contribution, but was not a contribution and did not beach any of the contribution standards.

The Commissioner was asked to rule on some matters and held that a low or zero rate interest loan did not breach section 109 of SISA 93. Section 109 prevents the Trustee of the Fund entering into a non-arm's length arrangement so that the Trustee is worse off. But if the Trustee did not have to pay a market rate of interest then the Trustee and Fund members are better off. What happens then?

In 2016, the Commissioner released guideline PCG 2016/5 stating his formal opinion on the matter:

"When a SMSF acquires an asset under a LRBA, the non-arm's length income (NALI) provisions in section 295-550 of the ITAA 1997 may apply to ordinary or statutory income generated from the asset, if the terms of the LRBA are not consistent with an arm's length dealing. This Guideline sets out the 'Safe Harbour' terms on which SMSF Trustees may structure their LRBAs consistent with an arm's length dealing. That is, for income tax compliance purposes, the Commissioner accepts that an LRBA structured in accordance with this Guideline is consistent with an arm's length dealing and that the NALI provisions do not apply purely because of the terms of the borrowing arrangement."

In simple terms the Commissioner is stating that the LRBA is a trust structure which receives income and from that expenses are deducted with the resultant net income distributed to the Trustee of the Fund. Where interest rate payments are less than market value the income received is higher than it would be under an arm's length interest. The NALI income is taxed at 45%.

Accordingly, where the Trustee enters into a related party LRBA then they can provide evidence that the loan is arm's length or use the safe harbour provisions as published by the Commissioner. Use of these terms and conditions means the Commissioner will not audit the LRBA for NALI purposes.

ATO: PCG 2016/5 Safe Harbour Provisions

Safe Harbour for Property

	ATO Acceptable Terms
Interest Rate	Reserve Bank of Australia Indicator Lending Rates for banks providing standard variable housing loans for investors. Applicable rates: • For the 2015-16 year, the rate is 5.75% • For the 2017 it is 5.8% and for later years, the rate shed published for May (the rate for the month of May immediately prior to the star of the relevant financial year)
Fixed and Variable Interest Rates	Interest rate may be variable or fixed: • Variable – uses the applicable rate (as set out above) for each year of the LBRA • Fixed – Trustees may choose to fix the rate at the commencement of the arrangement for a specified period, up to a maximum of 5 years. The fixed rate is the rate published for May (the rate for the May before the relevant financial year). The 2016-17 rate of 5.8% may be used for LRBAs in existence on publication of these guidelines, if the total period for which the interest rate is fixed does not exceed 5 years (see 'Term of the loan' below)

Term of the Loan	• Variable interest rate loan (original) – 15 year maximum loan term (for both residential and commercial)
	• Variable interest rate loan (re-financing) – maximum loan term is 15 years less the duration(s) of any previous loan(s) relating to the asset (for both residential and commercial)
	• Fixed interest rate loan – a new LRBA commencing after publication of these guidelines may involve a loan with a fixed interest rate set at the beginning of the arrangement. The rate may be fixed for a maximum period of 5 years and must convert to a variable interest rate loan at the end of the nominated period. The total loan term cannot exceed 15 years.
	• For an LRBA in existence on publication of these guidelines, the Trustees may adopt the rate of 5.8% as their fixed rate, provided that the total fixed-rate period does not exceed 5 years. The interest rate must convert to a variable interest rate loan at the end of the nominated period. The total loan cannot exceed 15 years.
Loan to Value Ratios	• Maximum 70% LVR for both commercial and residential property
	• If more than one loan is taken out to acquire (or refinance) the asset, the total amount of all those loans must not exceed 70% LVR.
	• The market value of the asset is to be established when the loan (original or re-financing) is entered into.
	• For an LRBA in existence on publication of these guidelines, the Trustees may use the market value of the asset at 1 July 2015.
Loan Security	A registered mortgage over the property is required
Personal Guarantee	Not Required
Repayments	Each repayment is of both principal and interest Repayments are monthly
Is a Loan Agreement Required?	A written and executed loan agreement is required

Safe Harbour for Listed Shares and Managed Funds

LRBA Condition	ATO Acceptable Terms
Interest Rate	Reserve Bank of Australia Indicator Lending Rates for banks providing standard variable housing loans for investors plus 2%. Applicable rates: • For the 2015-16 year, the interest rate is 5.75% + 2% = 7.75% • For the 2016-17 it is 7.8% and later years, the rate published for May plus 2% (the rate for the month of May immediately before the start of the relevant financial year)
Fixed and Variable Interest Rates	Interest rate may be variable or fixed: • Variable – uses the applicable rate (as set out above) for each year of the LBRA • Fixed – Trustees may choose to fix the rate at the commencement of the arrangement for a specified period, up to a maximum of 5 years. The fixed rate is the rate published for May (the rate for the May before the relevant financial year). • The 2015-16 rate of 7.75% may be used for LRBAs in existence on publication of these guidelines, if the total period for which the interest rate is fixed does not exceed 5 years (see 'Term of the loan' below)

Term of the Loan	• Variable interest rate loan (original) – 7 year maximum loan term • Variable interest rate loan (re-financing) – maximum loan term is 7 years less the duration(s) of any previous loan(s) relating to the collection of assets • Fixed interest rate loan – a new LRBA commencing after publication of these guidelines may involve a loan that has a fixed interest rate set at the beginning of the arrangement. The rate may be fixed up to for a maximum of 3 years, and must convert to a variable interest rate loan at the end of the nominated period. The total loan term cannot exceed 7 years. • For an LRBA in existence on publication of these guidelines, the Trustees may adopt the rate of 7.8% as their fixed rate, provided that the total period of the fixed rate does not exceed 3 years. The interest rate must convert to a variable interest rate loan at the end of the nominated period. The total loan cannot exceed 7 years.
Loan to Value Ratios	• Maximum 50% LVR • If more than one loan is taken out to acquire (or refinance) the collection of assets, the total amount of all those loans must not exceed 50% LVR. • The market value of the collection of assets is to be established when the loan (original or re-financing) is entered into. • For an LRBA in existence on publication of these guidelines, the Trustees may use the market value of the asset at 1 July 2015.
Loan Security	A registered charge/mortgage or similar security (that provides security for loans for such assets).
Personal Guarantee	Not Required
Repayments	Each repayment is of both principal and interest Repayments are monthly
Is a Loan Agreement Required?	A written and executed loan agreement is required

viii) Related Party Loans - Questions and Answers

Q: Can I apply the safe harbours in PCG 2016/5 to assets other than real property or listed units and shares?

A: The safe harbours provided in PCG 2016/5 only apply to LRBAs that are used to acquire real property or stock exchange listed shares or units. SMSF Trustees who use an LRBA to acquire other assets – such as shares in an unlisted company or units in an unlisted unit trust – will need to be able to demonstrate that the arrangement was entered into and maintained on terms consistent with an arm's length dealing when considering the application of the non-arm's length income (NALI) provisions.

One example of how a Trustee may demonstrate this is by obtaining evidence that shows their particular arrangement is established and maintained on terms that replicate the terms of a commercial loan that is available to them in the same circumstances. A printout from a bank's website of general loan terms is not sufficient to meet this requirement.

Where, for example, an LRBA is over an asset for which the SMSF could not find a commercial third party lender to provide finance to acquire that asset and so entered into a related party loan, the Trustee will be unable to demonstrate that the LRBA has been made on arm's length terms. For the SMSF to be assured that it won't be selected for an income tax review for the 2014–15 year or earlier years purely because the SMSF entered into an LRBA, the LRBA will need to be brought to an end by 31 January 2017.

Q: If by the 31 January 2017 deadline a taxpayer has not satisfied PCG 2016/5, will the ATO give taxpayers a further opportunity to rectify the loan arrangement?

A: Where SMSF Trustees have not satisfied all the criteria of the PCG 2016/5, it does not mean that the arrangement will necessarily be deemed to be non-arm's length. This only means that the Trustees are unable to be assured that the Commissioner will accept the arrangement to be consistent with an arm's length dealing.

PCG 2016/5 states that we will not select an SMSF for an income tax review for the 2014–15 year or earlier years purely because the SMSF has entered into an LRBA. However, this is conditional on the Trustee ensuring that any LRBA that their fund has, is on terms consistent with an arm's length dealing by 31 January 2017 or, alternatively, is brought to an end by that date. In addition, payments of principal and interest must be made under the LRBA terms, consistent with an arm's length dealing by 31 January 2017.

Following this deadline, if it is considered that the NALI provisions apply to a particular LRBA and no reasonable attempt has been made to bring the arrangement in line with an arm's length dealing, the NALI provisions will apply from the commencement of the arrangement.

Q: Can refinancing of an existing loan be with a related party lender?

A: There is no prohibition on the refinancing of an existing loan with a related party lender. However, to ensure that the NALI provisions do not apply, SMSF Trustees will need to provide evidence that the refinanced loan is established and maintained on terms consistent with an arm's length dealing; for example, by applying the safe harbour guidelines in PCG 2016/5 if applicable.

Q: Do the NALI provisions apply to all of the income generated by the asset or just the non-arm's length portion?

A: An amount of income either has the character of being NALI or it does not. When an amount of income is NALI, the whole amount is NALI. An amount of income that is characterised as NALI cannot be divided between an amount that is NALI and an amount that is not NALI. The amount of income that is NALI is not only the amount by which an amount of income is greater than the amount that might have been derived if the parties had been dealing at arm's length; it is the whole amount of income derived, including any capital gains (refer to Taxation Ruling TR 2006/7, paragraphs 10 and 12).

12.5 Checklist and Steps for Related Party LRBA with Existing SMSF

1. Determine the amount to be lent and taking into account the safe harbour provisions in PCG2016/5. This would include the purchase price – any associated costs as well as current and possible future repairs.

2. Assess where the Funding for the purchase and costs are coming from and in terms of the related party loan which entity is to carry the loan – family company, members, relatives, family trust and even other SMSFs.

3. Establish the Trustee of the LRBA Holding Trust and ensure it is not the same as SMSF – generally best to use a company as this is required for a commercial loan. The Trustee of the Holding Trust may be an existing company and can be used for multiple LRBAs however the financials need to be kept very separate. Check with the proposed Holding Trust accountant and tax agent around the tax file number and any lodging requirements.

4. Get a legal firm to prepare the Holding Trust documentation and ensure only one Holding Trust per LRBA.

5. Ensure SMSF has a special purpose corporate Trustee not a shelf company with standard association and articles. With property there is a danger of litigation for accidents on the property so Trustee protection is required and thus a company is crucial.

6. Prepare change of Trustee documentation if required to change from an individual Trustee to a corporate Trustee. This can be completed as part of the entire LRBA package undertaken by a legal firm or facilitated by the Fund's specialist SMSF accountant, planner or adviser.

7. Review and upgrade the SMSF trust deed to cater for the latest SMSF legal changes and also flexibility in LRBA arrangements. Be careful and read the deed to see what is possible regarding the LRBA and there are no limitations. Any deed that is pre-2016 will not suffice and preference is a very current one that caters for 2017 changes and reserving.

8. The Fund's Trustee to prepare an investment strategy resolution in relation to property purchase and ensure that the investment strategy covers property and in the right proportions plus the extent of the Fund's potential liabilities and cash flows as required under SISA 93.

9. Sign and exchange the contract on the proposed property purchase in the right name – this will depend upon the state in how it is set up legally. Make sure that you get a strong SMSF conveyancing lawyer to facilitate the transaction.

10. Assess whether the property needs any current and on-going repairs to ensure that it can be facilitated from any related party borrowing.

11. Deposit to be paid from the SMSF by the Trustee of the SMSF.

12. Stamp duty to be paid from the Super Fund - does holding trust need to be stamped – check the State the property is in. This should be completed by the Fund's lawyer.

13. Sign and execute documentation to establish the Holding Trust - other States may be different.

14. Borrower to have meeting for LRBA and if a company or Family Trust – then ratify and agree to the loan

15. Related party Loan documentation to be completed by the legal firm and ensure that it meets the Commissioner safe harbour guidelines in PCG2016/5.

16. Loan advance can be to cover stamp duty, legal fees and other professional costs if required and these should be built into the LRBA agreement

17. The LRBA may include a draw down facility that includes future repairs. If not then any repairs will have to be Funded from the SMSF bank account.

18. First mortgage to be taken over the property and registered as per PCG2016/5.

19. Lease to be in the name of Holding Trust Trustee.

20. Rental income to be deposited into SMSF bank account or cash management trust.

21. Loan repayments to paid to lender as per the loan agreement.

22. Register for land tax if applicable.

CHAPTER THIRTEEN

Accessing Superannuation

"The desire to access super is so great that there have been so many schemes and crazy ideas promoted to get hands on a member's super early. Each has failed and rightly so as the whole idea of super is to provide for those golden days when no money is coming in. Protection of balances has never been more important."

13.1 **The Objectives of Superannuation**

It has long been said that the purpose of superannuation is to provide for the retirement of members of superannuation funds. This can be found in section 62 of SISA 93 dealing with the sole purpose test. To enshrine this purpose the Government introduced the Superannuation Objective Act 2016 which states as its preamble:

"The Objective Bill enshrines the primary objective and subsidiary objectives of the superannuation system in legislation. The primary objective of the superannuation system is to provide income in retirement to substitute or supplement the age pension" (section 4, subsection 5(1)).

This objective clarifies that the role of the superannuation system is to assist individuals to support themselves by providing income to meet their expenditure needs in retirement, rather than being a concessionally taxed investment vehicle for tax minimisation and estate planning. Superannuation, through a combination of requiring compulsory employer superannuation guarantee contributions and allowing voluntary contributions, supports the other pillars of the retirement income system — the age pension and other savings. *Its purpose is not to allow for tax minimisation or estate planning.*

The subsidiary objectives of the superannuation system will be prescribed by regulation. (See section 4, subsection 5(2)) They are to:

- facilitate consumption smoothing over the course of an individual's life;

- manage risks in retirement;

- be invested in the best interests of superannuation fund members;

- alleviate fiscal pressures on Government from the retirement income system; and

- be simple, efficient and provide safeguards.

13.2 The Rollover – Crucial to Starting a SMSF

Unless you have access to a parent's SMSF, 99.9% of Australian workers and superannuation recipients start their super life in a non-SMSF. This may be a retail superannuation fund run and owned by one of the big banks or insurance companies – an industry superannuation fund that is primarily for the needs of members of a specific trade or industry (such as the Care Super Fund which is for health care workers) and then there are various State and Commonwealth Government funds.

It's a simple system – an employee works and their employer contributes 9.5% of their salary (SGC) into a superannuation fund. Under the superannuation laws an employee can choose their SGC fund or if they don't choose, the employer SGC contribution is made into a default low cost fund chosen by your employer. The benefits of a SMSF is that you run the Fund, not someone you don't know or potentially trust.

If you are switching to a SMSF you need to get your money out of your old fund and move it into the SMSF. This means the fund must be set up before you start the transfer or rollover process. You can change super funds by filling out a rollover form and sending it to your new fund or by logging on to your MyGov account.

Check your life insurance cover before moving funds

If you change super funds you may not get the same death, total permanent and disability or income protection cover that you had in your old fund. Be particularly careful if you have a pre-existing medical condition or are aged 60 or over. Seek financial advice if you are unsure.

13.3 Accessing Superannuation Benefits

One of the key benefits of a SMSF is that the Trustee of the Fund can pay a wide variety of benefits where a specific condition is met during the life of the member. It is much like a contract for benefit payments – you meet a term under the contract and it triggers a payment in a particular way, shape or form. For example, when a member of a fund retires or reaches age 65, they have full access to their superannuation benefits and can take them as a lump sum or enter into an agreement with the Trustee of the Fund, to pay a pension or some other income stream.

However, it is not only retirement benefits that are payable to members. For example, it is not well known and certainly not offered by the industry or retail superannuation funds, but if the SMSF's trust deed allows, a member may be able to access sickness and accident benefits from their member's account (known as temporary incapacity). This can be in circumstances where a small business owner has an accident and is off work for a few weeks. It can also be where an employee takes accident leave from work and is not adequately compensated by the employer for the time taken off – either through salary, insurance or workers compensation. A temporary incapacity strategy such as this, only available in a well-constructed SMSF can make all the difference to working members of the Fund, particularly younger members. Of course, there are a number of requirements to ensure the strategy works – but if you have a good deed and a great SMSF adviser – possibilities are endless.

13.4 The Preservation Rules

Under SISA 93 and SISR 94 superannuation benefits are locked into the system until retirement, or in some cases, if another legislated condition for release of the benefits, is met. The following table summarises the key conditions of release and is taken from Schedule 1 of the SIS Regulations 94. *I apologise here for reproducing the actual laws themselves but the reasoning is two-fold:*

1) To be able to provide advice in SMSFs under the Corporations Act 2001, it is a requirement that the adviser be able to read, understand

and apply the law. Below is the law in its full glory – no spin – just the real law, real time and in black and white.

2) By understanding and moreover applying the law, I have found as Australia's pre-eminent teacher of SMSF law, that knowing the law provides confidence for advisers and Trustees alike. It is very hard for people to challenge the actual law and say it is wrong – the law is the law!

O—⚷ Grant's Key Point

When looking at the chart below – the cashing restriction is the *key*. Importantly where the cashing restriction is Nil this means that the benefits may be used to fund or acquire a pension (provided the Pension Transfer Balance Limits are not exceeded) or taken as a lump sum. Where there is another cashing restriction, then this needs to be followed, but a Nil cashing restriction is the golden key.

Preservation Chart – Schedule 1 of the SIS Regulations

Note: Some less relevant conditions have been extracted as well as the release authorities provided by the Commissioner of Taxation in terms of accessing excess non-concessional contributions.

Column 1	Column 2	Column 3
Item	Conditions of release	Cashing restrictions
101	Retirement	Nil
102	Death	Nil
102A	Terminal medical condition	Nil
103	Permanent inca-pacity	Nil

105	Severe financial hardship	For a person taken to be in severe financial hardship under paragraph 6.01(5)(a)—in each 12 month period (beginning on the date of first payment), a single lump sum not less than $1,000 (except if the amount of the person's preserved benefits and restricted nonpreserved benefits is less than that amount) and not more than $10,000. For a person taken to be in severe financial hardship under paragraph 6.01(5)(b)—Nil.
106	Attaining age 65	Nil
107	Compassionate ground	A single lump sum, not exceeding an amount determined, in writing, by the Regulator, being an amount that: (a) taking account of the ground and of the person's financial capacity, is reasonably required; and (b) in the case of the ground mentioned in paragraph 6.19A(1)(b)—in each 12 month period (beginning on the date of first payment), does not exceed an amount equal to the sum of: (i) 3 months' repayments; and (ii) 12 months' interest on the outstanding balance of the loan
108	Termination of gainful employment with an employer who had, or any of whose associates had, at any time, contributed to the regulated superannuation Fund in relation to the member	1. Preserved benefits: Noncommutable life pension or noncommutable life annuity 2. Restricted nonpreserved benefits: Nil

109	Temporary incapacity	A noncommutable income stream cashed from the regulated superannuation Fund for:
		(a) the purpose of continuing (in whole or part) the gain or reward which the member was receiving before the temporary incapacity; and
		(b) a period not exceeding the period of incapacity from employment of the kind engaged in immediately before the temporary incapacity
110	Attaining preservation age	Any of the following:
		(a) a transition to retirement income stream;
114	Any other condition, if expressed to be a condition of release, in an approval under subparagraph 62(1)(b)(v) of the Act	Restrictions expressed in the approval to be cashing restrictions applying to the condition of release

13.5 What do the Legal Words Mean?

It is no secret that there are more than 3,000 pages of legislation and rulings that relate specifically to SMSFs. And believe it or not another 500 were added, with Explanatory Memorandum and ATO guidelines for the changes of the $1.6 million pension Transfer Balance Cap.

I have been blessed to be there from the start – reading, understanding, applying - and best of all - teaching SMSF law. This means that when any new law is introduced, I know where it fits, what is being sought to be achieved by the law, and more importantly what is caught and what is not caught.

Importantly for strategies, what is *not* caught, is generally where the strategy lies. I do empathise with anyone starting in this industry afresh – the laws are now so big and complex, the idea of Simpler Super is broken. It is an impossible dream to be on top of it, but I (and maybe you?) have been one of the lucky ones. Having said that, I hope new industry participants have the heart and mind to learn as much as possible, starting with the current laws and strategies in this book.

The Preservation Table above covers some important terms on the release of a member's benefits so let's study those, to see what they mean:

1) What is Preservation Age?

Preservation age is important as a member may retire when they reach preservation age or if not retired they may access a Transition to Retirement Income Stream (TRIS). Under the laws Preservation Age depends on a member's birthdate:

Date of birth	Preservation age (years)
Before 1 July 1960	55
1 July 1960 – 30 June 1961	56
1 July 1961 – 30 June 1962	57
1 July 1962 – 30 June 1963	58
1 July 1963 – 30 June 1964	59
After 30 June 1964	60

The TRIS, as it is commonly known, enables a member to access their superannuation while still working full or part time, provided it meets the following conditions:

- the member has reached preservation age;

- the TRIS is an income stream allowed under the governing rules of the Fund;

- there must be at least one income stream payment per year and for members under age 65 (the majority for TRIS members), the minimum is 4% of the account balance of the TRIS at the start of the income year, and no more than a maximum of 10%;

- the TRIS cannot be commuted or taken as a lump sum;

- it is not tested under the Pension Transfer Balance Rules.

A properly drafted TRIS will see it converting to an account based pension when the member retires or reaches age 65. Importantly it can be like having your cake and eating it too.

STRATEGY **The TRIS Washing Machine**

A core tax planning tool for financial planners and accountants for many years has been the "TRIS strategy" which saw an employee or business owner contribute super to a super fund and at the same time take out concessionally taxed benefits by way of a TRIS. For some there were immediate PAYG tax savings as the employee's salary was sacrificed into the super fund. However, the salary sacrificed contribution is assessable income for the Trustee of the Fund, which with good tax planning and investments, tax on these contributions may be able to be reduced below 15%. In tandem, the member transferred their accumulation super benefits to commence a TRIS – these were placed into the tax-exempt pension side of the fund. The member could then take, as a TRIS income stream, up to 10% of their TRIS benefits which were then taxed at their marginal tax rate but with a 15% tax offset. If the TRIS member was over age 60 then the TRIS payments were tax-free. The goal was to budget living expenses firstly from TRIS income and then salary with any surplus salary contributed into the employee's superannuation fund.

This *was* a great strategy - but nohing lasts and the Government made changes from 1 July 2017. Now, the TRIS can no longer be counted as part of the fund's exempt pension income and deductible concessional contributions (a must for salary sacrifice) have now been limited to $25,000 per annum. The strategy still works, but just not as good as it once was.

2) The Meaning of Retirement

The definition of retirement can be found at SIS Regulation 6.01(7) and for any Fund member over age 60 retirement is:

(b) in the case of a person who has attained the age of 60 — an arrangement under which the member was gainfully employed, has come to an end, and either of the following circumstances apply:

   (i) the person attained that age on or before the ending of the employment; or

   (ii) the Trustee is reasonably satisfied that the person intends never to again become gainfully employed, either on a full time or a part time basis.

So, let's test our application of the law.

John Jones will be 60 on 15 November 2017. On 1 December 2017, John leaves a Board role that he had with a small company for which he was paid director's fees. John continues to work full time in his consulting company and carry on as company director in another three companies. Has John met the "retirement" condition of release so he can access his superannuation benefits?

Answer: As John has ceased an employment arrangement after age 60 then all of his benefits become non-preserved. This is the case even though he continues on in other employment including directorships. Importantly, any contributions made by employers *after this time* will be preserved and another condition of release – such as complete retirement or termination of another employment arrangement – is needed to release those benefits. However, once the benefits become non-preserved they are always non-preserved. Strategically for those turning aged 60 and still working, ensure that you give up an arrangement post turning age 60 even if it is a short term one.

STRATEGY Age 60 is not the turning point it once was. I am writing this whilst on a golf trip in Thailand and there are a number of aged 70+ participants who are still working in their family businesses. They don't really need that much of their super as they are still working BUT they can access it as they have reached age 65 – see Item 106. The sensible strategy is to live off as much tax free super as is possible and salary sacrifice unneeded income into their Fund.

3) The Meaning of Financial Hardship

Item 105 of Schedule 1 of the SIS Regulations 1994 provides that where a condition of release being "severe financial hardship" is met, then the Trustee of the fund may release:

"For a person taken to be in severe financial hardship under paragraph 6.01 (5) (a) — in each 12 month period (beginning on the date of first payment), a single lump sum not less than $1,000 (except if the amount of the person's preserved benefits and restricted non-preserved benefits is less than that amount) and not more than $10,000.

For a person taken to be in severe financial hardship under paragraph 6.01 (5) (b) — Nil."

Adviser Question

A client received a letter from a lawyer stating that they faced real financial concerns and the client has then gone and withdrawn an amount from his SMSF. Unfortunately, this has come to my attention after the event and the client is only aged 40 and well under preservation age.

I believe the client has to be in severe financial hardship to access funds from SMSF, not simply facing financial hardship. If the member could be found to be in financial hardship, do they have to be on social security benefits for 6 months and is it limited to $10,000 a year?

Answer – Let's go to the Law

Severe financial hardship is defined in SIS Regulation 6.01(5)(a) to be where:

"(a) the trustee of a superannuation entity is satisfied:

(i) based on written evidence provided by at least one Commonwealth department or agency responsible, for administering a class of Commonwealth income support payments, that:

(A) the person has received Commonwealth income support payments for a continuous period of 26 weeks; and

(B) the person was in receipt of payments of that kind on the date of the written evidence; and

(ii) that the person is unable to meet reasonable and immediate family living expenses."

If your client is under age 55 firstly - you are correct - they need to produce evidence to the Trustee that they meet the various conditions of severe financial hardship which is 26 weeks of Commonwealth income support and that they cannot meet reasonable and immediate living expenses. Even if this first condition is met, the maximum that can be paid as a single lump sum in any 12 month period, is $10,000. The Commissioner has been extremely hard on cases where a person has sought to access their superannuation benefits via a SMSF. As such the potential compliance breach needs to be sorted out immediately.

To complete the financial hardship story , sub-regulation 6.01(5) (b) provides that where the person is over age preservation age, is in receipt of a Commonwealth income support payments for a cumulative period of 39 weeks and is not gainfully employed (part or full time) at the time of seeking release of the superannuation benefits, then all the member's preserved and restricted benefits, may be cashed. As a final point, sub-regulation 6.01(6) of the SIS Regulations 1994 provides that the evidence under sub-regulation 6.01(5)(a) must be no later than 21 days from the date of making a claim for severe financial hardship.

4) Temporary Incapacity Benefits

At the outset of this chapter we noted that temporary incapacity is not often used in practice and generally not offered within an industry or retail based superannuation fund. For the Trustee of a SMSF, provided the Fund's trust deed and governing rules allow, income style benefits can be paid out to a member that has met the condition of release known as temporary incapacity.

The cashing restriction for temporary incapacity is the payment of a non-commutable income stream for the period of temporary incapacity and an amount of income no greater than the member was receiving before the temporary incapacity event. A non-commutable income stream in SISR 6.01 is an income stream where

a) the income stream cannot be commuted (taken as a lump sum cash payment): and

b) is paid at least monthly; and

c) does not have a residual capital value, meaning a lump sum payment at the end of the temporary incapacity; and

d) for the monthly income the total amount paid each month is fixed or varies only:

i) for the purpose of complying with the Act and these regulations; and

ii) during any period of 12 months by a rate not exceeding either:

(A) 5% per annum; or

(B) the rate of increase in the last Consumer Price Index (All Capital Cities) for a quarter to be published by the Australian Statistician before the end of that period of 12 months compared with the Consumer Price Index (All Capital Cities) published for the same quarter in the preceding year.

This means that if a member of a fund has an accident or is sick, from falling off a bike, having a stroke, being involved in a car accident, or undergoing chemotherapy – the Trustee of the Fund may pay a monthly replacement income to compensate the member for what they were receiving before the sickness or accident.

Procedurally the amount has to come from the member's account, although this may be bolstered with reserve allocations if the Trustee has any reserves. Importantly this benefit is not a superannuation benefit and is just ordinary income for the member. This means that the payment is fully assessable to the member. Tax wise the Trustee may get a tax deduction for some of the income paid to the incapacitated member.

STRATEGY **When to Use** – Temporary incapacity benefits cease when the member goes back to work, retires, moves into permanent incapacity or dies. As such it may go on for some time and will be heavily dependent upon the amount of benefits the member has and any reserves the Trustee of the Fund may have in place. It is certainly a good strategy for younger members of the fund if workers compensation or their sickness and accident policy does not fully compensate them for all loss of earnings.

5) Paying Benefits on Death

When a member dies, their benefits may be paid to their dependants or their legal estate. Dependants this is defined under SISA 1993 to includes the spouse, children – both infant and adult, other persons interdependent on the member and also all persons who are financially dependent on the deceased member. Generally, the payment can include a lump sum or pension – although there are strict limitations on making pension payments. For example, an income stream cannot be paid to an adult child unless they are disabled or financially dependant, and under age 25.

If there is no planning in terms of the payments of death benefits it is generally up to the Trustee to decide what to do with the payment of the benefits. This has seen a number of cases where the surviving Trustee has taken full advantage of the lack of planning and directed the deceased's members benefits to themselves ignoring the member's wishes in their will. In simple terms those that do not plan their SMSF estate may end up seeing their estate going to places they did not expect. After all how important is it that your bloodline keeps your super on your death. No planning and you don't know where it could go.

Given the importance of SMSF estate planning we have dedicated a complete chapter to it later in *The Guru's Guide to SMSFs*.

CHAPTER FOURTEEN

Taking Money from a SMSF - Superannuation Benefits

"Now the fun starts and retirement dreams beckon but wait – there is a blip on the horizon. There is a over 50% chance that one of you may live over the age of 90 – will you have enough given your current balance, spending and projected investment returns?"

14.1 Introduction – Tax Free Lump Sums and Pensions on Retirement – Simple Choice

"Hooray" – we are finally down to the place where we can take money out of our SMSF. Once we are retired, we can run two types of accounts in our SMSF:

1) The Lump Sum Withdrawal Account

This is essentially an accumulation account run for a retiree member. All withdrawals from this account are lump sums and if over age 60 they are tax free in the hands of the retiree. The benefit of a lump sum withdrawal account is that the member has access to it at any time but there is no requirement to withdraw anything from it. A member may decide in an income year not to take anything because they have a bit of cash saved up outside of the fund and want to conserve and grow their capital. Alternatively, a member may want to access 50% or more of their account balance as a lump sum – there is no maximum limit on lump sum withdrawals.

For the Trustee, any income earned on the assets and investments held in the member's accumulation account is taxed at 15%. Capital gains are included in the Fund's assessable income but are entitled to a 33 1/3% discount. Importantly, a member may only run one accumulation account per fund, but at retirement, a member may access lump sums from their Lump Sum Withdrawal account while still contributing to the fund. Both the lump sum withdrawals and contributions are booked and accounted for in the member's accumulation account.

2) The Pension Account

This is an account used by the Trustee to pay regular income payments to a retired member. There are no general laws stating how many payments are required for a pension, but it is safe to say that at least a regular payment, or at least once a year is required. Of course, it could be weekly, monthly or quarterly. It is up to the terms and conditions of the pension created and contracted for between the member and the Trustee of the SMSF. However, a requirement under SISA 93 is that the member must take a minimum pension payment. Again, if the member is over age 60 then the pension payments are tax free. Importantly any income or capital gains earned on pension assets within the fund is tax free.[24] Unlike the accumulation account, a member may have more than one pension in a Fund (which we will discuss in more depth as part of SMSF Estate Planning).

14.2 A Short Course on SMSF Retirement

When retirement hits, what should a member do? Now if you remember from earlier in this book, retirement can happen even if the member is still working full time. All they have to do is prove to the Trustee of the Fund that at some time after age 60, they have given up one form of gainful employment -such as part time work or a paid directorship of a family company. Once retired, all of a member's super benefits become unrestricted unpreserved which is a legal way of saying that they may be accessed as a lump sum or pension.

So what exactly should a member do once retired?

1) Pay Down Debts at Retirement

The smart superannuation strategy advocated by most financial planners is to use super to pay off all mortgages, credit cards and other debts. I would go one further and say it is time for a well-deserved holiday with loved ones. Let's face it - you have worked way too long not to have some enjoyment – even if it is a trip around Australia.

But once the holiday is done? Well reality will hit. No wages or salary are coming in, and it is time to budget. Look around and witness the retirees who continue to spend lump sums like there is no tomorrow.

---

24 We will see in the taxation of SMSFs that the Trustee of a Fund can run segregated investment strategies where tax is dependent on whether the income or gains are derived from the accumulation or pension accounts. However most Trustees run the Fund's investments based on a pooled basis which means that there are no separate accumulation or pension account assets for tax purposes – rather a proportional basis is used. So any sale of an asset will have a proportional tax liability dependent upon the percentage of accumulation/pension assets across the whole fund.

THE GURU'S GUIDE TO SELF-MANAGED SUPER FUNDS

A holiday here, renovation there, lend a bit here and there to the children, travel first class, buy a business and the list goes on. Fun at the time but with no salary or wage income, and when interest rates are low, there will come a time to pay the piper.

Capital diminishment is the fear of most retirees and the prospect of having to sell the family home - rears its ugly head. There is nothing wrong with downsizing and it makes sense. After all the Government has introduced new laws that blow the contributions rules apart by allowing a home owner, of any age, with or without super, to contribute up to $300,000 into super upon the downsizing of their home.

2) The Needs and Values of a Retiree

During my many talks to retirees over the years, I ask them to grab a piece of paper (and maybe you want to try this simple exercise with me now) and write down what comes into their mind when I ask the following question:

"What is important to you about your retirement?"

If you are retired, it is a great question to focus your mind and time. I have found from seeing responses from more than 5,000 retirees, that the following three responses always pop up – in no certain order:

1. Health.

2. Having a secure income for life.

3. Family and being able to look after them financially, as well as spending quality time with them.

3) Income Security

I have found that income security is one of the most important things for most retirees. For many this means budgeting, for others getting the Age Pension, and for some getting a good income stream product to support their account based pension in the SMSF.

You may recall the story about my Dad constantly harassing my Mum about making long distance phone calls and only giving her $50 per week spending money. It was probably a bit over the top but that frugality enabled his superannuation savings of $400,000 in 1988 to still be in excess of this balance even today. In fact, Mum tells me they still have more than $500,000 in super, they are both in their mid-80s, still own their own home and Dad is in a retirement home that costs $80,000 per annum. So income, security and budgeting are a big deal in retirement – as of course are smart investment choices.

For most in retail or industry based superannuation funds where balances are much lower, budget management means getting access to the Centrelink Age Pension. However, for a SMSF member with (generally) a larger super balance - don't expect social security anytime soon[25]. For those in a SMSF, the main income driver is a private SMSF pension known as an account based pension.

In short when a SMSF member retires, they ask the Trustee to transfer monies (and the Trustee may transfer assets) from their accumulation account to their pension account. Once there, the Trustee of the Fund must ensure that the member is paid a pension equivalent to a designated minimum amount. For a pension account member under age 65, the minimum is 4% of the pension account balance at the start of the income year. This minimum pension requirement increases over time with age such that by age 90 it is 11%. Naturally a member can draw down more than the minimum but the minimum must be taken otherwise the Commissioner will assess that there is no Pension and the account is an accumulation account. *Importantly (as we have already seen) after age 60, like the payment of a lump sum - it is tax free.*

---

[25] The Age Pension is important for all retirees but the continual restriction means it cannot be guaranteed to anyone. It's great to have but as many SMSF members found out in the last few years, the Government continues to significantly reduce the assets and incomes threshold and for many, that means taking their entitlements away. It is better not to budget for it if you have retirement assets in excess of $800,000. The day will come when you will get it – but probably not right now.

On the investment side, as my Trustee parents have found, the current low interest rate environment means that their minimum pension withdrawal and budgeted income needs are well in excess of the return on their term deposit investments. This means their capital is eroding before their eyes.

So what is the solution? An income producing product (such as a bond or annuity) that the Trustee of the Fund can buy to use to produce the desired budgeted income in order to pay out the member's pensions. Currently these products generally have low interest rates, but things are changing and there are more and more income products coming into the market for Trustees to provide income to pension members.

4) Grant's Strategy Tip - Retirement means just that

When you retire make sure that you do. Don't get involved in a business that you know nothing about – it will lead to stress and potential loss of capital. I can give you many instances from my experience where a well to do retiree has left their job and, to feel useful, has invested in a franchise or other business. This is not a smart move as it puts mental health and capital at risk. My suggestion? If you want to keep "useful" - work out what you are passionate about and write a book. Self publish it and then consult to others on your passion. It could be something as simple as executive travel, time management, handling children or divorce, best Australian fishing spots, tapestry. Who knows what it is, but if you have a passion, it will get you up and out of bed in the morning – give you a purpose in life and it won't cost anything. Plus you can publish books on Amazon for nothing and also get them printed on demand for very little cost. Who knows, you may find that you sell a few books and land some consulting work – sweet! Now that is a cool thing to do at retirement and is exactly what I plan to do while travelling the world.

14.3 **Beware SMSFs – The Brakes on Tax Concessions are on**

For those in SMSFs – don't you pity your retired friends and family living on investments outside of super – having to pay tax at marginal tax rates and lodge income tax returns? How droll and cumbersome! Superannuation has to be one of the best tax based investment vehicles around. I have even given talks on SMSFs overseas - and to say people are jealous of the virtual tax haven status of SMSFs is an understatement!

Where the Trustee of the Fund maintains member accumulation accounts, then the income the Fund earns on those assets is taxed at 15%. Capital gains earned on these assets is discounted by a third and taxed at the same rate with a resultant tax rate of 10%.

So if a member has $1M in an accumulation account, and the Trustee earns $50,000 on the assets set aside for this account, then the tax attributable and payable on that income will be $7,500. And remember for those over aged 60 there is no tax on lump sum withdrawals. But as we have seen before, things get better where the Trustee holds assets to pay an account based pension (excluding a Transition to Retirement Income Stream) where income and capital gains are exempt from tax. On the same $1M in the member's accumulation account, when it is shifted to commence an account based pension, the Trustee of the Fund does not have to pay any tax on the $50,000 it earns. A great system really for someone over age 60 – no tax on income earned in the fund and no tax on the accounts based pension income taken out of the fund. Imagine getting social security as well – Nirvana but it is getting harder to dip into the public purse too many times.

Grant's Comment: I made a call in my 2015 SMSF Strategies Roadshow that we were at the high point of SMSFs – things were too good to be true. It had become quite clear that with some SMSF members having accounts as large as $2M or more, the loss to the Government's budgeted revenue created huge angst in the corridors of Treasury and so the 2016 Budget by Treasurer Morrison started attacking super benefits. Thanks to those changes, super fund members can only commence a pension with $1.6M from their accumulation account – anything more must be left in the fund's accumulation account with income taxed at 15%. This is still a good deal, as we have to remember that withdrawing lump sum benefits from the accumulation account post age 60 are tax free[26].

Transferring superannuation monies from the accumulation side to the pension side for a member requires a test against the member's $1.6M personal Transfer Balance Cap. Importantly, once a pension is commenced there is no further test of that pension irrespective of what it grows to. *The best strategy that I can give to anyone is build your super up to $1.6M by age 60, meet the retirement condition of release and then invest wisely thereafter.*

STRATEGY **The Family Pension Cap:** The $1.6M pension transfer balance limit is a concern for many SMSF members, but the cap is not $1.6M per fund – **it is $1.6M per member.** For spouses combined it is effectively $3.2M per family. Let's face it - any family with that much in super is probably not reading this book but paying a fortune to advisers to look after their investments, taxation and also estate planning – *the family drama maker.* [27]

---

26 Both sides of Parliament have said on numerous occasions that they will not impose tax on lump sum or pension payments made after age 60. And I am here to tell you – that may be now but it will happen at some time. Mark my words – there is simply too much money in super for a future Government to ignore the impact it can have on the bottom line.

27 BUT Remember the Access Rules: The beauty about SMSFs is that members are Trustees and have control of the Fund – its investments, what contributions it can accept and when to pay out benefits. That has seen a number of promoters offering to set up SMSFs for employees and then once their superannuation is rolled into the fund, allow them to access their super in breach of the access rules. We have seen previously that a deliberate breach of the rules – including the fund's trust deed, may result in instant fines, the fund losing its complying SMSF status and the parties involved in the breach subject to criminal penalties. In fact, the ATO has taken over 20 criminal actions against parties involved in "early access" schemes.

14.4 **Lump Sums – the SMSF Way**

You may have realised that the beauty of SMSFs is their wide range of choices, strategies and options compared to their cousins – the industry, public and retail super funds. We have already seen this when it comes to investment choice, such as early stage innovation companies and when benefits can be paid including salary continuance benefits – now let's look at the **lump sum possibilities** of taking money from the Fund. upon retirement

1) **Take it ALL Out**

This lump sum strategy is for those who don't trust super with the Government changing the rules all the time. Once retired, some members take all their super out of the fund and close their account down. This doesn't happen often in SMSFs if the members have made it to retirement.

Now lets go back to our case study earlier where the member has $1M in their accumulation account. For those members not trusting super, they would take the $1M out, wind up the Fund and invest in probably the same assets - BUT now income and capital gains tax must be paid at the member's marginal tax rate. In addition, personal income tax returns will need to be filed and all the hoo-ha that goes along with that. So probably not a good choice if you ask me!

Do you Trust Super? On a scale of one to ten – with absolute trust scoring a 10, how well do you trust super? If you are five or above, then you are one of the lucky ones and will tend to put more than your fair share of non-concessional and salary sacrifice contributions into super. If you don't, and you are saving for your retirement outside of super, you will probably end up with a portfolio of negatively geared properties. These will give you a tax headache, until the loans are repaid and the capital gains tax bill once you sell one of the properties is horrendous. *Mark my words* – a portfolio of three properties in a SMSF worth $1.5M is worth a lot more in terms of after tax dollar receipts than the same properties outside a SMSF.

2) The SMSF Bank Account

There is no requirement to start up a pension in a SMSF. After all, paying a lump sum from a fund post age 60 is tax free. The only difference is that income in the fund upon assets held for pension purposes, is tax free, but in the Trustee's accumulation account income is taxed at 15%.

However, with low interest rates or a recessionary market where income is hard to come by, consideration should be given to keeping things simple. Pensions are not the final game for some. Perhaps run a simple lump sum accumulation account and don't worry about a pension. The big plus about holding a simple lump sum accumulation account is that there are no minimums and the member only needs to draw upon the account as needed. If the fund has a bank account, the member could use a debit card straight off the back of the fund's account with each drawdown, being a lump sum withdrawal. I like to call this strategy "the SMSF Bank Account".

3) Lump Sum Accounts beyond $1.6M – For Estate Planning and Aged Care Purposes

We may have planned our retirement well and invested very wisely along the way, only to find out that our accumulation balance exceeds the $1.6M pension cap[28]. This means that any amount over the member's TBC is to stay in the accumulation account indefinitely, or taken out to meet expected or unexpected lump sum costs.

With $1.6M in an account based pension paying regular income, a member could generally expect to provide the bulk of their lifestyle income by way of an income stream. However, if a member gets to $3M (thanks to great investments) and transfers $1.6M to their pension account, then a very healthy $1.4M will be left in the accumulation account for investing.

---

28 Remember the growth in the member's account based pension, once it is tested, is not tested for the cap again so it is vital whenever possible and subject to the access laws, to start a pension as soon as you can. Not a transition to retirement income stream as that is not a tested pension, but a real account based pension. Of course, you have to be at least age 60 to make that magic mark.

But for what purpose?

If the $1.6M meets all of the member's budgeted income needs each year, what is the purpose of the growing accumulation balance? Certainly, it is good emergency money – for the children, lavish holidays with the family, or an unexpected health problem - but $1.4M is a lot of emergency money.

It can be applied to pay for aged care accommodation at a high quality aged care facility – generally requiring a refundable accommodation deposit of $500,000 or more but again, this is contingency funding and not guaranteed. One thing that can be absolutely guaranteed is that the member will die. There is nothing contingent about that.

For me, the real purpose of the money and assets in the excess accumulation account is SMSF Estate Planning. After the death of the member, its purpose is to be passed on to the spouse and then to the next generation, or the generation after that. In some cases, the member may leave wishes or, as we will see, demands in a SMSF Will, that the spouse or one or more of the next generation be excluded from their SMSF assets. With SMSF Wills, unlike normal wills, it is up to the Trustee of the Fund to enforce the member's estate planning demands.

We will look at SMSF Estate Planning in a later chapter – again a "must do" strategy for anyone upon entering a SMSF.

At this point however, any excess held in the accumulation account should be focused primarily on estate planning, with the advantage that it may also be used for aged care purposes down the track. An account based pension, as we will see, should be made a reversionary pension - that is, passed onto the surviving spouse with continuing income payments (provided their pension TBC is not breached in the process).

STRATEGY The **Lump Sum Investment Strategy:** Barring any disasters, the money in the accumulation account should not be needed to fund day to day living expenses of the member. That is the purpose of the account based pension. So if no income is needed, the Trustee of the Fund should look at maximising growth in this part of the fund – the more the better to pass on to the next generation. This means capital growth investments with little taxable income. Of course, it would be great to have capital growth upside with concessionally taxed income – such as franked dividends that are reinvested into growth assets. It makes sense to maximise the amount in the excess accumulation account for the benefit of the children and grandchildren – of course with strings attached!

4) Lump Sums not in Cash

In some cases, a member may wish to take an asset from the fund rather than a cash lump sum such as shares or property. This is called an "in-specie" lump sum. To do this, the Trustee of the Fund will need to value the asset, put in place the correct documentation to effect the lump sum/asset transfer, and implement it correctly. The in-specie lump sum asset transfer is particularly effective when using a SMSF Will for estate planning purposes – enabling the member of the Fund to transfer specific assets to spouses, children or financially dependant grandchildren. The beauty about this specific transfer is that, as we will find in our later SMSF estate planning chapter, it generally cannot be challenged if it is done according to the Superannuation Laws.

For the most part, many members may not see value in making in-specie lump sums or death benefit lump sums, but for those farmers with their farming land inside their super (a great strategy), it enables the deceased member to pass on their farm to the spouse and only those children that work on the farm. But - when passing any asset out of a SMSF to a related party, be ultra-careful as there are many pitfalls along the way - such as losing tax concessions where death benefits are not paid out in cash. The in-specie transfer is still an option but must be executed in a certain way.

5) Lump Sum Taxation

At any time, provided the member meets the relevant condition of release, the member may take out a lump sum. For SMSFs the process is as follows:

- The member requests the Trustee of the Fund to withdraw a lump sum amount – in cash or in-specie;

- The Trustee has a meeting to discuss the ability of the member to withdraw a lump sum including the relevant condition of release and the taxation of the lump sum benefits;

- The Trustee makes the lump sum payment less any requisite withholding taxes according to the table below.

In determining the tax on any lump sum benefit, it is vital for the Trustee to assess the relevant components of the lump sum at the exact time of making the payment. In short there are three types of components – tax free, taxable and untaxed taxable component[29].

The tax-free component whenever received by a member is always, as the name says tax free. In an accumulation account, it is a fixed amount referable to non-concessional contributions made by a member as well as the CGT exempt component of any contribution made by a member to the fund on the disposal of a small business asset. This means that in an accumulation account all employer contributions, salary sacrifice contributions and any other concessional contribution *plus all earnings and growth credited to a member*, will be taxable component.

Untaxed taxable component is very rarely seen in a SMSF and is more the preserve of Government funded pensions. However, if a member dies and part of the member's death benefit payments includes an insurance component, a portion of this may be untaxed taxable component. For any insurances, a SMSF insurance expert and SMSF lawyer should be called upon to assess the componentry upon death of a member.

It is important to note that any lump sum payment is included in the member's assessable income but, courtesy of tax rebates, the maximum

---

29   For a SMSF, it is highly unlikely that the member will have an untaxed component as this is the preserve of unfunded superannuation schemes such as Government super. These sort of funds are known as untaxed plan funds. The one case where it may come about in a SMSF, is when a life insurance payment is received and this is paid to the beneficiaries of a deceased member.

tax rate is limited to the amount seen in the Taxation of Lump Sum table below. For example, a 58 year old member of a Fund who has retired and is paid a $500,000 lump sum on 1 April 2018 consisting entirely of taxable component, would have the first $200,000 tax free – which is the low rate cap amount for the 2018 income year - with any remainder subject to tax at a rate of 17%. However, if the retired member has $1M in carry forward capital losses, then the lump sum amount will be reduced by tax losses so there will be no tax payable on the lump sum payment.

Type of payment and tax component	Age of person at the date the payment is received	Amount subject to PAYG withholding	Rate of withholding
Member benefit – taxed element of the taxable component	Under preservation age	Whole amount	22%
	Preservation age to 59 years	Amount up to low rate cap	Nil
		Amount above the low rate cap	17%
	60 years and above	Whole amount	Nil
Member benefit – untaxed element of the taxable component	Under preservation age	Amount up to untaxed plan cap	32%
		Amount above untaxed plan cap	47%
	Preservation age to 59 years	Amount up to low rate cap	17%
		Amount above the low rate cap up to the untaxed plan cap	32%
		Amount above untaxed plan cap	47%
	60 years and above	Amount up to untaxed plan cap	17%
		Amount above untaxed plan cap	47%

Taxation of Lump Sums – Withholding Taxes payable by the SMSF Trustee[30]

---

30 Table courtesy of www.ato.gov.au and Sub-division 301-B of the ITAA 97

14.5 Income Streams and Pensions – the SMSF Way

Once a member is retired, income to replace salary and wages is vital. From a SMSF point of view, the best income stream or pension to provide, is the account based pension. For those interested in looking at what a pension is at law, SISR 1.06 provides the keys for all pensions in a superannuation fund including SMSFs. Some pensions such as lifetime pensions, known as defined benefit pensions, cannot be offered by a SMSF and are a hangover from a different time and era.

Old School Pensions – RBL Style: Most SMSF trust deeds enable the Trustee to offer old school pensions such as fixed term pensions and market linked pensions, which were used prior to 2007 for the purposes of reasonable benefit limits (RBL). RBLs are the old limits applied by the Commissioner of Taxation to limit the amount of concessionally taxed benefits taken out of superannuation by a taxpayer. Any excess benefits in this case were taxed at the member's marginal tax rate – a real super downer and certainly limited the desire for many to build up too much in super[31]. Where a member's benefits were in a non-commutable (i.e. not able to be turned into a lump sum) pension – such as a fixed term or market linked, then a higher RBL could be used.

Be warned: If you have one of these old school pensions then you are at least 70 years of age and with the changes to the transfer balance limits, you need to seek expert SMSF professional legal advice. The new laws around these old school pensions are beneficial – if structured in the right way.

---

31 Can you imagine what would happen if the Government had put in place a system where any excess over the $1.6M pension transfer balance cap had to be taken from super and tax paid on it at 47%.? There would be screams all the way to the elections.

14.6 **Must know Account Based Pension Rules**

Let's discuss the basic accounts based pension rules. The Trustee and member must know these.

1) The Pension cannot be added to

A pension commences when the documentation setting the pension up states it is to start. Once commenced a member cannot transfer an amount from their accumulation account or contribute directly to the pension. Once started, it continues until the pension runs out or the member ceases the pension by commuting it in full as a lump sum withdrawal or transferring it to the accumulation account – otherwise called a rollback. So, if a member wants to add to the pension with an amount in their accumulation account, then a new pension must be established. The process for doing this is:

i)   Cease the pension by commuting it and rolling it back to the member's accumulation account. The accountant to the SMSF will need to work out the pension account balance at the time of roll back. They will also need to determine the tax free and taxable components - $ value at that time as well.

ii) The rollback amount will be credited to his Personal Transfer Balance Account (PTBA) at that time – see later on how this account works.

iii) Commence a new account based pension for the member with their entire or a designated amount sitting in the member's accumulation account. The pension amount will be debited and tested against the member's PTBA – so make sure there is no excess or the excess will need to be commuted! The accountant to the SMSF will need to assess the % of tax free/taxable component at the time of commencement of the pension.

DIY Pension Danger: Rolling back the pension and aggregating it with existing accumulation benefits – commonly termed as "refreshing a pension" can have diabolical consequences. Quite apart from the complexity of what happens from a Pension Transfer Balance point of view, the estate planning consequences for adult children can be a tax disaster. How so?

Let's say John, a 61 year old member sets up a pension in August 2017 with $1.2M pension transfer balance when they retire. They have a spouse and adult daughter who will share in any superannuation benefits on the death of the member. The pension is set up with 100% taxable component. If this is passed to the spouse as a death benefit on the death of the member it is tax free. Whereas if it goes to the daughter, in whole or part then it is taxed at 17%.

In April 2018, John's mother dies and leaves him a cash legacy of $250,000 which John contributes to the fund as a non-concessional contribution (NCC), using the three year bring forward rule. The NCC is treated as a tax free component. However, in May 2018 John, on the advice of his accountant, refreshes the pension by rolling it back to the accumulation account to pick up the NCC. The Trustee rolls back the pension and the member's accumulation account is now $1.4M being $1.15M from the pension, following a pension payment to John and the $250,000 NCC. The Trustee then commences a new pension with the entire accumulation account. Sounds simple and smart. No way – a silly strategic move for the family. Why?

The new pension will be tested for tax free/taxable component percentage at the time the pension is commenced. With $1.4M in the accumulation account consisting of $250,000 of tax free component being used for the new pension, the components would be 17.8% tax free/82.2% taxable component. This means that if John dies and leaves $1.2M to his spouse it will be tax free. However, if he leaves $200,000 to his daughter then the taxable component of the lump sum payment is $164,400 and would be taxed at 17% = $27,948. I am not sure if the daughter will be happy to pay that tax bill.

The better strategy would have been to leave the existing pension as is and set up pension No 2 with the $250,000 tax free component. The $200,000 lump sum to be paid to the adult daughter should come from pension No 2. It would all be tax free component and thus not taxable in her hands.

2) Minimum Pension Amount

The pension payments in any year must be at least the minimum having regard to the members age and the value of the pension account at the commencement of the pension or the start of the income year.

The current minimum pension amounts and the minimum withdrawals for each age limit:

Age Group	Minimum Pension Percentage %	$1M Pension Account Payment Amount	$2M Pension Account Pension Amount
Under 65	4	$40,000	$80,000
65—74	5	$50,000	$100,000
75—79	6	$60,000	$120,000
80—84	7	$70,000	$140,000
85—89	9	$90,000	$180,000
90—94	11	$110,000	$220,000
95 or more	14	$140,000	$280,000

Account Based Pension - Minimum Pension Payments

Make the Minimum Pension Payment or Else: If the Trustee does not make the minimum pension payment in any income year then the Commissioner of Taxation will treat the pension as having ceased during the income year when the minimum was not made. This can be a disaster as it means the pension is automatically rolled back to the member's accumulation account. This creates three problems;

i)   Loss of tax exemption for pension assets;

ii)   The member's Personal Transfer Balance Account will be debited with the rollback but any new pension will have to be tested again. If the account has risen over the course of the year, whilst it is in pension, this could have Transfer Balance Cap problems;

iii) If there has been any estate planning built into the pension, such as having a tax free Pension No 2 for the purposes of making a tax free lump sum payment to an adult daughter, then this strategy is terminated as well.

So by all means and methods possible - ensure the minimum pension payment is made on all pensions.

3) Reversionary Pensions

As part of establishing the pension, the member may establish an auto-reversionary beneficiary. This means that upon the death of the pension member, the pension transfers automatically to the auto-reversionary beneficiary. However, the death benefit rules which cover the transfer, limit the persons to whom the pension can be transferred upon the death of the pension member. SISR 6.21 provides that the pension can only be transferred to a spouse, dependant or if a child of the deceased – the child dependant must be under age 18 or, if financially dependant upon the deceased member – under the age 25. For child pensions, if allowed, they can only remain to be paid until age 25 whereupon a lump sum, equal to the remaining pension account balance, must be paid to the child pension beneficiary.

So how do reversionary pensions work in practice?

John Smith has an accumulation account with a $1M balance. He is 60 years old and has just retired. John commences an account based pension with all of his accumulation account with an auto-reversionary beneficiary being his wife Susan.

John dies at age 62 with $1.1M in his pension account. At the time of death, Susan is aged 52 and is alive. Immediately on John's death pension transfers to Susan and she commences to receive pension payments from the Trustee of the Fund. Importantly the Trustee needs to ensure that Susan takes a minimum pension payment for that period of the year that she holds the pension – this is to be 4% x (No of pension days/365). Remember - no minimum pension payment and there is no pension.

If Susan is not alive at the time of John's death the auto-reversion does not apply and the pension will cease and head back to the accumulation account, awaiting the distribution by the Trustee according to any nominations or requests by the deceased member (in a SMSF Will or binding death benefit nomination).

As an auto-reversionary pension, the pension will not be tested for Susan's Transfer Balance Caps for 12 months. A non-reversionary pension is tested when the pension commences in Susan's name. For Susan - well this means a significant TBC balance to her credit well before her retirement.

4) Commuting the Pension

Where a member has an account based pension, at any time they may elect to commute the whole or part of the pension into a lump sum. A commutation is the turning of an income into a lump sum. This could be by way of a payment to the member as a lump sum or alternatively, a roll back to the accumulation account. A roll back is also a commutation. If the pension is commuted in part, so at least $1 remains in the pension account, then the pension remains in force. However, if a pension is commuted in its entirety, then the pension ceases and all components of the pension and any estate planning is terminated. For example, if John with his pension account above, seeks to refresh his pension by rolling it back to his accumulation account, then the pension and auto-reversionary built into the pension for Susan ceases.

The taxation consequences of commuting to a lump sum are the same as the withdrawal taxation table shown earlier. On the death of the member, a SMSF Will created by the member may require the commutation of the deceased member's pension to a lump sum for the benefit of a dependant. The taxation consequences in relation to any SMSF estate planning and in particular, a SMSF Will, should be discussed with a qualified SMSF adviser.

14.7 The Pension Transfer Balance Caps

From 1 July 2017 the total amounts used to *commence a pension* cannot exceed $1.6M.

Every time a pension is commenced, a credit of the amount used to commence a pension is made to the members Personal Transfer Balance Account (PTBA). This is then tested against the General Transfer Balance Account – currently $1.6M and if excessive, then the excess must be withdrawn voluntarily by the member or the Commissioner of Taxation will step in and commute the excess amount.

The excess can be withdrawn as a lump sum commutation or rolled back to the fund's accumulation account. Any roll back creates a debit in the member's PTBA. The roll back amount may see the member's PTBA go into a negative.

In the Commissioners guideline on Pension Transfer Balance Accounts – LCG 2016/9 – he shows the transfer balance rules in action as illustrated in the following example:

"Example 1 – Transfer balance account credits and debits

On 1 July 2018, 61 year old Darius commences an account-based pension (pension A) with a $1.1 million value. His transfer balance account commences on this date. Investment returns and payments made to Darius to meet minimum drawdown requirements change the value of the superannuation interest supporting his pension. Because of this, the value of his superannuation interest at 1 July 2019 is $1.05 million. These changes, however, do not cause a credit or debit to arise in his transfer balance account and his transfer balance remains $1.1 million.

On 1 July 2020, Darius decides that he is unhappy with the investment returns from his provider and instructs his superannuation fund to fully commute his pension. Darius' superannuation fund commutes pension A on 7 July 2020 to a superannuation lump sum of $1 million on that day. Accordingly, a debit equal to this amount arises in his transfer balance account on this day.

The following table details Darius's transfer balance account and the debits and credits arising from the above transactions.

Transfer balance account

Date	Description	Debit/Credit	Transfer balance
1 July 2018	Commence pension A	$1.1 million	$1.1 million
7 July 2020	Commutes pension A	*$1 million*	$0.1 million

STRATEGY **Negative Transfer Balance Limits – a Strategic Opportunity**

The Explanatory Memorandum (EM) to the Transfer Balance Limit laws states that there may be cases where a member's personal transfer balance limit is negative. This could arise if investment earnings meant that a superannuation income stream is worth more when it is commuted from retirement phase, than its initial value when it commenced. The EM provides the following example:

"On 1 July 2017, Taylor purchases a pension worth $1.6 million. On 1 June 2018, the superannuation interest that supports the pension is valued at $1.7 million because of investment earnings. Taylor fully commutes the pension on this day and receives a $1.7 million superannuation lump sum. Taylor's transfer balance account is debited by $1.7 million to reach a balance of — $100,000. Taylor is entitled to start a new pension worth up to $1.7 million without breaching his transfer balance cap."

By now you should be well and truly SMSF Strategy Smart – how could you use this rule to benefit you and when would you use it with a roll back in a falling investment market?

14.8 The Taxation of Pensions

1) Trustee Taxation

Where a SMSF Trustee is paying a pension to a member, the Trustee is entitled to a tax exemption on income and capital gains arising in relation to assets set aside to meet the Fund's SMSF pension liabilities. This is different to the lump sum accumulation stage of a SMSF where income is taxed at a rate of 15% and capital gains 10% (effective after a 331/3% discount).

Where the Trustee runs a pooled investment strategy, meaning the assets of the Fund are pooled to pay all member benefits including pensions, then the Trustee will obtain a proportional tax exemption on income and gains earned by the Fund. This is generally the case with most SMSFs paying a pension. The exemption proportion is to be determined by reference to the liabilities to pay current pensions, versus the Fund's total superannuation benefit liabilities and is determined each year by an actuary. The cost for actuarial services is commonly $300 per annum.

In contrast, where the Trustee of the Fund runs a separate investment strategy for any SMSF pension (segregating assets from the rest of the Fund), then any income or gains earned on these assets is tax free. The segregation of assets is a simple book keeping exercise that can be undertaken by the accountant or administrator to the Fund. Importantly, if the assets have accrued capital gains in the lump sum side of the SMSF, then the transfer of the assets to a separate pension investment strategy in the Fund will not create a tax liability at the time of transfer. Furthermore, provided the assets funding the pension are disposed of by the Trustee at the time the SMSF pension has commenced, there will be no capital or income tax consequences in respect of the disposal of the assets. However, if a member of the Fund is receiving a pension and any member of the Fund has exceeded their General Transfer Balance Account limit – for 2017-2018 of $1.6M[32] then the Trustee must use the proportionate method.

As a final point - where the Trustee of the SMSF holds Australian shares (as part of the fund's pension assets) paying imputation credits, no tax is payable on the dividend. However, the Trustee may claim the imputation credits to reduce overall tax payable in the Fund. If there are excess credits in an income year, these will be refunded by the Commissioner of Taxation to the Trustee of the Fund.

As can be seen there are significant taxation advantages in running a separate investment strategy for pension assets of the Fund, subject to the General Transfer Balance Account limitation detailed above.

2) The Taxation of Pension Members

For pension members any income received from the pension is tax free:

a) If the pension is received by the member post age 60 except where the pension consists of untaxed taxable component – an unlikely event in a SMSF[33];

---

32 The General Transfer Balance Account includes superannuation benefits sitting in any super fund and both accumulation and pension account balances.

33 Section 301-10 ITAA 97

b) If the pension consists of tax free component. This is important for a member in receipt of pension income below age 60 such as a person who has reached their preservation age and retired[34].

For any other pension income, it is assessable income to the member however there is a 15% tax offset[35]. This includes a disability pension, one where the member has met the permanent incapacity condition of release and the Trustee has decided to use their benefits to pay a pension. An income payment by way of salary continuance under a temporary incapacity income stream, does not receive any tax benefits in the Fund nor in the hands of the member – it is fully taxable as ordinary income and is not part of the Fund's tax-exempt pension assets.

14.9 The Transition to Retirement Income Stream

So far, we have looked at lump sums and pensions but there is one little addition - the transition to retirement income stream (TRIS). We have looked at the TRIS when reviewing the preservation laws and saw that purpose of the TRIS is to enable members to access their superannuation whilst in the workforce.

As such, once a person reaches their preservation age, they can access all or part of their superannuation benefits as an income stream - provided the income stream is not able to be commuted to a lump sum. The income stream has the same terms and conditions as an account based pension, meaning that capital cannot be added to the TRIS once commenced and a minimum pension payment must be made each and every year. Importantly, a TRIS can convert to an account based pension when the member retires.

The key terms and conditions of a TRIS are as follows:

---

34 Section 301-15

35 Section 301-20 and for a disability pension – section 301-40

1. it is not a pension for the purposes of SISA 93 or the ITAA 97 and thus is not taken into account for the purposes of the tax exemption of pension assets inside the Fund;

2. the maximum income stream that may be taken each year is no more than 10% of their account balance in any income year;

3. the TRIS cannot be taken as a lump sum but can be rolled back into a member's accumulation account;

4. like an account based pension, where the person is over age 55 the income stream will generally attract a 15% tax offset. Once the member is 60 years of age or older the income from the transition to retirement income stream will be tax free.

CHAPTER FIFTEEN

The Taxation of a SMSF

"SMSFs are a low, low taxation vehicle. However, I see so many Trustees (alone and with advisers) not really care about tax strategy. Seriously, if you can legally reduce contributions tax then why not go for it? In the long run, as any investor will tell you – a 5% difference over time can make a huge difference thanks to compounding. With SMSF tax – get advice, get strategic, plan and implement."

15.1 **Tax rules in a nutshell**

The following rules are an overview of how SMSFs are taxed:

1) Income and capital gains earned on assets held by the Trustee of the Fund for the purposes of accumulation are subject to a maximum tax rate of 15% (although capital gains accrue a CGT discount of 33 1/3%).

2) If the Fund is paying out pension benefits to members and the pension meets the requirements for pensions - under SISR 1.06 - then section 295-385 of the Income Tax Assessment Act 1997 (ITAA 97) provides that any income or capital gains earned on assets held by the Trustee specifically for the purposes of paying current pensions, will be tax free.

3) If the SMSF is a non-complying Fund, then a penalty tax rate of 45% will apply to any income and gains earned by the Fund.

4) For tax and investment strategy purposes, the 15% rate of tax in the Fund may be reduced by imputation credits paid to the Fund. Imputation credits payable at the rate of 30% would result in an excess credit being available to the fund. This excess credit may be used to offset tax payable by the fund on capital gains, rent, interest or even assessable contributions. Imputation credits paid on shares held for the purposes of paying current pensions can be used by the Fund to reduce tax, even though no amount of the franked dividend will be subject to tax. Excess credits cannot be carried forward to future income years but are refundable.

5) Contributions made on behalf of another person, generally deductible employer and individual contributions known as concessional contributions, are assessable income of the fund – s 295-160 of ITAA 97. This means any so-called contributions tax can be reduced by legitimate deductions in the Fund, such as interest costs arising from a Limited Recourse Borrowing Arrangement (LRBA), capital allowances and depreciation on rental property investments in the Fund - and for any tax payable, the Trustee may apply any imputation credits.

15.2 Capital Gains Tax in a SMSF

Where the Fund acquires an investment asset which is not a security (such as bonds and 90 day bank bills), any gains realised upon disposal of the asset will generally be subject to capital gains tax (CGT) (s 295-85 of ITAA 97). This is important for when the Trustee trades shares and develops property. Ordinarily these profits would be fully assessable and not subject to CGT, meaning the Trustee would miss out on the tax reduction for CGT purposes. The only exception is if the assets are trading stock of the Trustee of the Fund.

15.3 Deductible Life Insurance Premiums

If a Trustee of the Fund elects to take out life insurance, then any premiums paid by the Fund to secure the life insurance coverage on behalf of a member will be tax deductible pursuant to s 295-465 of the ITAA 97. A deduction is also allowed for premiums paid by the Fund for temporary and permanent disability insurance for a member.

SISR 4.07C provides that the Trustee of a regulated superannuation fund is prohibited from providing members with insured benefits other than those that satisfy the conditions of release at Schedule 1 of the SISR for death, terminal medical condition, permanent incapacity and temporary incapacity. As such, trauma insurance cannot be acquired by the Trustee of a SMSF as trauma is not a condition of release.

In relation to some life insurance policies, Table 4 of s 295-465 ITAA 97 provides that a certain percentage is deductible. The proportion that is deductible can be seen in the following table:

For an insurance policy that provides...	the fund can deduct...
Total and Permanent Disability (TPD) any occupation cover	100%
TPD any occupation cover with one or more of the following inclusions: > activities of daily living > cognitive loss > loss of limb > domestic (home) duties	100%
TPD own occupation cover	67%
TPD own occupation cover with one or more of the following inclusions: > activities of daily living > cognitive loss > loss of limb > domestic (home) duties	67%
TPD own occupation cover bundled with death (life) cover	80%
TPD own occupation cover bundled with death (life) cover with one or more of the following inclusions: > activities of daily living > cognitive loss > loss of limb > domestic (home) duties	80%

15.4 Taxable Contributions

As noted above, where the Fund receives an employer contribution, or a contribution where the member has made a declaration to the Trustee under s 290-150 of the ITAA 97 that it is deductible to the member, then s 295-160 requires that the contribution will be included in the Fund's assessable income. Assessable contributions also include contributions made on behalf of another *excluding* child contributions, spouse contributions and the Government Co-contribution.

15.5 Non-Arms Length Income (NALI)

Private company dividends and income received by the Fund which is earned on a non-arm's length transaction (only income in excess of an arm's length value) will be classified as non-arms length income of the Fund (s 295-550 of ITAA 97). Non-arm's length income is subject to tax at the rate of 45% in the Fund. Distributions from a Family Trust are also included as NALI.

In addition, we have already seen in the SMSF Borrowing chapter that the Commissioner has also released an LRBA guideline – PCG 2016/5 where he stated that a zero or discounted related party loan would see the holding trust established under the LRBA receive more income that would be expected if an arm's length rate of interest was used. As such this income would be NALI and taxed at a rate of 45%.

15.6 Unit Trust Investments taxed as Companies

Certain unit trusts are taxed as companies under the Tax Act. Where a super fund invests in a unit trust, it will be taxed as a company, unless the unit trust carries on eligible investment business pursuant to s 102M of the ITAA 36. Eligible investment business means investment in shares, units, debentures, options, futures and in property which is held for rental purposes only. So, investment by a Fund in a unit trust that carries on a business, or is developing land for sale, will result in the trust being subject to tax as a company.

> **Warning**
>
> As with any transaction or development it is important to get advice in relation to the transaction – particularly if the $ amount is significant – see some consequences in ATO IT 2010/128.

15.7 Death Benefit – Future Service Element

Where a member of a SMSF dies or becomes permanently disabled, and the Trustee of the Fund has been paying insurance for the member, the Trustee may elect not to deduct the insurance premiums in that income year, but instead claim a deduction for the future service element of the death benefit payment (s 295-470 of ITAA 97). The Commissioner looked at this specific tax-deductible claim for the Trustee of a super-annuation fund in ATO ID 2015/17.

STRATEGY **Future Service Element Case Study:** Let's consider an example of Sarah Smith's SMSF. The Trustee of the Fund has been claiming a tax deduction for life insurance premiums and in April 2018, Sarah dies at the age of 45 - leaving her husband, Francis, and two teenage daughters. The Trustee of the Fund receives a life insurance payout of $500,000 and with her existing superannuation benefits of $200,000, makes a $700,000 tax free lump sum payout to Francis.

In the 2018 income year, the Trustee elects not to claim the insurance premium deduction but a s 295-470 deduction. This is worked out by looking at the super benefits paid out: $700,000 multiplied by a proportion of that part of her future working life which bears to her entire working life. Assuming Sarah started work at age 25 and with a normal retirement age of 65, then her death at age 45 results in a future service percentage of 50% or a $350,000 deduction for the Trustee of the Fund.

This can be carried forward to the extent it is not used in the current income year by the Trustee of the Fund, and may be applied in future years against contributions included as the Trustee's assessable income for Francis and Sarah's daughters.

15.8 **Complying to Non-Complying - A Tax Disaster**

Section 295-325 of the ITAA 97 deals with a case where a superannuation fund turns from a complying to a non-complying super fund in a year of income. In the year that this occurs, the Fund's assessable income will include the total market value of the assets of the Fund, less any non-concessional contributions. As a non-complying Fund, this will be subject to tax at a 47% tax rate. This also includes the situation where an Australian superannuation fund becomes a foreign superannuation fund at any time.

ATO Case Study – Foreign SMSF Consequences

Bob and Betty were Trustees and members of a SMSF. Bob worked outside of Australia for two years and eight months. As a result, the SMSF failed to meet the residency rules and no longer met the definition of an Australian superannuation fund (under section 295-95(2) of the ITAA 97). Because the SMSF is not an Australian superannuation fund, it cannot be a complying superannuation fund (under subsection 42A(1) of the Superannuation Industry (Supervision) Act 1992 (SISA)).

Bob and Betty voluntarily told us about their SMSF's situation. We started an investigation as a result of their voluntary disclosure.

Result

Usually a SMSF would lose its complying status if it stopped being an Australian superannuation fund. As a result:

- its assessable income would be taxed at a rate of 47%; and

- it would lose almost half its assets in a one-off additional tax bill in the year that it became non-complying.

However, in this case we did not make the SMSF non-complying because of a number of mitigating factors:

- ✓ Bob and Betty voluntarily disclosed the breach to us before we took action;

- ✓ Bob was terminally ill; and

- ✓ Bob and Betty were divorced and their super benefits were subject to a Family Court order.

We allowed the SMSF to retain its complying status and receive concessional tax treatment until it could be wound up. Bob and Betty were required to roll over all the benefits and wind up the SMSF.

CHAPTER SIXTEEN

SMSF Estate Planning

"At my seminars I ask the question – is it important that your money and assets stay within your bloodline? And you know what? 99% of the attendees put their hand up and the 1% who don't – don't have bloodline or don't understand the question. Then I look at their SMSF estate plan and bloodline is nowhere to be seen. Whose fault is that? Why is this happening in million and multi-million dollar SMSFs? Something is going seriously wrong in SMSF land."

16.1 **Introduction**

"The payment of death benefits from a superannuation fund is determined in accordance with the governing rules of the superannuation fund and not in accordance with the terms of the deceased's will."

The Commissioner of Taxation - SMSFD 2008/D1

Estate planning is the process of planning and documenting a person's wishes for the distribution of all assets owned and controlled by the deceased at the time of death. But take a look at the Commissioner's statement above – look hard! If you have a SMSF, then any normal will or estate planning that you may have completed has no impact on a SMSF. So, let's compartmentalise SMSF estate planning – what exactly is it?

SMSF Estate Planning is the process of planning and documenting a member's wishes in relation to the distribution of *a deceased member's superannuation interests, both accumulation and pension to their dependants — including non-dependant children, as well as their legal estate.*

Case study — SMSF Estate Planning Disaster

The father of a family died of a sudden heart attack at age 70 in November 2017. There was no pain, and according to his family he lived his life to the fullest. The funeral was attended by a wide circle of friends and family, but only close family were invited to the reading of the father's legal will. The father left behind a house that was jointly owned with his wife, a portfolio of $200,000 in blue chip shares and an account based pension in the family SMSF which had a balance of $850,000. His wife was the only other member of the family SMSF with a small accumulation account balance.

In his will, which had been recently made by the family lawyer who claimed his estate planning expertise, the eldest of his three sons was appointed as executor, essentially the person to carry out the wishes of his will. His wishes were that his wife be able to live in the house for the rest of her life or for as long as she desires. The executor was also to provide financial support to her for life — any assets remaining after she dies were to be split equally among their children. The father had not made any directions regarding his superannuation, believing upon the advice of his lawyer that his superannuation would automatically pass to his legal estate for distribution as part of his estate via the will.

In effect, the will has pitted the children against his wife and left one of the children in full control of his estate. If the child executor looks after his mother like his father wanted, he and his brothers may see their inheritance being spent. Or, the executor may decide to provide his mother with very little money by investing in capital growth assets so he and his brothers receive more on her death. Is it possible to create a balance where everyone is happy?

What happens when one of the boy's spouses becomes involved?

What happens if one of the boys feels that his father should have looked after him more because of his financial predicament and takes the matter to the Supreme Court?

Unlike the Commissioner of Taxation, many people (including Lawyers!) don't understand that the father's superannuation benefits cannot be dealt with in a will.

In terms of the distribution of the father's superannuation benefits, it is a matter for the Trustee of the SMSF solely to handle the superannuation benefits of the deceased in line with what is in the governing rules of the Fund, and any SMSF Will or Binding Death Benefit Nomination (BDBN) made by the father and held by the Trustee. If a SMSF Will or other direction has not been lodged with the Trustee, the Trustee has complete discretion to deal with the benefits as they see fit including giving it to themselves if they are a non-dependant adult child — see *Katz v Grossman* [2005] NSWSC 934.

In the current case, the remaining Trustee upon the member's death is the deceased member's wife[36]. With no SMSF Will in place, she as Trustee has full power over the disposition of his superannuation benefits. In this instance, she could convert the deceased member's account based pension into a lump sum and pay it to the estate where the executor could look after it. Alternatively, she could continue paying her husband's pension to her in line with his desire to look after her for life. On her demise, she may pass all of her superannuation benefits to charity and there is little her children can do about it, despite their father's wishes.

The children have almost no rights of legal redress against the Trustee. Outside of a SMSF, the Superannuation Complaints Tribunal (SCT) provides dependants with a legal forum to challenge a Trustee's decision. However, this is not the case with SMSFs that are excluded from the jurisdiction of the SCT.

This scenario is an example of many family SMSF estates. Moreover, SMSF estate planning can become extremely complicated if second and third marriages, as well as de facto relationships are involved (and especially where there are children from different relationships).

16.2 **Key elements of an effective SMSF Estate Plan**

Creating an effective SMSF estate plan can be a long and drawn out task, requiring great skill of a SMSF adviser, as well as ensuring that all contingencies and wishes are covered. Great care and time needs to go into developing any SMSF estate plan and, more importantly, designing and documenting it[37].

---

36 As a sole trustee of the family SMSF, she has six months to appoint another trustee or change the trustee to a corporate trustee to remain a SMSF for the purposes of SISA.

37 SMSF estate planning relates only to the distribution of a member's superannuation interests in the event of the member's death. At the same time, as a SMSF estate plan is being prepared, a review or the creation of a will is necessary to cater for the distribution of non-super assets or superannuation interests where the member has elected to pass their superannuation interests to their legal estate in the event of their death.

The key elements of an estate plan are to:

- determine what is important to a person in relation to looking after their family and dependants in the event of their death;

- determine who is going to control the distribution of the deceased member's superannuation interests as superannuation benefits upon the person's death;

- create a blueprint to deliver the desired SMSF estate planning goals using the right combination of vehicles and life insurance if need be;

- make sure the plan is simple, certain and easy for all parties to understand before the person dies;

- ensure the person or persons left in charge of implementing the plan on behalf of the deceased know what they are doing or use experienced advisers to deliver the plan. For a SMSF, this is the Trustee of the Fund;

- ensure the SMSF estate plan is tax effective; and

- ensure that it complies with the laws and any chance of legal disputation is minimised.

16.3 Payment of Death Benefits

For the most part, SMSF estate planning can be carried out via the direct transfer of a deceased member's superannuation interests from their family SMSF. This may be by way of a lump sum or pension — although there are legal limitations for the Trustee of a Fund paying an income stream or pension. The SMSF strategic possibilities for a member of a Fund in terms of their SMSF estate planning are seen in the following Table:

Beneficiary	Allowable Superannuation Benefit
Spouse	Lump sum, income stream and/or both
Dependant child under the age of 18	Lump sum, income stream and/or both. However, any income stream must cease by age 25
Dependant child between the ages of 18 and 25	Lump sum, income stream and/or both. However, any income stream must cease by age 25
Dependant grandchild	Lump sum, income stream and/or both
Non-dependant grandchild	Lump sum via the legal estate
Dependant child over the age of 25	Lump sum
Non-dependant child over the age of 18	Lump sum
Non-dependant (not a child of the member)	Lump sum via the legal estate
Legal estate	Lump sum

Table 1: The Payment of Death Benefits to a Member's SMSF estate

16.4 Who is a Dependant?

The sole purpose test provides that the Trustee of a SMSF can pay death benefits to a "dependant" upon the death of a member. There are different definitions of dependant for SISA and ITAA 97. Under SISA, all children are dependants, as is seen in the table above. However for tax dependency which guarantees tax free death benefit payments, only minor or financially dependent children under the age of 25 are considered dependants. This is explained further below.

A death benefits dependant[38] for taxation purposes includes:

---

38 Section 302-195 of ITAA 97

- a deceased person's spouse or former spouse[39]; or

- a deceased person's child, aged less than 18; or

- any other person with whom the deceased person had an *interdependency relationship* just before he or she died; or

- any other person who was a dependant of the deceased person just before he or she died — that is a *financial dependant.*

It also includes someone receiving a super lump sum because the deceased died in the line of duty as a member of:

- the defence force;

- the Australian Federal Police;

- the police force of a state or territory;

- a protective service officer; or

- the deceased member's former spouse or de facto spouse.

The meaning of "interdependent relationship[40]" has been described as "one of continuing mutual commitment to financial and emotional support between two people who reside together. The definition will also include a person with a disability who may live in an institution but is nevertheless interdependent with the deceased. For example, two elderly sisters who reside together and are interdependent will be able to receive each other's superannuation benefits tax-free. Similarly, an adult child who resides with and cares for an elderly parent will be eligible for tax-free superannuation benefits upon the death of the parent."

The Meaning of Financial Dependence

The issue of who is a financial dependant has occupied the court's mind for more than a century in relation to workers compensation,

---

39 Spouse in relation to a person includes another person who, although not legally married to the person, lives with the person on a genuine domestic basis as a couple and also includes, where the Superannuation Laws allow, members of the same sex or any other relationship between two persons.
40 s 302-200 of ITAA 1997; s 10A of SISA

taxation and superannuation matters. There have been two significant cases concerning the meaning of financial dependant for the purposes of the Superannuation Laws — *Malek v FC of T* 99 ATC 2294 and *Faull v Superannuation Complaints Tribunal* [1999] NSWSC 1137.

In Malek's case, Antoine Malek was aged 25 when he died. He was single, had no children and, prior to his death, he and his widowed mother lived together. Mrs Malek received a disability support pension of approximately $153 per week, but her accountant estimated that Antoine Malek contributed approximately $258 per week to Mrs Malek's living expenses for food, mortgage payments, taxi fares, medical expenses and other bills.

The tribunal reviewed the cases on financial dependence and in its decision cited the following authoritative statement from Gibbs J of the High Court:

Gibbs J said in Aafjes v Kearney (1976) 180 CLR 1999 at page 207:

"… In Kauri Timber Co. (Tas.) Pty. Ltd. V. Reeman (1973) 128 CLR 177 at pp 188–189, I accepted that one person is dependent on another for support if the former in fact depends on the latter for support even though he does not need to do so and could have provided some or all of his necessities from another source. I adhere to that view."

In the end, the Administrative Appeals Tribunal held that Mrs Malek was a financial dependant because the financial support she received from her son maintained her normal standard of living. Moreover, she was reliant on the regular continuous contribution of the other person to maintain that standard.

In Faull's case, the Court held that the mother of 19-year-old Llewellyn Faull was a financial dependant of his at the time of his death, and determined that his death benefit in its entirety should be paid to her. At the time of her son's death, Mrs Faull had regular employment that earned her income of $30,000 pa. Her wages were supplemented by an amount of $30 per week paid by her son as board and lodging. Although the sum paid to Mrs Faull every week by her son was small, the court stated that "the payment of that amount augmented her other income and, to that extent, she was dependent upon the deceased for the receipt of some of her income. Accordingly, she was partially dependent upon the payments made by the deceased".

The courts have looked at financial dependence in the broad sense of the meaning, and concluded that partial dependence and reliance is enough to establish financial dependence for the purposes of SISA, provided the payment is ongoing and recurring.

Regulator Guideline

APRA has considered the issue of financial dependence as part of the payments standard guideline — APRA Guideline No.I.C.2 stated the following:

"There is no need for one person to be wholly dependent upon another for that person to be a 'dependant' for the purposes of the payment standards. Financial dependency can be established where a person relies wholly or in part on another for his or her means of subsistence. Nor must the recipient show a need for the money received from the deceased member in order to qualify as a dependant. Moreover, since partial financial dependency can generally be sufficient to establish a relationship of dependence, it is possible for two persons to be dependent on each other for the purposes of the payment standards."

Given the significance to the Commissioner of Taxation of the meaning of financial dependence, expect this area of the superannuation laws to be hotly contested in the courts over the next decade or more. Remember a financially dependant child can receive death benefits comprised of taxable component and not have to pay 17% tax on the taxable component.

16.5 Why a Lump Sum may not be suitable for some Beneficiaries

A lump sum can be extremely popular to the recipient, but it can also prove a financial disaster. Consider whether a parent, on their death, should provide a lump sum to the following children:

- A child under age 18, resulting in the remaining parent or guardian having full control of where and how the lump sum is invested, and how much is to be dedicated to looking after the child. This may be exacerbated if the remaining parent had a dysfunctional relationship with the deceased member as a consequence of a divorce or relationship split.

- An adult child who is currently in a dysfunctional or concerning relationship. On death, any lump sum payment will become part of matrimonial property if the child is married (or joint property if they are in a de facto relationship). Is this what the deceased member wanted?

- A child with a history of alcohol, spending, drug or criminal problems — irrespective of their age. Is it appropriate to leave a lump sum with someone who may just spend it on the wrong things?

- A child with a business. The danger of the lump sum payment is that the child may use it for the business — although this may be good for business expansion it may place the lump sum at risk. An income stream may mean that the business does not need to pay out as much cash flow to the owners, and has a better chance to survive and flourish.

- A child or person with no financial common sense.

However, the superannuation laws limit the payment of an income stream to some dependants and also non-dependants of a deceased member. As such, the provision of an income stream needs to be by way of a lump sum death benefit payment to the legal estate for allocation to a testamentary trust. This is a case where you need to have a lawyer that is very experienced at wills, estate planning and also, *SMSF estate planning*.

16.6 **Testamentary trust v SMSF**

Testamentary trusts created with superannuation benefits have their legitimate place in SMSF estate planning - as do direct payments from a SMSF. However, they both have their unique advantages and disadvantages.

The Testamentary Trust

A testamentary trust is commonly used by estate planning lawyers to protect the assets of the family from creditors, family law actions and, at the same time, provide flexibility in relation to the distribution of the estate. In essence, a testamentary trust is a trust that arises from the estate of the deceased and is contained in the deceased's will. As such, the terms and conditions of the trust, including the appointer, income and capital beneficiaries, Trustee and so on, are to be designated in the will of the deceased. The benefits and limitations are discussed below.

Advantages

a) Control is held by the Trustee of the testamentary trust and obviously the person who has the power to appoint and remove the Trustee — the appointor of the trust.

b) It is built for the purpose of looking after the family and others on the death of a family member, with income and capital distributed by the Trustee to a group of family or non-family beneficiaries. Generally, the testamentary trust will require the Trustee to look after family members in a specified way, rather than provide the Trustee with complete discretion.

c) It is possible to create income streams from the testamentary trust — although with difficulty and certainly not the tax certainty of a pension in a SMSF.

d) The Trustee is able to look after capital and income beneficiaries differently. The Trustee may distribute a capital gain to one beneficiary, a dividend to another, while a third may receive property income, depending on the terms of the testamentary trust deed.

e) A capital gains tax discount of 50% applies to any assets disposed of by the Trustee, provided the Trustee has held them for more than 12 months. Although the Trustee claims the discount, they distribute the pre-tax capital gain to the beneficiary. This enables the beneficiary to claim the discount in their own hands and, more importantly, offset the capital gain with any capital loss that they may have from the disposal of assets in the current or prior years.

f) Assets are protected from creditors. Any assets in the testamentary trust may be protected from creditors of the potential family beneficiaries.

g) Minor beneficiaries are not subject to penalty taxes and are taxed just like any other ordinary taxpayer.

h) In terms of divorce and family break-ups, testamentary and other trusts have proved their effectiveness in sheltering assets from the Family Court and courts in general, although this is becoming more difficult.

i) Some part of the testamentary trust can be used to house a deceased's superannuation benefits. If these benefits are held solely for the use of dependants of the deceased, then no tax is payable on receipt by the executor of the deceased's estate on these amounts. If the benefits are to be applied for the benefit of non-dependants, then the tax on the lump sums received is 17%. Any income or gains earned in the testamentary trust on these partitioned superannuation proceeds are taxed as ordinary trust income.

Disadvantages

a) Testamentary trusts are complex structures, particularly when different types of income and capital are distributed among beneficiaries under a wide-ranging trust deed. This means the costs of running a testamentary trust may be substantial.

b) Where specific requirements are built within the trust deed (eg each child to receive a set amount of income each year), the drafting of the legal document can become quite complex and only a skilled estate planning lawyer, with SMSF skills, should attempt.

c) All income and capital gains must be distributed annually or the testamentary Trustee pays tax on the income at the top marginal tax rate of 47%. In the case of a trust with different income and capital beneficiaries, this means that, in terms of capital gains made by the trust, it must choose one of the following options and still balance between both types of beneficiaries:

- distribute capital gains to capital beneficiaries whenever made which reduces the asset base for the income beneficiary;

- distribute capital gains as part of the income of the trust to the income beneficiary if the income of the trust includes assessable capital gains;

- keep it in the trust with the Trustee paying tax at 47%, and

- keep it in the trust with the capital beneficiary paying tax with distributions recapitalised.

d) Income distributed from the trust is subject to tax at the beneficiaries' marginal tax rate, although imputation credits on dividends received and passed through to a beneficiary will shelter some of the tax payable. There are no tax concessions provided to beneficiaries of a testamentary trust except that minors are taxed as ordinary taxpayers.

e) Testamentary trusts are subject to the "rule against perpetuities" and must be wound up no later than 80 years from the date of establishment. This may impact estates seeking to pay long term income benefits to a family line including children and grandchildren.

2) SMSFs as an Estate Planning Vehicle

SMSFs have the tax benefits of a superannuation fund as well as the flexibility of the family and testamentary trust (subject to income stream limitations). Each SMSF is different, as each must be tailored to the specific and changing needs of the family through the use of a strong and flexible set of governing rules - particularly when it comes to estate planning. The limitations of income stream estate planning for adult children has lessened the estate planning attractiveness of the SMSF, but it still has significant tax and legal advantages over the testamentary trust. More importantly, it has built a platform for the introduction of the SMSF Will — found in good SMSF trust deeds.

Advantages

a) SMSFs can be family SMSFs built for lifetimes and provide long term estate planning solutions, including laying down income streams for future generations, where possible. While death benefits may be paid directly to all dependants as defined under the SISA 93, income streams are limited to dependants - but if a child of the deceased member, only a minor, permanently incapacitated, or child under the age of 25 who is a financial dependant.

b) If a SMSF Will is used, specific actions and requests by a member of a Fund may be put in place in respect of their superannuation benefits in the event of their death.

c) Control — like the family trust, the Trustees of the Fund have control of the Fund. Under SISA 93 there is a requirement that all members of the Fund, generally the family, must also be Trustees of the Fund or directors of the Fund's corporate Trustee. This means shared control among members of the Fund. Although it is wise to put in place proportional voting where Trustees have votes at a Trustee meeting based on their account balances;

d) A wide range of investment choices. Where the member is using a SMSF Will, the member may designate specific assets to pass to dependants and non-dependants upon their death. If an income stream option is used, then the Trustee may invest the assets of the Fund for the benefit of the dependant income stream recipient.

e) Assets remaining in the Fund are protected from creditors.

f) SMSFs have a significant advantage over other entities in terms of taxation.

g) SMSFs are simple in terms of administration, with a professional administrator recording all transactions that the Trustee has made, although compliance with SISA 93 does add to the cost of delivering a Fund that complies with all the laws.

h) The penalty tax rates that apply for investment income paid to a minor do not apply to income paid from a superannuation fund or SMSF.

i) If the deceased member had an auto-reversionary pension and was over age 60, then the dependant receiving the pension will not pay tax on the pension - ever. If the deceased member was not in receipt of a tax free income stream or was not receiving a pension, then the beneficiary will include the pension income as assessable income with a 15% tax offset until age 60 when it will be tax free.

Disadvantages

a) If a SMSF Will or valid binding death benefit nomination is not used, the passing of superannuation benefits of the deceased member is at the mercy of the remaining Trustee of the Fund — see *Katz v Grossman* [2005] NSWSC 934.

b) SISA 93 weighs heavily on the Trustee of the Fund and, as a result, the Trustee and member must consult a specialist SMSF adviser or lawyer to ensure that the SMSF estate plan not only delivers what is required but also complies with the laws. There are significant financial penalties for breaching the laws and the Commissioner of Taxation may replace and disqualify a person as Trustee.

c) The cost of establishing a SMSF estate plan will depend on the size of a SMSF estate.

d) SMSFs cannot be viewed in isolation but are part of an entire estate plan.

e) Benefits in a superannuation fund are part of spousal property and may be split in the event of divorce. This may be of a concern where superannuation benefits are paid as a lump sum to children.

f) If the deceased member does not want to pay a lump sum to an adult child but rather an income stream with capital protection, then the structure of choice is a testamentary trust.

The Best of All Worlds – the TT and SMSF

STRATEGY SMSFs have income limitations for adult children. For parents who don't want to see their child with an income stream, the use of a testatmentary trust via the legal estate running *alongside* a SMSF is ideal. But be careful - one mistake in the documentation of the Will, TT or SMSF governing rules and the whole estate plan can fail.

16.7 SMSF Estate Planning Taxation

Where superannuation benefits are paid as a lump sum or income stream to a dependant, non-dependant or the legal estate of a deceased beneficiary, they may be subject to tax. The differentiating tax treatment will depend upon the recipient and the component of the superannuation benefit paid. As we have seen previously, these components may consist of a:

- tax-free component;
- taxable component; and
- untaxed element of the taxable component.

Where the recipient of the superannuation benefit is the Trustee of the deceased member's legal estate, the taxation of the benefit or part of the benefit will relate to the intended distribution by the Trustee of the benefit or part of the benefit. The taxation of the benefit will follow the intended or actual distribution to a dependant or non-dependant of the deceased[41] as shown in the following tables:

Table 2 — The Taxation of Death Benefit Lump sums

Benefit component	Dependant*	Non-dependant
Tax-free component	Nil	Nil
Taxable component	Nil	17%
Untaxed element of the Taxable component[1]	Nil	32%

Dependant means a tax dependant

Table 3 — the Taxation of the Taxable Component of Death Benefit Pensions

Benefit component	Deceased died aged 60 or above or dependant aged 60 or above	Deceased died aged under 60 and dependant aged under 60
Tax-free component	Nil	Nil
Taxable component	Nil	Assessable income + 15% tax offset
Untaxed element of the taxable component	Assessable income + 10% tax offset	Assessable income

Warning: A reversionary income stream can only be paid to dependants of the deceased member and only until age 25 where the dependant is a child, after which time the income stream must be commuted[42].

---

41   s 302-10 of ITAA 1997

42   R 6.21 of SISR

Pension Transfer Balance Limits and Death Benefits

A member in receipt of a pension may make a pension auto-reversionary meaning that upon their death, it transfers automatically to a spouse or dependant, as allowed under SISA 93. If there is no auto-reversionary the member or Trustee may have directions via a SMSF Will, BDBN or Trustee's discretion to pay a reversionary beneficiary a pension.

As the beneficiaries will be in receipt of a new pension, sourced from the deceased member, it is to be tested against their Personal Transfer Balance Amount just like any new pension. However, for auto-reversionary beneficiaries the testing is delayed - see Commissioner's LCG2017/3:

"If you are the recipient of a reversionary death benefit income stream, you are a reversionary beneficiary and a transfer balance credit arises in your transfer balance account. The time at which the credit arises is:

a) for death benefit income streams commencing before 1 July 2017 - the later of 1 July 2017 or 12 months from the day the death benefit income stream first became payable; and

b) for death benefit income streams commencing on or after 1 July 2017 - 12 months from the day (the starting day) when you started to be the retirement phase recipient of the death benefit income stream."

16.8 Binding Nominations in a SMSF

The Commissioner has stated, on a number of occasions, that the super laws that establish binding death benefit nominations - do not apply to SMSFs. In particular he has stated at SMSFR 2009/3 that:

"Section 59 of the Superannuation Industry (Supervision) Act 1993 (SISA) and Superannuation Industry (Supervision) Regulations 1994 (SISR) regulation 6.17A do not apply to SMSFs. This means that the governing rules of a SMSF may permit members to make death benefit nominations that are binding on the Trustee."

This means that before any death benefit nomination is made, the Trustee of the Fund, the member concerned and their advisor should review the current SMSF deed and governing rules to assess what type of death benefit nominations, *if any apply*. Remember if the trust deed is silent on the matter, no death benefit nomination is applicable. In addition, if the trust deed provides that the Trustee may make a binding death benefit nomination in accordance with the SISA 93, then as the death benefit nomination rules under SISA do not apply to SMSFs, this clause has no meaning and once again, the Trustee cannot offer a member a binding death benefit nomination.

An acceptable SMSF trust deed would have (as a bare minimum) rules enabling a BDBN and more importantly specific governing rules that allow a SMSF Will (as discussed below).

16.9 SMSF Wills

a) Introduction

As we have discussed, the opportunity of legal challenge is dramatically reduced when death benefits are not paid or payable to the legal estate of a deceased member by the Trustee of a complying SMSF - but directly to a beneficiary as specified by the deceased member. The payment of superannuation death benefits are not subject to the provisions of the member's Will, but should be catered for in a SMSF Will.

b) What is a SMSF Will?

A SMSF Will is an important legal document that becomes part of the governing rules of the Fund, detailing how a member seeks to provide superannuation death benefits to their dependants, non-dependants or legal estate in the event of their death. There are several possibilities in a SMSF Will:

- the provision of a superannuation lump sum — by way of cash or specific assets to dependants and/or the deceased member's legal estate;

- the payment of a superannuation income stream to dependants under SISA 93, but for child dependants it is limited to a child under the age of 18, a permanently incapacitated child and any child under the age of 25 who is a financial dependant

- the payment of a reversionary superannuation income stream to a dependant subject to SISA 93, and subject to the child limitations immediately above

- where a member of a SMSF has more than one superannuation interest in a Fund consisting of varying tax-free/taxable components — the choice of allocating from these interests to various dependants and non-dependants.

Note: A SMSF Will is a defined set of procedures and requirements purpose built into a SMSF trust deed to allow a member to provide specific benefits, assets, and otherwise direct what is to happen to their superannuation benefits in the event of their death. Not all superannuation fund trust deeds have the capacity to offer comprehensive and strategic SMSF estate planning or a SMSF Will.

c) Creating a SMSF Will

The process of creating a SMSF Will is as follows:

- provide the member with a product disclosure statement regarding the strategic death benefit possibilities under the Fund's trust deed[43];

- determine how the member proposes to distribute their superannuation interests — income stream, lump sum to dependant, non-dependant or through the legal estate;

---

43 Both trustees and advisers are required to issue a PDS to a member of a SMSF wherever a superannuation interest in the fund is involved, including a death benefit interest.

- determine the key components of the member's existing super-annuation interests, both accumulation and income stream. The determination should include the tax-free and taxable components;

- provide specific instructions to a qualified SMSF Will lawyer. Remember that the distribution of a member's superannuation interest is only part of their total estate planning. It is crucial for all facets of their SMSF estate plan to be put in place — both the deceased's Will and SMSF Will. It is also important to employ a lawyer capable of handling both SMSF and non-SMSF estate planning; and

- obtain SMSF Will and get member to execute. The SMSF Will should reside on the Fund's compliance file for action when a member dies.

16.10 SMSF Estate Planning Strategy

STRATEGY Adviser Question: SMSF Will or Auto-Reversionary Pension?

Our client is 61 years of age and has $1 million of superannuation benefits with $400,000 tax-free component. He has recently retired due to poor health and will commence an account based pension during this current year. He has a de facto spouse who is 66 years of age and in the event of his predeceasing her, wants his superannuation interest to pay her an income stream for the rest of her life. She has only $200,000 in an AMP super fund and is currently taking an account based pension. Upon her death, he wants any remaining benefit to form part of his estate to be distributed to his children from his first and only marriage.

The Fund has a corporate Trustee of which he is the sole shareholder and director. His de facto spouse is not a member of the Fund at present. Upon his death, can his executor become the sole shareholder and director of the Trustee company or does his spouse as the recipient of the pension have to be appointed a director also?

Grant's Strategic Response

Most lawyers receive numerous requests for SMSF estate planning advice and further the provision of SMSF Wills for clients in blended marriages — where couples have co-joined families following earlier divorces or spousal separations. Blended marriages create some interesting SMSF estate planning strategies and complexities — getting it just right among the numerous options — is a challenge. And SMSF estate planning is ever-changing. We have thrown out binding nominations following the Commissioner's guidelines on the fact that BDBN laws do not apply to SMSFs and replaced them with the SMSF Will. It is the same concept as a Will (that sits outside the fund) but deals with only superannuation interests in a SMSF, sits independently of the person's normal Will, resides with the Trustee and is acted upon by the Trustee /executor after the death of the member.

Where a member holds only a lump sum superannuation interest, there are a range of choices including the provision of income streams and lump sums to dependants and/or lump sums to non-dependants.

However, if a member is about to commence an account based pension as is the case here, then a SMSF Will or the pension itself can be used to create the SMSF Estate Plan. Both can be drafted with strength, certainty and providing a wide range of options. For example, a SMSF adviser concerned about a spouse withdrawing a lump sum can put in place terms and conditions that reverting income stream is non-commutable (no lump sum) with limited payment options – no more than 8% (as an example) of the pension account balance during any income year.

One strategy to be reviewed in light of the question above is to run auto-reversionary income streams with estate planning built in. This is estate planning by the terms and conditions of the income stream, rather than the SMSF Will. Like the SMSF Will, it is binding on the Trustee.

Strategy note: The term reversionary beneficiary and auto-reversionary pension are terms used when considering SMSF estate planning strategies. A reversionary beneficiary is that person entitled to be paid a lump sum or income stream in the event of the death of a member of the Fund. An auto-reversionary pension is an income stream that automatically reverts to the next recipient (if alive) upon the death of a member of a superannuation fund. At the time of death, the deceased member's income stream ceases and passes to the next recipient.

Possible Auto-Reversionary Pension Strategy

Looking at the circumstances of the client, ideally we can create an account based pension that has the following terms and conditions that are binding upon the Trustee of the Fund:

1) An accounts-based pension payable to the member for his life.

2) This pension is to revert to his spouse for her life with conditions including non-commutability and payment restrictions — much the same conditions as in a transition to retirement income stream (otherwise she will be able to withdraw all of the benefits as an income stream or lump sum payment). Generally, this means she cannot ever turn it into a lump sum, must receive an income that is at her choosing but capped at say 10% of the account balance so that the capital is not withdrawn excessively as a pension payment.

3) A reversionary income stream payable to whoever of his children/grandchildren that remain alive on her death provided that they were dependant upon the pension member at the time of death. If the child dependant is over age 25 at the time of the death of the spouse, their reversionary pension entitlement must be paid out as a lump sum or into a Testamentary Trust.

In order to create this multi-generational reversionary pension, we need to have the following parts in place:

1) A flexible, strategic SMSF trust deed;

2) Review of SISA 93 and SISR 94; and

3) The ITAA 1997.

1) Review of the SMSF trust deed

The first place to start any strategy development is with the SMSF trust deed. The Trustee must be able to offer a member an income stream where allowed under the Superannuation Laws. An income stream should be defined to include an account based pension with multi-generational reversionary pension members.

2) Review of SISA 93 and SISR 94

As the client has retired, he can access his superannuation interest and take either a lump sum superannuation benefit or an income stream superannuation benefit. SISR 1.06(1) provides that a pension is considered a pension for the purposes of the SISA provided that it complies with the following minimum rules:

- a minimum payment is made annually according to Schedule 7 of the SISR 94;

- the pension may not be topped up with further capital; and

- if the pension is commuted in whole during the income year, a proportional minimum income stream is taken prior to any commutation payment.

These are minimum requirements and thus, the broad nature of these provisions should not be underestimated. Provided we commence an income stream and make minimum income payments according to Schedule 7, then there are opportunities, via the governing rules of the Fund to make further additions to layer on top of the minimum requirements. As there are no limits as to who can be a reversionary income stream member under the SISA, a multi-generational SMSF estate planning income stream can be created for the client.

Strategy note: It is interesting that the limitations on paying an income stream on death under SISR 94 relates only to a child of the deceased member not another person who may be a financial dependant such as a grandchild, brother or other family member.

3) The ITAA 97

The difference between the two types of superannuation benefits is found in s 307-5 of ITAA 1997:

Superannuation benefit type	Superannuation member benefit	Superannuation death benefit
Superannuation Fund payment	A payment to you from a superannuation Fund because you are a Fund member.	A payment to you from a superannuation Fund, after another person's death, because the other person was a Fund member.

The pension, in the hands of the auto-reversionary beneficiary is a death benefit. As for the Transfer Balance Caps, the beneficiary has 12 months to credit the amount to their Personal Transfer Balance Account.

Conclusion

The multi-generational reversionary pension — with no commutation and a limitation on income stream payments — is an important SMSF strategy tool. However, the Trustee must ensure that any reversionary beneficiary is a dependant of the original pension member at the time of their death. If the beneficiary is a child when the reversionary pension moves into their hands then the pension must be commuted.

At this time, the safer option may be to provide a reversionary to the spouse with no commutation and a limitation on income stream payments, plus no ability to vary the income stream. As an income stream member, she must become a Trustee but if she is the only member, then an additional Trustee may be put in place. This may be one of the children. The rules of the Fund could have voting power in respect of any income stream payable on reversion placed in the hands of the alternative Trustee (say one of the children who is acting as an additional Trustee). The problem however is that on her death, no benefits may be paid to the children from her account directly as they are not her dependants under the wider SISA 93 sole purpose test. This means that the money will find its way into her estate, where it may be paid to the children. However, this will require delicate negotiation to incorporate such a clause in her will and ensure that she does not vary it.

CHAPTER SEVENTEEN

SMSF Terms and Meanings

"An important addition for The Guru's Guide to SMSFs are some common terms that are used when dealing with SMSFs generally and throughout this guide. Ideally these terms would form part of the Fund's trust deed and governing rules. They are in alphabetical order and where in capitals are defined elsewhere in the terms."

STRATEGY The SMSF Terms and Meanings section is the hard part of *The Guru's Guide to SMSFs*, but the strategic rewards in understanding these and how the whole SMSF system fits together, is a lifetime of challenge, strategy and fulfillment.

Accounts means those accounts, including trust accounts established by the Trustee for the Fund, a Member's Superannuation Interest or Interests, a group of Members' Superannuation Interests, a Reserve Account and any other account of the Fund.

Accounts Based Pension includes a Pension where capital cannot be added to the Pension except to create a new Pension and that the standards in SISR 1.03(1), 1.06(1), 1.06(9A) and 1.06(9B) apply or such other standards as prescribed for Accounts Based Pensions in the Superannuation Laws.

Active Member is a Member of the Fund that meets the criteria for active membership under the Superannuation Laws including the making of continuous contributions on behalf of the Member to the Fund. This is important as part of determining an Australian super Fund compared to a Foreign Super Fund.

Actuary is any professional actuary authorised under the Superannuation Laws to carry out the role of actuary to a Complying SMSF and which may include an actuary who is a practising Member of the Institute of Actuaries of Australia. It is a necessity to obtain a tax exemption where the Trustee of the Fund is seeking a proportionate tax exemption for pension assets of the Fund.

Additional Trustee is a person who is a non-Member of the Fund but is appointed as a Trustee of the Fund, as a consequence of the Fund having only one Member.

Assets of the Fund include, but are not limited to real, personal or intellectual property, shares, futures, collectables, businesses or business interests, any assets or property transferred or contributed to the Fund plus income, earnings and profits arising from those assets or property interests as well as any other asset that a Superannuation Fund may lawfully hold on behalf of a Member, Fund Superannuation Interest, Member Superannuation Benefit, for Insurance purposes, as well as for the Dependants and the Legal Estate of a Member or deceased Member, but excludes Cash.

Auditor is an auditor authorised under the Superannuation Laws or by the Regulator to be an auditor of a SMSF. The Trustee of a SMSF must appoint a licensed auditor each and every year to complete a compliance return for the Fund.

Australian Superannuation Fund means a Superannuation Fund that meets the conditions of an Australian Superannuation Fund under the Superannuation Laws or is otherwise held to be an Australian Superannuation Fund by the Regulator.

Authorised Contribution made on behalf of a Member or Members of the Fund means a Contribution, whether by way of Cash, Asset or in-kind (including a Fund expense payment or the forgiveness of a debt), made to the Fund by a person, entity, government, Regulator, Employer Sponsor where the Trustee is satisfied that the Contribution has met the requirements for making a superannuation Contribution under the Superannuation Laws and that the acceptance of the Contribution by the

Trustee of the Fund will not result in the Trustee of the Fund breaching the Superannuation Laws, but does not include an allocation from a Reserve Account of the Fund.

Auto-Reversionary Income Stream or Pension means an Income Stream or Pension where a person including a Dependant (the auto-reversionary beneficiary) is included in the Income Stream or Pension documentation as the recipient (if alive) of the Member's Income Stream or Pension upon the death of the Income Stream or Pension Member or beneficiary. Where the Superannuation Laws do not allow an auto-reversionary beneficiary to continue, the auto-reversionary beneficiary's share of the Income Stream or Pension is to be commuted to a Lump Sum.

Bare/Holding Trust is a Trust and includes a Holding Trust established by the Trustee or some other party which holds one of more Assets on bare trust for the Trustee of the Fund. The Trustee of the Bare Trust or Holding Trust is to hold any Asset of the Fund for the absolute entitlement of the Trustee of the Fund. A Bare Trust may be used for the purposes of the Trustee entering into any Limited Recourse borrowing arrangement (LRBA) under the Superannuation Laws or a traditional instalment warrant arrangement or limited recourse lending arrangement pursuant to s 67, 67A and 67B of the SISA 1993 or such other Superannuation Laws that allow the Trustee of a SMSF to borrow.

Benefits in Kind are Superannuation Benefits allowed to be paid under the Superannuation Laws that are neither Cash nor an Asset of the Fund and includes a set-off. The value of any Superannuation Benefit in Kind is to be determined by the Trustee of the Fund who may engage the services of a valuer in that regard.

Cash includes any currency, cheque, promissory note and any amount held by the Trustee in a bank account, cash management trust, deposit account or similar account where cash may be held on deposit for the Trustee.

Cashing Restriction is any restriction in the Superannuation Laws that may apply where a Member satisfies a Condition of Release in respect of one of more of their Superannuation Interests.

Child in relation to a person, includes an adopted child, a step child or an ex-nuptial child of the person or any other person as defined under the Superannuation Laws.

Company includes any entity incorporated pursuant to CA 2001 or the Superannuation Laws and is important for SMSF Trustee companies to meet the special conditions of those types of companies.

Compassionate Grounds includes those grounds listed under the Superannuation Laws authorising the Trustee, subject to direction by the Regulator, to pay a Superannuation Lump Sum to Members based on Compassionate Grounds.

Complying SMSF means a superannuation Fund that meets both the definition of a SMSF and the conditions of a complying SMSF under the Superannuation Laws or as otherwise determined by the Regulator.

Commutation is the conversion of a pension to a lump sum. The commutation amount may be paid out of the Fund to a member or a dependant of a deceased member or rolled back to a member's accumulation account.

Concessional Contributions are those Contributions and allocations defined as Concessional Contributions in the Superannuation Laws.

Condition of Release includes those conditions of release of Superannuation Benefits in the Superannuation Laws and in particular Schedule 1 of the SISR1994.

Contract of Life Insurance includes any policy as defined under the Superannuation Laws and in addition a policy for the Temporary Incapacity, Permanent Incapacity, Death or any other event dependent upon the life of a Member of the Fund and allowed under SISR 4.07C.

Contribution includes a payment, distribution or transfer of Cash or an Asset to the Fund or payment in kind on behalf of a Member of the Fund or the Trustee of the Fund that the Trustee or Regulator is of the opinion is a Contribution but does not include an allocation from a Reserve Account on behalf of a Member.

Contribution In Kind includes a deemed Contribution as declared or notified by the Trustee or the Regulator and would include a person meeting an expense or other legal obligation of the Trustee of the Fund including the forgiveness of a loan.

Contributions Reserve includes a Reserve of the Fund where unvested Contributions are made on behalf of a Member or a specific group of Members.

Contributions Splitting Notice is, subject to the Superannuation Laws and the Fund retaining its Complying SMSF status, a Notice provided to the Trustee by a Member requesting an amount to be Allotted, Rolled Over or transferred as a Transfer Superannuation Interest to a Member's Spouse from benefits in the Fund where a Member has applied to the Trustee and the Trustee has accepted to Allot, Rollover or transfer the amount as requested.

Corporate Trustee is any Trustee of the Fund who is a constitutional corporation, including a company constituted for the purposes of acting as a Trustee of a SMSF under the Superannuation Laws.

Death Benefit includes, subject to the Superannuation Laws and the Fund retaining its Complying SMSF status, a payment, including by way of in-specie asset transfer, of a Superannuation Lump Sum or Superannuation Income Stream to a Dependant, the Legal Estate of the deceased Member of the Fund or any other person however excludes any on-going pension or income stream payment to a Reversionary Pension Beneficiary under an Auto-Reversionary Pension.

Dependant includes, subject to the Superannuation Laws and the Fund retaining its Complying SMSF status, a Spouse of or a Child of a Member of the Fund or a person in an Inter-Dependant Relationship with a Member of the Fund or any financial dependant of a Member of the Fund irrespective of age and any other person the Trustee is of the opinion is a Dependant of the Member of the Fund at the relevant time. However, the Trustee may limit those persons who may claim or receive a Death Benefit upon the death of a Member including any Dependant.

Excess Contributions Tax includes an amount assessed by the Regulator for a period as being excessive in terms of Non-Concessional Contributions and/or Concessional Contributions in relation to a Member of the Fund under the Superannuation Laws and is at a rate of 47%.

Excess Contributions Tax Release Authority is an authority issued by the Regulator under the Superannuation Laws for the payment of Excess Concessional Contributions Tax and/or Excess Non-Concessional Contributions Tax.

Excess Transfer Balance is when the balance of the member's transfer balance account exceeds their personal transfer balance cap on a particular day.

Family Law Payment Splitting Notice is a notice issued to the Trustee of the Fund under the Superannuation Laws requiring the Trustee to split a Member's Superannuation Interest with the Member's Spouse or ex-Spouse.

Foreign Superannuation Fund means a Superannuation Fund that is not an Australian Superannuation Fund for the purposes of the Superannuation Laws.

Fund means this Fund established and maintained as a Complying SMSF under the Fund's Rules.

Gainfully Employed means employed or self-employed for gain or reward in any business, trade, profession, vocation, calling, occupation or employment.

General Transfer Balance Cap is $1.6 million for the 2017-18 financial year and is subject to indexation in $100,000 increments on an annual basis in line with the CPI.

Incapacity includes Temporary and Permanent Incapacity and Terminal Illness as well as those conditions under the Superannuation Laws that amount to incapacity.

Incapacity Superannuation Benefits include those Superannuation Benefits authorised under the Superannuation Laws or the Regulator to be paid to a Member, their Dependants, Legal Estate or other person in the event of a Member's Incapacity or for some other reason.

Income Stream Benefit includes any Pension, income stream or member's benefit that is not an accumulation superannuation interest.

Income Year is any year commencing 1 July and ending 30 June unless otherwise allowed by the Regulator.

In-House Assets Test is the requirement under the Superannuation Laws that limits the percentage of Assets a Trustee of a Fund may hold in Related Party and Related Trust investments and loans by the Trustee of the Fund.

Initial Trustee is the first Trustee or Trustees of the Fund.

Inter-Dependant Relationship is any relationship that meets the conditions of an inter-dependant relationship under the Superannuation Laws for the purposes of being a dependant.

Investment Reserve includes a Reserve that may be established by the Trustee for the purposes of smoothing investment returns amongst Member Superannuation Interests, allocating investment returns to specific Member Superannuation Interests and allocating to other Reserves of the Fund where the Superannuation Laws allow.

Investment Strategy includes, subject to the Superannuation Laws and the Fund retaining its Complying SMSF status, a written document formulating the investment objectives and includes the Insurance Strategy and a plan for investing the monies and Assets of the Fund or Superannuation Interest as required which has regard to all of the circumstances surrounding the Fund including, but not limited to:

a) The risk involved in making, retaining and realising Fund investments. Such decisions are determined by the prospective return from the Fund's or Member's investments having regard to the investment objectives of the Fund and the expected cash flow requirements of the Trustee;

b) The composition of the Fund's investments as a whole including the extent to which the investments are diverse or involve the Fund being exposed to risks from inadequate diversification;

c) The liquidity of the Fund's investments considering its expected cash flow requirements; and

d) The ability of the Fund to discharge its existing and future liabilities.

Legal Estate includes, subject to the Superannuation Laws and the Fund retaining its Complying SMSF status, a trust established or created under a trust deed, will, Bare trust, Enduring Power of Attorney, by way of Court order or in any other way for the purpose of holding a Member's Assets in the event that a Member lacks legal capacity or in respect of a deceased Member's Assets in the event of their death for distribution to Dependants, the Legal Estate or any other beneficiary.

Legal Personal Representative means upon the death of a Member the executor of a will or person who will be formally appointed as executor upon probate or administrator of the estate of a deceased person. It also includes the Trustee of the estate of a person under a legal incapacity or a person who holds an Enduring Power of Attorney granted by a Member of the Fund and includes any other person the Superannuation Laws allow as a Member's Legal Personal Representative.

Limited Recourse Borrowing Arrangement is a loan to a SMSF for the purpose of acquiring, or repairing an asset. Trustees of SMSFs are prohibited from borrowing under the SISA except when borrowing under an LRBA.

Member is a person who has applied for Membership or been automatically appointed as a Member under the Rules of the Fund and has been accepted by the Trustee of the Fund as a Member and has become a Trustee or director of a Corporate Trustee unless the Member is able to appoint a Replacement Trustee or Additional Trustee under the Rules of the Fund and the Superannuation Laws. There is no requirement for the Member of the Fund to have a balance in their Member Accumulation Account. For the sake of clarity, a Member also incorporates a person's

Legal Personal Representative in their position as Legal Personal Representative of the person even where the person has died.

Member Income Stream Superannuation Interest includes, subject to the Superannuation Laws and the Fund retaining its Complying SMSF status, a Superannuation Interest established by the Trustee under the Fund Rules for the purpose of paying a Superannuation Income Stream or Pension, including a Superannuation Income Stream that is currently payable or one that is to commence at some time in the future. A Member Income Stream Superannuation Interest remains in force provided that there is an account balance including $1 or more.

Member Income Stream Superannuation Interest Roll Back means the commutation in whole or part of a Member Income Stream Superannuation Interest in the Fund and the subsequent transfer to a Member Lump Sum Superannuation Interest in the Fund.

Member Lump Sum Superannuation Interest includes, subject to the Superannuation Laws and the Fund retaining its Complying SMSF status, a Superannuation Interest established by the Trustee under the SMSF Strategies Rules for the purposes of paying a Lump Sum to a Member or some other person.

Member SMSF Living Will includes a formal or informal set of directions made by the Member or the Trustee under these Rules to benefit a Member, their Dependants or Legal Estate where the Member suffers Temporary Incapacity, Permanent Incapacity, mental infirmity, loss of mental capacity or terminal illness.

Member SMSF Will includes a formal or informal set of directions made under these Rules by a Member dealing with their SMSF Legal Estate to benefit a Member's Dependants or Legal Estate in the event of their death by way of the payment of Death Benefits.

Non-Binding Death Benefit Nomination is a nomination made by a Member in relation to the distribution of their Superannuation Benefits in the event of their death which is not a Binding Death Benefit Nomination or a Death Benefit Rule.

Non-Concessional Contributions are those Contributions defined as Non-Concessional Contributions in the Superannuation Laws.

Non-Lapsing Binding Death Benefit Nomination includes, subject to the Superannuation Laws, a nomination in writing, as accepted by the Trustee that states:

a) the persons Legal Estate or other authorised entity specified in the notice that may receive the Member's Death Benefits;

b) the terms and conditions of the Superannuation Benefit that will be paid or transferred to that person or to each of those persons;

c) how and the amount of the benefit to be paid to that person or to each of those persons;

d) the notice is in effect; and

e) must be signed and dated by the Member and accepted by the Trustee of the Fund.

The notice is effective, until such time, as the Member revokes a notice unless the Superannuation Laws otherwise allow.

Pension includes a Superannuation Income Stream Benefit under these Rules or a pension under the Superannuation Laws.

Pension Reserve includes a Reserve established by the Trustee of the Fund for the following purposes:

a) to pay any Income Stream or Pension liability of the Trustee of the Fund whether by way of a payment of an amount or asset to a Member's Income Stream Superannuation Interest or directly to a Member with an Income Stream Superannuation Interest, such payment in satisfaction in whole or part of the Trustee's Income Stream liabilities in respect of that Member Income Stream Superannuation Interest:

b) to be used to commence a new Income Stream where an Income Stream Superannuation Member has commuted an Income Stream;

c) to pay a Death Benefit where a Member holding an Income Stream Superannuation Interest has died; or

d) such other payments as the Superannuation Laws allow in respect of Superannuation Income Streams.

Permanent Incapacity is, subject to the Superannuation Laws and the Fund retaining its Complying SMSF status, any condition that the Trustee determines amounts to Permanent Incapacity including in relation to a Member, means ill-health (whether physical or mental), where the Trustee is reasonably satisfied that the Member is unlikely, because of the ill-health, to engage in gainful employment for which the member is reasonably qualified by education, training or experience.

Personal Transfer Balance Cap begins as the general transfer balance cap at the time when the pension member has a transfer balance but is then modified by the proportional indexation of their cap.

Preservation Age is the age specified under the Superannuation Laws according to when the Member is born. The preservation age for a Member is:

a) for a person born before 1 July 1960 – 55 years;

b) for a person born during the year 1 July 1960 to 30 June 1961 – 56 years;

c) for a person born during the year 1 July 1961 to 30 June 1962 – 57 years;

d) for a person born during the year 1 July 1962 to 30 June 1963 – 58 years;

e) for a person born during the year 1 July 1963 to 30 June 1964 – 59 years;

f) for a person born after 30 June 1964 – 60 years.

Relative includes, in relation to an individual, the following:

a) a parent, grandparent, brother, sister, uncle, aunt, nephew, niece, lineal descendant or adopted child of that individual or of his or her spouse;

b) the spouse of that individual or of any other individual specified in paragraph (a).

Regulated Superannuation Fund is a superannuation Fund, including a SMSF that has elected to become a Regulated Superannuation Fund under the Superannuation Laws.

Regulator is the Commissioner of Taxation, APRA, the Australian Securities Investment Commission or any other governmental body that has jurisdiction for regulating the Superannuation Laws as it applies to circumstances of the Fund.

Replacement Trustee is a person who has been appointed as Trustee of the Fund on behalf of a Member or deceased Member according to the Rules of the Fund or pursuant to the Superannuation Laws including the Legal Personal Representative of a deceased Member of the Fund, the Legal Personal Representative of a Member where the Member is under a legal disability because of age, mental incapacity or for some other reason, the Legal Personal Representative of a Member who holds the *Member's Enduring Power of Attorney* or any other person who may act as a Replacement Trustee under the Superannuation Laws.

Retirement and Retired includes, subject to the Superannuation Laws and the Fund retaining its Complying SMSF status, where a Member of the Fund who has reached preservation age and no longer intends to work again. It also includes:

a) where a Member of the Fund is over their preservation age and the Trustee is satisfied that the Member will never again be engaged in part-time or full-time gainful employment;

b) the Member is over age 60 and an arrangement under which the Member is gainfully employed has come to an end on or after that age or the Trustee is satisfied that the Member will never again be engaged in part-time or full-time gainful employment;

c) at any other time according to the Superannuation Laws.

Roll Back includes the transfer of part or all of a Member's Income Stream Superannuation Interest to a Lump Sum Superannuation Interest in the Fund established for the Rollback Member's benefit.

Rollover means paid as a Superannuation Lump Sum (other than by way of being transferred) between Superannuation Funds within the superannuation system including an Employer Rollover Superannuation Benefits where the Superannuation Laws allow.

Rollover Superannuation Benefit includes the payment of a Superannuation Lump Sum, a Superannuation Income Stream or any other Superannuation Benefits or Superannuation Interests between Superannuation Funds allowed under the Superannuation Laws.

RSE Licensee is a Trustee or other party that has been issued a license by the regulator of non-SMSFs under the Superannuation Laws.

Self-Managed Superannuation Fund and SMSF is a superannuation Fund that meets all of the terms and conditions of a Self-Managed Superannuation Fund as that term is defined under the Superannuation Laws.

Severe Financial Hardship is financial hardship that the Trustee is of the opinion is severe and includes conditions as described under the Superannuation Laws for Severe Financial Hardship.

SISA 1993 is the Superannuation Industry Supervision Act 1993.

SISR 1994 are the Superannuation Industry Supervision Regulations 1994.

SMSF Adviser is a person who is recognised by a professional association, educational institution or the Regulator as a specialist in providing advice to Trustees or other professionals on the Superannuation Laws as they apply to a SMSF.

SMSF Legal Estate means the whole of the Superannuation Interests of the Member at a time determined by the Trustee including any allocation from a Reserve of the Fund to a Member Superannuation Interest.

SMSF Will includes any document accepted by the Trustee of the Fund dealing with the transfer of a Member's Superannuation Benefits, including any Reserve Benefits in the event of a Member's death.

Spouse in relation to a person includes another person who, although not legally married to the person, lives with the person on a genuine domestic basis as a couple and also includes, where the Superannuation Laws allow, members of the same sex or any other relationship between two persons.

Superannuation Benefit includes a payment, the transfer of an Asset or a payment in kind, whether by way of a Superannuation Lump Sum or a Superannuation Income Stream from the Fund to a Member or other person or Legal Estate on behalf of a Member or deceased Member, provided the Superannuation Laws allow.

Superannuation Fund includes a provident, retirement, welfare or benefit Fund both within and outside Australia and for the sake of removing any doubt - the Fund.

Superannuation Income Stream includes, subject to the Superannuation Laws and the Fund retaining its Complying SMSF status, a series of periodical payments created by the Trustee for the benefit of a Fund Member or any other person and shall include conditions relating to the term of the Income Stream or pension, the quantum of payments, any indexation or other factors to be applied to the periodical payments and when or whether the Income Stream is commutable to a lump sum, has an automatic reversion or is capable of being transferred upon the death of the Member including a Conditional Reversionary Pension or a pension that has a residual capital value. A Superannuation Income Stream also includes, amongst other periodical payments, the following (subject to the terms and conditions of a Trustee of a SMSF offering the following Income Streams under the Superannuation Laws) which may or may not have an auto-reversionary:

a) Any pension or income stream whose terms and conditions comply with SIS Regulation 1.06(1) including the requirement that the pension or income stream cannot be added to by way of capital;

b) A lifetime complying pension [SISR 1.06(2)];

c) An Accounts Based Pension;

d) An allocated pension [SISR 1.06(4)];

e) A market-linked pension [SISR 1.06(8)];

f) A fixed-term complying pension [SISR 1.06(7)];

g) A non-commutable life pension [SISR Schedule 1 – Item 108];

h) A non-commutable allocated pension [SISR 6.01(2)];

i) A Transition to Retirement Income Stream [SISR 6.01(2)];

j) A non-commutable pension [SISR 6.01(2)];

k) A Temporary Incapacity Superannuation Income Stream – non-commutable income stream [SISR 6.01(2)];

l) An Assets Test Exempt Pension within the meaning of that term under the Social Security Act 1991 including, but not limited to sections 9A, 9B and 9BA; and

m) Any other pension or Superannuation Income Stream under the Superannuation Laws.

Superannuation Interest is any interest in a Superannuation Fund created under the Superannuation Laws and the Rules of the Fund including but not limited to a Member Lump Sum Superannuation Interest, a Member Income Stream Superannuation Interest and a Reserve Account.

Superannuation Interest Entitlement is the amount determined by the Trustee, subject to the Superannuation Laws and the Fund retaining its Complying SMSF status, at any particular time that is the amount, which if paid in either cash or Assets of the Fund, would discharge the Trustee's liability in relation to the particular Superannuation Interest.

Superannuation Laws mean the Commonwealth of Australia Constitution Act 1900, Superannuation Industry (Supervision) Act 1993, the Superannuation Industry (Supervision) Regulations (1994), the Income Tax Assessment Act 1936, the Income Tax Assessment Act 1997, the Income Tax Regulations, the Corporations Act 2001,the Corporations Regulations, the Social Security Act 1991 (C'th), the Social Security Regulations, the Veterans Entitlement Act 1986 (C'th), the Veterans Entitlement Regulations, the Family Law Act 1975, the Family Law Regulations, the Bankruptcy Act 1966, Superannuation (Departing Australia Superannuation Payments Tax) Act 2006, Superannuation (Excess Concessional Contributions Tax) Act 2006, Superannuation (Excess Non-concessional

Contributions Tax) Act 2006, Superannuation (Self Managed Superannuation Funds) Supervisory Levy Amendment Act 2006 and any other law dealing with an Australian Superannuation Fund as amended from time to time.

Superannuation Lump Sum is a Superannuation Benefit that is not a Superannuation Income Stream and includes, subject to the Superannuation Laws and the Fund retaining its Complying SMSF status, an amount paid out, an Asset transferred from the Fund or a payment in kind according to the Rules of the Fund to a person entitled to be paid a Superannuation Lump Sum or the payment of a Lump Sum upon the commutation of a Member Superannuation Income Stream.

Tax Free Component is that part of a Superannuation Benefit that is a Tax-Free component as determined under the Superannuation Laws.

Taxable Component is that part of a Superannuation Benefit that is not a Tax-Free component.

Temporary Incapacity is, subject to the Superannuation Laws and the Fund retaining its Complying SMSF status, any condition that the Trustee determines to be Temporary Incapacity for the purpose of these Rules and includes where a Member has ceased to be Gainfully Employed (including a Member who has ceased temporarily to receive any gain or reward under a continuing arrangement for the Member to be Gainfully Employed) due to ill health (whether physical or mental) that caused the Member to cease to be Gainfully Employed but does not extend to Permanent Incapacity.

Temporary Incapacity Superannuation Income Stream is a Superannuation Income Stream payable by the Trustee of the Fund under the Superannuation Laws for a Member that is Temporarily Incapacitated and includes a Superannuation Income Stream that:
a) cannot be commuted or turned into a Superannuation Lump Sum;
b) is paid at least monthly;
c) does not have a residual capital value; and
d) is such that the total amount paid each month is fixed or may be indexed provided that the indexation component, during any 12

month period, does not exceed the greater of 5% per annum or the Consumer Price Index for the previous 12 months.

Terminal Illness includes where:

a) two registered medical practitioners have certified, jointly or separately, that the person suffers from an illness, or has incurred an injury, that is likely to result in the death of the person within a period (the certification period) that ends not more than 12 months after the date of the certification;

b) at least one of the registered medical practitioners is a specialist practicing in an area related to the illness or injury suffered by the person;

c) for each of the certificates, the certification period has not ended.

Transfer Balance Account operates in a similar way to a bank account balance or the balance of a general account ledger. Amounts an individual transfers to the retirement phase give rise to a credit (increase) in their transfer balance account. Similarly, certain transfers out of the retirement phase give rise to a debit (decrease) in the individual's transfer balance account.

Transfer Balance Cap is the limit the amount of capital individuals can transfer to the retirement phase to support superannuation income streams. This, in turn, limits the amount of superannuation fund earnings that are exempt from taxation.

Transfer Superannuation Interest includes, subject to the Superannuation Laws and the Fund retaining its Complying SMSF status, the transfer of part or all of one or more of a Member's Superannuation Interests from a Superannuation Fund (including a Foreign Superannuation Fund and the Fund itself) to a Superannuation Interest of a Member, their Spouse or any other person in the Fund or another Superannuation Fund.

Transition to Retirement Income Stream means an Income Stream Superannuation Interest that meets the terms and conditions of a Transition to Retirement Income Stream and a Non-commutable Allocated Pension or non-commutable pension under the Superannuation Laws.

Trustee is the Trustee of the Fund and includes a Replacement Trustee appointed for a Member or an Additional Trustee where the Member is the only Member and Trustee of the Fund.

Trustee Law means whichever of the Trustee Act (NSW) 1925, the Trustee Act (Vic) 1958, the Trustee Act (SA) 1936, the Trustees Act (WA) 1962, the Trusts Act (Qld) 1973, the Trustee Act (Tas) 1898, the Trustee Act (ACT) 1957 and the Trustee Act (NT) 1907 applies and any other Commonwealth, State or Territory legislation that relates to the duties, role and investment powers of a Trustee of a trust including a trust that is a SMSF or Superannuation Fund.

Trustee Meeting is a meeting of the Trustee as required by the Rules of the Fund and the Superannuation Laws or where matters regarding the Fund are discussed.

Value of Assets of the Fund is the value of any asset of the Fund as determined by the Trustee of the Fund, subject to the Superannuation Laws, Audit Standards and any direction by the Regulator, which may include the Asset's historical cost, the replacement cost of the Asset, the market value of the Asset as at last accounting balance date or the current market value of the Asset. The Trustee may change valuation principles applicable to different Assets of the Fund unless the Superannuation Laws provide otherwise. However from 1 July 2012 the Trustee is to use market value for all valuations of the Assets of the Fund.

Value of a Member's Superannuation Interest is the value the Trustee determines in respect of a Member Superannuation Lump Sum Superannuation Interest or Member Superannuation Income Stream Superannuation Interest and if there is no such determination by the Trustee it is the value of the Member's particular Superannuation Interest at the time of the last audit of the Fund plus any additions made to the Superannuation Interest less any deductions to the Superannuation Interest up to the time of the determined value of the Member's Superannuation Interest. However, where the Superannuation Laws require a specified valuation or provide a formula the Trustee is to apply that valuation or formula to the calculation of the value of a Member's Superannuation Interest.

www.ingramcontent.com/pod-product-compliance
Lightning Source LLC
Chambersburg PA
CBHW061129220326
41599CB00024B/4216